S OF VIENNA

A study in Allied Unity: 1812-1822

by

HAROLD NICOLSON

Nothing appears of shape to indicate
That cognisance has marshalled things terrene,
Or will (such is my thinking) in my span.
Rather they show that, like a knitter droused
Whose fingers play in skilled unmindfulness,
The Will has woven with an absent heed
Sure life first was; and ever will so weave.
THOMAS HARDY, *The Dynasts*

Historic sense forbids us to judge results by
motive, or real consequences by the ideals and
intentions of the actor who produced them.
VISCOUNT MORLEY

GROVE P
New York

Originally published in 1946 by
Harcourt, Brace and Company, New York

The quotation from Thomas Hardy on the title page is made with the
permission of The Macmillan Company, publishers.

Printed in the United States of America

FIRST GROVE PRESS EDITION

Library of Congress Cataloging-in-Publication Data

Nicolson, Harold George, Sir, 1886–1968.
    The Congress of Vienna : a study in allied unity, 1812–1822 / by
Harold Nicolson.
        p.   cm.
    Originally published: New York : Harcourt Brace Jovanovich,
1946.
    Includes bibliographical references and index.
    ISBN 0-8021-3744-X
    1. Congress of Vienna (1814–1815). 2. Napoleonic Wars, 1800–
1815—Treaties. 3. Europe—Politics and government—1789–1815.
I. Title.

DC249 .N5 2000
940.2'7—dc21   00-041709

Grove Press
841 Broadway
New York, NY 10003

01 02 03 04   10 9 8 7 6 5 4 3 2 1

THIS BOOK IS DEDICATED
TO
ANTHONY EDEN

Contents

Introduction

THIS STUDY of the grouping and regrouping of the United Nations between 1812 and 1822 makes no claim to original research. There remain, indeed, many references which I should have wished to consult but which, owing to the war, were unavailable. In Appendix II will be found a list of the main published works upon which this narrative has been based. It would be ungenerous none the less not to mention specifically Sir Charles Webster's classic work upon *The Foreign Policy of Castlereagh*. It is from this huge quarry that so many of us have gathered our little heap of stones.

There is a prefatory warning which I wish to give. The analogies between the events described in this volume and those which we are now experiencing are so frequent that they may mislead. Then as now Great Britain (at first alone and thereafter assisted by powerful allies) had destroyed a totalitarian system which threatened to engulf the world. Then as now the common purpose which had united the Nations in the hour of danger, ceased, once victory had been achieved, to compel solidarity. Some members of the Alliance sought to exploit their power by extending their former frontiers or by establishing fresh and alarming zones of influence; the realism of their methods was at first obscured by the idealism of their professions. Other peoples, being wearied by long years of effort and adventure, hoped through isolation to devote themselves undisturbed to the problems of internal reconstruction. Then as now there were those among the older generation who were saddened by the fear lest, having made their sacrifice to preserve against an external enemy the world they knew and loved, they had allowed an internal enemy, an inner illness, to sap the vigour of the State. Then as now there were those who felt that in destroying one menace to the peace and independence of nations they had succeeded only in erecting another and graver menace in its place.

To accept such analogies too readily—to identify Great Britain, for instance, with the old Austria, or the United States with Great Britain—would be to surrender to what Professor Arnold Toynbee has called "the egocentric illusion." We can learn little from history unless we first realise that she does not, in fact, repeat herself. Events are not affected by analogies; they are determined by the combinations of circumstance. And since circumstances vary from generation to generation it is illusive to suppose that any pattern of history, however similar it may at first appear, is likely to repeat itself exactly in the kaleidoscope of time.

Whether or no one adopts the determinist view of history, whether or no one believes that events are influenced by individuals or individuals by events, it must be recognised that the combinations of circumstance are governed as much by invisible as by visible factors, as much by the unapparent as by the apparent.

Thus if we reject the "apathetic fallacy" and assume that individual character, ambition or genius can either accelerate or retard the march of events, we are still left with the conclusion that even the most dominating individuals are subject to invisible change. No man can have possessed greater resilience than Napoleon, yet after 1812 some hidden fault in his secretions, some unaccountable decline in his energy and willpower, came to falsify all expectation. Alexander of Russia, again, appeared in 1814 as the arbiter of the world's destinies, as the Great Liberator possessed of vast military power and dynamic ideas. Yet in him also influences were at work, almost hidden from his contemporaries, which combined to deflect his ambition and to cloud his mind and will. No British statesman has ever possessed the calm consistency, the cool independence, of Castlereagh, yet he also unexpectedly lost his reasoning powers and died a sudden death. Such secret changes should convince us of the mutability of the individual mind.

INTRODUCTION

If, on the other hand, we believe that history is determined by the spirit of the age, then this narrative should warn us that the *Zeitgeist* also is subject to invisible mutations and delays. How came it that the younger generation in Germany, who at the time of the *Tugendbund* and the War of Liberation, displayed so resurgent a spirit, should have been snuffed out so lastingly by the Carlsbad Decrees? How came it that the partisan movement in Spain, which had manifested such heroic activity during the French invasion, should thereafter have so surprisingly declined? How came it that the Italian *Risorgimento*, which seemed so imminent in the days of Murat and Lord William Bentinck, should have been so long deferred? How came it that the general rising so confidently predicted in 1820 should have been postponed till 1848? These questions are not answered by ascribing the pause which ensued to the ingenuity of Metternich or the potency of the Holy Alliance. They can be explained only by the hidden interplay of challenges and responses, of energy and exhaustion, of enthusiasm and apathy, of youth and middle age.

"I am left with the impression," wrote Gentz after attending all the conferences of his time, "that nobody is ever quite right all through." If he was referring to the accuracy of human prediction, then I agree with his conclusion. But if he was referring to the efficacy of moral principles, then I refuse to subscribe to so defeatist a doctrine. I believe in fact that certain principles are absolute and must in the end prevail. But I admit that their functioning is obscure, that no single interpretation of the combinations of circumstance can ever be a valid interpretation, and that if history can teach us anything it can teach us the folly of prophecy and the wisdom of patience.

H. N.

Sissinghurst,
September 1, 1945

1. The Retreat from Moscow

[October 18-December 18, 1812]

The 29th Bulletin—Napoleon abandons his army and returns to Paris—His journey with Caulaincourt through East Prussia and Poland—His arrival in Dresden—He reaches the Tuileries at midnight on December 18—The Russian campaign might have proved decisive—What would have happened if a Cossack patrol had noticed the ford at Studienka?—If ·the Tsar had captured Napoleon, what sort of peace would have been made?—Estimate of the character and education of Alexander I—The influence of La Harpe—His weakness as commander in chief during the 1812 campaign—His consequent loss of popularity—Effect of these circumstances upon his subsequent policy and action—The balance of power as it existed in December 1812.

THE 29TH BULLETIN was issued from Molodetchno on December 3, 1812. In it Napoleon confessed that "an atrocious calamity" had befallen the *Grande Armée* and that his Russian campaign had ended in disaster. The Bulletin reached Paris on December 16 and was published on the following morning.[1] (*) Foreseeing the dismay which this news would occasion in France, Napoleon decided to leave the front and to return to his capital with all speed. Only his personal presence in the Tuileries could allay the consternation which the Bulletin was certain to provoke. At Smogorni, on the night of December 5, he abandoned his army and took the road to the west. He reached Paris at midnight on December 18.

The details of that secret journey have been preserved in the memoirs of Caulaincourt, Duc de Vicence.[2] In all the library of Napoleonic literature there are few passages which illustrate so forcibly the dominance which Napoleon's genius, insensitiveness

---

* See notes to the several chapters at end of book, p. 275.

and egoism exercised upon the minds and hearts of those who served him. Caulaincourt had no cause to love or trust his pitiless master. He can have had little doubt that Napoleon had sought deliberately to implicate him in the murder of the Duc d'Enghien in 1804. Although innocent of anything worse than the violation of the neutrality of Baden, the stigma of this incident weighed upon Caulaincourt throughout his honourable life. There is no doubt either that Napoleon, in selfish mischief, destroyed Caulaincourt's domestic happiness by forbidding his marriage to Madame de Canisy for ten long years; only at Fontainebleau in 1814, when he had already signed his abdication, did Napoleon accord the consent which he was then powerless to withhold; with superb devotion, Caulaincourt kissed the hand of his fallen master in gratitude for this empty boon.

For ten long years had Caulaincourt endured the perversity of Napoleon's temperament. Having been Ambassador to Russia, having enjoyed the intimacy of the Tsar Alexander I,[3] Caulaincourt was fully aware of Russian political and social conditions, of the menace of the Russian climate, and of the strain of obstinacy which flowed like some dark current beneath the gentle ripples of the Tsar's desire to please.[4] Again and again had he warned Napoleon against the dangers of a Russian campaign. "You have no knowledge of such things," his master barked at him, "you have no judgment in political affairs. You are more Russian than you are French; you have been mesmerised by Alexander's charm. A single victory, and the Tsar will come creeping towards me as he did at Tilsit. The great landowners will rise against him; I shall emancipate the serfs." Thus did he reject all warnings. And when they entered the Kremlin, and found the clocks there still ticking quietly in the saloons, Napoleon turned in scorn upon his Master of the Horse. "Well, My Lord Duke, what about this Russian climate of yours? It is mild as a September day at Fontainebleau." Caulaincourt bowed his head in silent apprehension.

Then followed the horrors of the retreat, the miracle of the Beresina. The corpses of those who during the advance had fallen at Borodino or outside Smolensk still littered the fields beside the roadway—hummocked now by snow, having the appearance in the dim light "of vast flocks of sheep." From time to time Napoleon would leave his carriage and ease his numbed limbs by stamping along the frozen track, a staff cut from a larch tree in his hand. The tattered stragglers from his army would stop and stare at his passage and then drop dead beside him on the road. Then followed Smogorni and the intimate drive across an uncertain Europe from Russia into France.

Caulaincourt travelled under his own name as Duc de Vicence. Napoleon appeared upon their passports as his secretary, under the name of Monsieur de Rayneval. The Emperor's travelling carriage proved too heavy for the snow-bound road and the horses slipped and struggled on the ice. On reaching Kowno Caulaincourt discovered an old covered sledge—a mere box on runners which had once been painted red. They abandoned the comfort of the travelling carriage; they abandoned the luggage; even Rustam the mameluke and the Emperor's dressing case were left behind. Unshaven and alone they pursued their journey day and night across the snow. At Tilsit they entered Prussian territory and the Emperor became afraid lest he might be recognised and seized; he cowered back into the recesses of the sleigh, pulling his fur cap down upon his eyes, muffling himself in the great green velvet bear-skin which he wore. They cut across East Prussia into Poland and on December 10 they reached the Hôtel d'Angleterre at Warsaw. The Abbé de Pradt, the French Ambassador, was summoned to the hotel sitting-room and upon him the Emperor discharged for a few hours the vials of his accumulated wrath. The Abbé de Pradt was one of those men who even at the best of times was apt to ruffle Napoleon's nerves. "He was extremely addicted," remarked the Emperor to Sir Neil Campbell when at Elba, "to descanting upon military subjects, which is very disgusting to military men." The interview in the parlour of the Hôtel d'Angleterre was thunderous; the Abbé de Pradt retired to his Embassy outraged and bewildered; he thereafter revenged himself upon his master by conspiring with M. de Talleyrand.

On again they drove through the night towards Germany

and the Rhine. Napoleon's spirits revived as soon as the Prussian danger had been left behind them. His rear guard under Murat would make a stand at Vilna; he would collect another army and rejoin them in the spring. And what would have happened to them had they been seized by the peasants or the *Tugendbund* in East Prussia? Would they have been handed over to the English? Would they have been exposed in wicker cages for the delectation of the London crowd? The picture of Caulaincourt, so dignified always and so austere, in such a position aroused Napoleon's sense of farce. He flung himself back in the hard and draughty sledge and laughed vulgarly. He stretched out his hand in order, as was his wont, to tweak the lobe of Caulaincourt's ear. But the Master of the Horse had swathed his face in bandages; the Emperor ceased from rummaging and tapped him amicably upon the nape of the neck.

During all those days and nights Napoleon talked and talked. Feverishly he talked about his former glories and his future plans. Three hundred and thirty thousand men of the *Grande Armée* lay hummocked in snow upon the plains of Russia, but he talked only of further armies, further campaigns, and further victories. His voice at times was almost jubilant; at other moments it would rise or fall into the scream or snarl of hatred. One name alone (since as a rule he was mild about his enemies) would rouse these paroxysms of rancour. That name was England. The insatiable enemy, who had defied him all these years, who had defied him even when she stood alone. "England! England! England!"—as the postillions lashed their tottering horses and the great red box slid and lurched across the snow.

[2]

At midnight on December 13, 1812, they reached Dresden. It was here, scarcely more than six months before, that he had celebrated in full pomp the apogee of his renown, and had appeared as Charlemagne among the tributary Princes of Central Europe. He had gone there "with all the display and apparatus of an Eastern potentate" in order to impress upon his satellites the magnitude of his power and the splendour of his pre-eminence.⁵ During those weeks of May the roads which led from France to Saxony had been thronged with long lines of vans and carriages bringing to Dresden the chamberlains and the maids of honour, the equerries and the pages, the silks, the velvets and tapestries, the gold plate and diamonds, the cooks and footmen, of the Court of France. The rulers of Germany and Austria flocked to do him homage. On the night of May 15 he arrived in Dresden and established his household in the palace of the King of Saxony. His lords in waiting, the ladies who formed the suite of Marie Louise, bore the oldest names in France: Turenne, Noailles, Montesquieu. The strictest etiquette was preserved. At 9 A.M. he held his own levée at which were present the Princes of Germany; at 10 A.M. came the levée of the Empress which he himself attended with the officers of State. Then followed a solemn Mass in the chapel of the palace and in the evening came a ceremonial banquet. The officers of the Imperial household would gather in the throne-room and two of the Lords Chamberlain would stand at the entrance to announce in loud tones the styles and titles of the guests. These formal entrances were planned by Napoleon upon a rigid and ascending scale and with precise regard for dramatic effect. First came the Ministers and Ambassadors each resonantly introduced; they were succeeded by the minor royalties; the Duke of Weimar, the Duke of Coburg, the Duke of Mecklenburg, the Grand Duke of Würzburg. After a short pause the Queen of Westphalia was announced. "Their Majesties, the King and Queen of Saxony"—the Chamberlain shouted, and Frederick Augustus with Queen Maria, abashed and benevolent, would enter their own drawing-room. "His Majesty, the King of Prussia"—the Chamberlain called, and into the room hesitated the hapless widower figure of Frederick William III looking like a bewildered major in some minor regiment. "Their Imperial and Apostolic Majesties the Emperor and Empress of Austria, King and Queen of Hungary"—and Francis the First entered giving his arm to his young and ailing wife. "Her Imperial Majesty the Empress of the French,

Queen of Italy," and Marie Louise, followed by her ladies and draped in diamonds, swept girlishly into the room. A long silence followed, while the assembled potentates waited uneasily. Then suddenly would come the single simple cry: *"L'Empereur!"* Dressed in his green uniform Napoleon would enter alone.

One pictures him bursting rapidly upon that accumulated silence,—so rapidly that the sound of his coming footsteps echoed to the assembled company upon the parquet of the adjoining galleries and saloons. One pictures him scowling for a moment with histrionic effect, one hand pressing the famous hat along his thigh, the other thrust deep into the buttons of his waistcoat. But it was not so: all observers agree that on such occasions Napoleon adopted another and more courtly mode. As if to mark the difference between his military and his imperial manner he would walk in hesitatingly, almost mincingly, and on the balls of his feet. The effect, it seems, was in no sense ridiculous; there was nothing about it of the dancing school or the academy of deportment. It was in its way more sinister. It gave the impression of a lion entering the arena, slowly, cautiously: on padded feet.

Night after night, while Paer's orchestra played gently in the anteroom and the crowds outside gazed up at the rows of lighted windows, these ceremonies were observed. On May 28 Napoleon left Dresden for the Russian frontier.

His return, at midnight on December 13, was less auspicious. The city was in complete darkness; there was not a soul in the streets. They could not find their way to the house of the French Minister and there was nobody whom they could ask. Seeing a lighted window, they shouted up at it. The window was opened and a man thrust out a nightcapped head. "The house of the French Minister?" they called up to him, "The house of le Comte de Serra?" The head popped in again and the window rattled down; it was an hour before they found their direction. Before retiring to rest Napoleon wrote long letters to the Emperor of Austria and to the King of Naples.

At seven next morning they were again on the road. They

abandoned their red sledge at Dresden, where it was subsequently acquired by an enterprising Englishman and exhibited as an object of curiosity. They left Dresden comfortably in a carriage placed at their disposal by the King of Saxony. Travelling by Leipzig, Mainz and Château-Thierry they reached Meaux where they were obliged, owing to a broken axle, to change into a decrepit posting chaise. That night, December 18, they drove under the Arch of the Carrousel and into the courtyard of the Tuileries. As they did so, the clock struck a quarter to twelve. They walked along the garden colonnade and tapped at the glass door which led to the Empress' apartments on the ground floor. The porter appeared in his nightgown with a candle. "It is I," shouted Caulaincourt, "the Duc de Vicence." The porter raised his candle to the glass and saw only a tall figure swathed in bandages and fur. He went back to his lodge and fetched his wife. The Emperor now left the shadow of the colonnade. He opened his heavy velvet cloak and showed his uniform. "It is the Emperor!" exclaimed the porter's wife. "It is he himself." Limping painfully on swollen joints, blinking with sore eyes in the glare of the lights which were brought hurriedly from inner rooms, Napoleon entered his palace. Her ladies rushed to rouse the Empress. "Goodnight, Caulaincourt," said the Emperor curtly, "you also must need some rest."

The Duc de Vicence had scarcely closed his eyes for fourteen days and nights.

[3]

By all the rules of warfare Napoleon and the *Grande Armée* should have been taken prisoner at the crossing of the Beresina on November 29. Three Russian armies, outnumbering the French by almost four to one, were converging for his capture. To the north Wittgenstein, to the south Tshitshagoff, were poised to cut him off from the river; already the solitary bridge at Borisoff was in Russian hands; and Kutusoff, with the bulk of the Russian armies, was lumbering up upon his rear. In all appearance, by all reasonable conjecture, the trap had closed upon him. To some extent Napoleon owed his escape to the

courage of Ney and the resource of Oudinot; to an even greater
extent he owed it to the devotion of the French sappers who,
waist-deep in icy water, constructed the secret pontoon bridges
at the ford of Studienka. But essentially he owed it to the speed
of his own genius and the slowness of the Russian mind.

Few historical speculations are more interesting than the
conjecture as to what would have happened had Tshitshagoff
realised in time that the apparent preparations south of Borisoff
were no more than a feint; that the real crossing was being
made at Studienka, four miles to the north. The French army
would have been forced to accept unconditional surrender upon
Russian soil; the Old Guard would have piled their arms to the
east of the Beresina; Napoleon would have been brought back
to Orcha or Smolensk where he would have handed his sword
to Alexander. And what would have happened then?

Austria, Prussia, the Germanies and England would, in such
circumstances, have counted for little. The decision would have
rested in Alexander's hands alone. How would he have decided?

It must be remembered that in November 1812 Austria and
Prussia, in theory at least, were Napoleon's allies; the rest of
the Continent (with the exception of Spain and Portugal which
were being maintained in a state of effervescence by the efforts
of the Marquis of Wellington) was under Napoleon's domination. The Tsar of Russia would have had before him a completely blank map upon which to sketch his design. It is curious
to reflect what he would have done to the map of Europe had
the Beresina marked the final downfall of Napoleon instead of
Waterloo.

Nor is this speculation wholly otiose. It provides a useful
conjectural basis from which to examine the Tsar's character,
which was in itself conjectural. The comparative simplicity of
such a speculation serves moreover as an illuminating contrast,
or foil, to the kaleidoscopic groupings and regroupings which
ensued and which it is the main purpose of this study to record,
and perhaps even to elucidate. The intricacy and confusion of
the two and a half years which followed blur the essential out-

lines: had unconditional surrender been imposed upon Napoleon at the Beresina those outlines would have been stark indeed.

Or would they? Alexander was certainly incalculable; but he was not inscrutable. "It would be difficult," said Napoleon to Metternich, "to have more intelligence than the Emperor Alexander; but there is a piece missing; I have never managed to discover what it is." A modern psychiatrist would experience no difficulty in deciding what, among the Tsar's great gifts and qualities, was the missing component; it was the faculty of co-ordination. Tainted as he was with his father's insanity, the Emperor Alexander was afflicted with split personality, or schizophrenia, which in his later years degenerated into depressive mania. Napoleon, in retrospect at St. Helena, attributed to duplicity or affectation the successive sincerities which had confused the Tsar's policies and actions: "A Byzantine of the decadent period," he called him, or again, "The Talma of the North." What Metternich described sententiously as the "periodic evolutions of the Tsar's mind," were none the less sincere phases of conviction. What renders his policy so difficult to interpret is that, although he would oscillate wildly between a given theory of action and its opposite, he sought always to remain constant to his word; and since the promises that he had made when under the influence of one set of theories were irreconcilable with the needs imposed upon him by another set of theories, he often tried, in almost pathetic confusion, to carry out the recently discarded and the recently adopted theory at one and the same time. As these successive impulses were contradictory, a marked impression of inconstancy and dissimulation was conveyed.

There are other factors which must be borne in mind, factors of education and temperament. The dominant influence of his early life, apart from that of his grandmother Catherine the Great, was the influence of his Swiss tutor, La Harpe. "All that I know," wrote Alexander in later life, "all that I am worth, is due to La Harpe." The latter had acquired from prolonged studies in the cantonal library at Lausanne, not only the liberal ideas which were fashionable at the close of the eighteenth century, but also a Platonic conception of political theory. Realising that complete democracy was not suited either to the condition of Russian society or to the Russian temperament, he decided to form his young and most malleable pupil into the semblance of the benevolent despot or philosopher king. It was he who had inspired the young Grand Duke with that consciousness of benign, or even divine, mission which, as will be seen, exercised so immense an influence upon his own actions and the fate of Europe. Napoleon, with his contempt for ideologues, never realised that the Tsar's idealism was the very mainspring of his soul.

His emotional instability was increased by other, and less avowable defects. It was not merely that the murder of his father had left upon his memory the impress of a night of horror, and upon his conscience a haunting sense of guilt; it was also that he was easily discouraged, constantly afraid. His subjective, sensitive, almost effeminate character, induced him (although he was not cowardly) to be terrified of cowardice; to dread the "haggard stare" with which, as Adam Czartoryski had frankly told him, he had been afflicted during the panic days of Austerlitz. His efforts to demonstrate his own virility would at times evoke in him, as after Lützen, moods of incomparable resolve; at other moments they would tempt him into showy unconvincing phrases as when his low voice would rise to a treble and he would scream at his attendant Ministers, "I hate civilians; I am a soldier; I only like soldiers."

But was he a soldier? The scorched earth policy which had brought the *Grande Armée* to disaster had not been the plan of Alexander; he himself had favoured a vast encircling movement by which Napoleon would be outflanked through Illyria and Italy. And where had Alexander been during the great days of Borodino and Moscow? He had been pacing the garden of his villa on Kammionyi island outside St. Petersburg, now shouting that he would retire to the uttermost recesses of Siberia; now giving instructions for the evacuation of the northern capital and the removal of the statue of Peter the Great; now seeking in his Bible those *sortes virgilianae* which would

give him sustenance and hope. He was well aware that it was
Kutusoff, and not he, the Tsar, who was regarded as the saviour
of the country. His sister the Grand Duchess Catherine, having
first told him to absent himself from the armies since he inspired
no confidence in the troops—was now writing sharp hysterical
letters to assure him that he had "lost his honour." Even the
Russian people had ceased to regard him as the Little Father.
At Kazan, on his name day, he had paid his annual visit to the
Cathedral: the citizens and peasants were grouped around the
entrance; it was in utter silence that he mounted the granite
stairway; his footsteps and those of his staff resounded in a
hush.

With such a temperament, in such a mood, how would the
Tsar have received Napoleon if brought to him, amid the ruin
of the *Grande Armée*, a prisoner to Smolensk? Might not his
chivalrous pity for a man so utterly fallen, might not the actual
magnetism which Napoleon's decisiveness exercised upon his
fluid character, have led him to forget what Russia had suffered
at the hands of her invader and induced in him a recurrence of
the Tilsit mood? A deal, even an alliance, was not impossible.
Alexander was under but slight obligation to England and none
at all to Europe as a whole. Napoleon would have offered him
the reconstitution of the Kingdom of Poland from Danzig to
Cracow: a Poland nominally independent but in fact so subservient to the Tsar's dictation as to bring the Russian frontier
almost to the Oder. The Tsar would have sought, and would
have obtained, the restoration of Prussia to her former power,
as a memorial to the dead Queen whom he had loved, and to
whom, upon the tomb of Frederick the Great, he had pledged
a solemn oath. But what need, what inducement,—apart from
his sense of mission,—was there to tempt him to further European effort? Napoleon would have distracted his errant mind
by dreams of Oriental splendour and have tempted him to
regain the love and admiration of his countrymen as the conqueror of Constantinople and the East. Hand in hand they
could march together through Turkey, Egypt, Mesopotamia,
Persia to the confines of India. Russia would fulfil her destiny;

and England, faced with this joint menace to her richest possessions, would at last be forced to accept an honourable peace.
How could Kutusoff, how could even Stein [6] himself, have
countered so romantic a temptation?

The merest chance, the presence of a single Cossack patrol
under an alert officer, might well have changed the fate of
Europe. It was the hidden ford at Studienka, the French sappers working half frozen through the night, which rescued
Alexander from this fantastic temptation.

All Europe and thirty months of arduous effort would now
be needed to complete Napoleon's overthrow.

"From Malo-Jaroslawetz to Smogorni," wrote Philip de
Ségur, "this master of Europe had been no more than a general
of a dying and disbanded army. From Smogorni to the Rhine
he was an unknown fugitive, travelling through a hostile country. Beyond the Rhine, he again found himself the master and
the conqueror of Europe. A last breeze of the wind of prosperity
once more swelled his sails."

[4]

These speculations, these conjectures, serve to emphasize the
fact that the Fourth Coalition [7] was formed almost fortuitously;
less by the deliberate planning of the several rulers and statesmen, than by the pressure of public opinion and the chain of
circumstance. Few men, considering the position as it stood in
December 1812, could have foreseen that another European
coalition was about to be created. Napoleon might well have
suffered a shattering reverse upon the plains of Russia, but his
potential power was still enormous and his potential enemies
were frightened, disunited, weak. The Emperor of the French
still controlled the whole of Germany, with the exception of
Prussia, and was still united to Austria by an alliance based upon
dynastic ties. He was still master of the Netherlands, of Italy,
of Illyria. From Moscow he had himself decreed the levy of
additional "cohorts" which had already brought him 80,000
men. He had decreed an additional levy of 137,000 conscripts,

and was planning a final levy which would, on paper, give him a fresh army of 650,000 men. He still garrisoned the fortresses of the Vistula, the Elbe and the Oder in unconquered might. He still retained the prestige, and was again to demonstrate the resourcefulness of the greatest military genius of all time. "I have made a great mistake," he informed his Ministers the day after his return from Russia, "but I possess the means of repairing it." There was little reason at the time to doubt his optimism.

For what, in fact, could his enemies muster against him? Russia had still at her disposal a field army of 110,000 with 30,000 cavalry. But her troops were exhausted, her generals hesitant, her equipment defective. Even when, in February 1813, the Emperor Alexander ordered the creation of further reserves, the machine worked slowly. By July of that year they amounted only to 68,000 infantry and 14,000 horse. England who, in defiance of her usual custom, had ventured to send an expeditionary force to Europe, was still heavily engaged in Spain. What did small battles such as Badajoz or Ciudad Rodrigo, what did even Salamanca, count in comparison with Napoleon's gigantic continental strides? The Peninsular War may well have proved, as Napoleon said, "the Spanish ulcer," but in December 1812 these Spanish skirmishes must have seemed to Alexander very distant from Smolensk. There was at that time no indication whatsoever that Francis I or Metternich had even contemplated changing sides against Napoleon. And what of Prussia? Tilsit had reduced Prussia to the status of a third-class Power. Her territory had been cut down to four provinces, her population to four and a half million, her armies to 42,000. She was riddled with debt, her population was impoverished, her King was weak, despairing and afraid. Who could foretell the great popular movement of the War of Liberation or forecast that within a few months Prussia would again count among the great military Powers? What sane person, in December 1812, could have prophesied that the armies of Alexander and his Allies would march across Europe, would pass the Rhine, would bivouac upon the heights of Montmartre?

Who could foresee that within a few short weeks the will to conquer, that unpredictable constituent of victory, would pass from the side of the French to the side of their enemies, their victims and their satellites; that confidence would be transferred?

Only by stages, only in sudden unexpected bursts of anger, hope and opportunity, was the Fourth Coalition formed. The will-power of the United Nations tautened rapidly and then gradually relaxed. It is the purpose of this study to examine the gradations by which a united front was constituted and how thereafter it slowly dissolved.

2. "The Revival of Prussia"

ON DECEMBER 19, 1812, therefore,—on the morning after his midnight return to the Tuileries—the position of Napoleon did not seem irreparable. He felt confident that the Emperor of Austria, the King of Prussia and his German or Italian satellites would not dare to move against him; he could for the moment discount the equivocal attitude being adopted by Bernadotte of Sweden; he had thus only two enemies in the field against him —Great Britain and Russia.

The British Army was at the moment fully occupied by the Spanish campaign. It was true that in the previous July Lord Wellington at Salamanca had defeated "40,000 Frenchmen in forty minutes" and had therefore occupied Madrid and driven King Joseph and the Spanish quislings in panic to Valencia; but in October the British had been checked at Burgos and only a few weeks later the French armies had reoccupied the Spanish capital. In spite of the heavy drains which he had made, and was still intending to make, upon his Spanish forces, Napoleon knew that he would be able to leave in the Peninsula a formidable French army of 200,000 men. He thus felt safe enough upon the Pyrenees.[1]

Russia, he knew, had suffered almost as severely in the 1812 campaign as he had himself. He was aware that Kutusoff and the generals, having won their victory and driven the invader from the soil of Holy Russia, had no desire at all to cross the Niemen and to extend the war into central or western Europe. He believed (too confidently perhaps) that court circles in St. Petersburg, together with the Russian landowners and merchants, were anxious only for peace and would restrain Alexander from any adventures beyond his own frontier. He hoped, and not unjustifiably, that under the threat of a spring campaign, and with the offer of the whole of Poland together with compensation for Prussia, he would be able to induce Alexander to make a peace such as would permit him to concentrate on driving the British out of Spain and Portugal and thereafter to achieve, with the help of Metternich, "a general pacification." Nor was this expectation unreasonable.

It is the misfortune of men of genius that they tend to underestimate, and therefore to ignore, the influence which people of lesser intelligence are able to exercise upon their fellows. The penalty of the cynic, who believes that human beings are actuated only by the motives of greed or fear, is that by his very cynicism he arouses passions of humiliation and resentment which in the end prove more potent than any logical calculation. The man of unflagging cerebral energy, the man of undeviating ambition, forgets moreover that glory also is subject to the law of diminishing returns, and that those who profit most by his success come in time to lose their sense of adventure, their desire for personal aggrandisement, and long only for the enjoyments of repose. And the person who has trained himself to take a purely mechanistic, or mathematical, view of life, fails to understand that what he so impatiently dismisses as "ideologies" are in fact ideas; and that what he discards as "sentiment" is the expression of deep and powerful feeling. There thus arrives a moment when "reasonable expectation" becomes too reasonable to be true. The assumptions which guided Napoleon's planning at the end of 1812 were mathematically correct assumptions; but mankind, in the last resort, is not moved by mathematics but by something else.

"Experience," writes Harold Temperley in his introduction to *The Foreign Policy of Canning*, "tends to diminish that certainty and confidence which a historian sometimes has when he judges from documents without regard to their human setting." Nobody, in fact, who has had occasion actually to witness history in the making, and to observe how infrequent and adventitious is the part played in great affairs by "policy" or planned intention, can believe thereafter that history is ever quite so simple, or quite so deliberate, as it seems in retrospect; or that the apparent relation between cause and effect was the relation which at the time, and in the circumstances, actually determined the course of affairs. Most documents are composed after the event and all too frequently they are designed, and even falsified, in the hope of giving to what was a chance or empirical decision the appearance of prescience, wisdom and intent. Nobody who has not actually watched statesmen dealing with each other can have any real idea of the immense part played in human affairs by such unavowable and often unrecognisable causes as lassitude, affability, personal affection or dislike, misunderstanding, deafness or incomplete command of a foreign language, vanity, social engagements, interruptions and momentary health. Nobody who has not watched "policy" expressing itself in day to day action can realise how seldom is the course of events determined by deliberately planned purpose or how often what in retrospect appears to have been a fully conscious intention was at the time governed and directed by that most potent of all factors,—"the chain of circumstance." Few indeed are the occasions on which any statesman sees his objective clearly before him and marches towards it with undeviating stride; numerous indeed are the occasions when a decision or an event, which at the time seemed wholly unimportant, leads almost fortuitously to another decision which is no less incidental, until, little link by link, the chain of circumstance is forged.

Some seemingly vast event may drop into the pool of time and arouse no more than a sudden momentary splash; a pebble may fall into the pool and create a ripple which, as it widens and extends, can stir the depths. Thus in the last days of 1812 it was questionable whether Alexander would decide to invade central Europe or to embark upon a crusade to liberate the Germanies from Napoleon's New Order. It was more than doubtful whether the King of Prussia would dare to defy his persecutor, or whether Metternich would wish in any circumstances to expose Austria to further hostilities. It seemed incredible that Great Britain would commit herself to an extended continental war or assume the vast responsibilities which the chain of circumstance thereafter imposed upon her. Nobody, in December 1812, can possibly have foreseen either Leipzig or Waterloo.

The pebble which set these vast waves in motion was in itself but a tiny little incident and not perhaps very creditable. It is called the "Convention of Tauroggen" and it was dropped suddenly into the pool of time on December 30, 1812.

[2]

It will be recalled that after the Treaty of Tilsit of July 1807 the Kingdom of Prussia had been reduced to a state of pitiful subservience to the French Empire. King Frederick William III [2] had in 1812 been forced by Napoleon to take sides against "his divine friend," the Emperor Alexander; it is true that he had been promised, in the event of the defeat of Russia, the acquisition of the Baltic States; yet he had entered this compact unwillingly and with a heavy heart. He was always able to display a dog-like, if somewhat bewildered, devotion to the winning side.

Under this arrangement a Prussian army corps, under General Yorck, was to assist the left flank of the French armies on the

Russian front. So soon as it became clear that the *Grande Armée* had been decisively defeated, and that all hope of acquiring the Baltic States was gone for ever, General Yorck entered into secret negotiations with his Russian opponent, General Diebitsch, and at Tauroggen on December 30, 1812, signed a convention under which the Prussian forces agreed henceforward to adopt an attitude of "neutrality" and to allow the Russian armies to march through Prussian territory. This sudden weakening of what remained of their left flank rendered it impossible for the French to make any further stand east of the Vistula. And Prussia thereby was irretrievably compromised.

Frederick William did his immediate best to repudiate General Yorck's action and to convince Napoleon that the Convention of Tauroggen had been concluded without his knowledge and consent. A legend has in fact arisen that General Yorck acted entirely upon his own initiative and in a burst of patriotic fervour. This is untrue. There is little doubt that the General had received verbal but precise instructions from his sovereign. Frederick William at the moment was striving desperately to place a foot in each camp. If we are to understand how so indecisive a man came to take so dangerous a decision we must examine for a moment the great surge of popular emotion which at the time was sweeping over Prussia and which in the end forced King Frederick William to bow before the hurricane of the *Befreiungskrieg*.

There exist in history few instances in which a victorious country has coerced and mulcted a defeated victim as ruthlessly as Napoleon exploited Prussia after 1806 and 1807. He bullied, he humiliated, he betrayed. He exposed the lovely Queen Louise—the very soul of her country's misery and courage—to insults so outrageous that the Prussian people ascribed to him responsibility for her early death. He retained his garrisons in the fortresses of the Oder; he induced the King of Saxony,² whom he had placed in nominal charge of the Grand Duchy of Warsaw, to confiscate all Prussian property in the Polish provinces; he exacted contributions from an impoverished Prussia to the extent of a thousand million francs; and by his Continental System he brought about the practical extinction of her maritime trade.

The indignities to which Prussia was exposed between 1806 and 1812 focussed upon her the sympathy of all the Germanies; it was her humiliation under Napoleon, rather than her triumphs under Bismarck, which rendered her the representative and symbol of the new Germanic spirit. Austria, with her heterogeneous Empire, with her unnatural dynastic adherence to the House of Bonaparte, appeared alien in comparison; the complacent, snobbish sneer of Metternich was contrasted with the tear-stained agonies of Queen Louise. Young Germany, in 1810, was already ripe for a profound spiritual and physical revival: a few gifted and determined men gave to this revival its peculiar impulse and direction.

All thinking Germans had been appalled by the apathy with which the German, and more specifically the Prussian, people had accepted the defeat of Jena. It became evident that the Prussians had lost, not their military confidence only, but their spiritual pride. Garrison after garrison would surrender to a mere platoon of French cavalry; the German people had abandoned all belief in themselves; they had almost abandoned their self-respect. There were men, however, who realised that the neurotic Prussian is congenitally subject to sudden alternations of extreme confidence and apathetic despair; who foresaw the ease with which the forlorn soul of Prussia could be transformed by moral rearmament, could be galvanised by a single compelling idea; and who understood how natural it was for the average Prussian, or indeed the average German, to pass (as it were in a night) from a sense of destiny to a sense of doom, and again from the helpless acceptance of doom to a feverishly active faith in destiny. What was needed, however, was the simple compelling idea: Fichte found it for them in the theme of selflessness.

In his *Reden an die Deutsche Nation of* 1807 he applied Kant's stern rule of duty to the conception of "the nation" as the one continuous reality to which each individual should devote his soul, his body and his life. The first practical symptom of the coming revivalism took an academic form and is marked by the founding of the Berlin University under Wilhelm von Humboldt in May 1809. From these beginnings there germinated with amazing rapidity what Fichte called "The blossoming of the eternal and divine in the world" but what we should call more prosaically an intensive youth movement, aimed almost consciously at acquiring physical through moral force. In June of 1808 was founded in Königsberg the *Tugendbund*, or, as it was officially called, "The Moral and Scientific Union," aiming at "the revival of morality, religion, serious taste and public spirit." The influence of the *Tugendbund* has been exaggerated, and Stein himself referred to their anti-French hysteria "as the rage of dreaming sheep." Yet there can be no doubt at all that it was the doctrine of Fichte which gave to the youth of Germany that union of purpose, that sense of personal dedication, without the discipline of which young Germans have always been apt to become ruminative, diffident, forsaken, lost.

It is an interesting fact that the founders of the Prussian revival were not themselves Prussians. Fichte and Gneisenau were Saxons; Hardenberg and Scharnhorst were Hanoverians; Stein was a Rhinelander; Arndt came from the little beech-clad island of Rügen; Niebuhr was partly Danish. It is useful moreover to recall that the older intellectual leaders of Germany had little sympathy with this new emphatic patriotism: Goethe and Wieland had been fascinated by Napoleon at Erfurt; they still believed in the old Olympian cosmopolitanism; it was the younger writers, Arndt, Kleist, Körner, Rückert, who stirred the imagination and the passions of German youth.

This intellectual and moral revival was accompanied by administrative and military reforms. It is to the credit of Frederick William III that under the influence of Queen Louise he introduced during those dark years a complete renovation of Prussian social and economic life. It was he also who in 1807 appointed a Commission for Military Reorganisation with Scharnhorst as its president and with Gneisenau as one of its members. It was this commission which devised the famous "shrinkage-system" (*Krumpersystem*) with the object of evading the provision of the Franco-Prussian convention of 1808 under which the Prussian army was to be restricted to 42,000 men for a period of at least ten years. By passing recruits rapidly through this narrow framework they provided themselves with a trained reserve of 150,000 men. It was these cadres which provided the non-commissioned officers for the new army which, with the calling up of the *Landwehr* in 1813, again rendered Prussia an important military factor in the final victory.

It was some time before Napoleon, who had a curious contempt for all Prussians, and who dismissed as doctrinaire the energies of Fichte or Humboldt, became alive to the danger. On December 16, 1808, he had, it is true, suddenly denounced *"le nommé Stein"* as an enemy of France and of the Confederation of the Rhine, confiscated his property, and ordered his arrest. Stein had been warned in time and escaped to Bohemia where he remained in hiding for three years. In May 1812, he joined the Emperor of Russia: to the chance presence of that fierce, dynamic personality at Russian headquarters in December 1812 must be ascribed, more perhaps than to any other single factor, the Tsar's decision to enter Europe and to devote his armies to the liberation of Germany.

From that moment the war ceased to be merely Franco-Russian or Peninsular: it became European.

[3]

In the last days of 1812 the disorganised remnants of the *Grande Armée* staggered across the Niemen into East Prussia. The German schoolboys, the young fanatics of the *Tugendbund*, received these splinters of a broken army with derision and delight. They danced around them in the streets of Königsberg yelling insulting songs:

> *Trommler ohne Trommel-stock,*
> *Kuirassier in Weiberock,*
> *Ritter ohne Schwert,*
> *Reiter ohne Pferd!*

*Mit Mann und Ross und Wagen
So hat sie Gott geschlagen!* *

Already the example of the Spanish partisans, who although unarmed and at first disorganised, had for years conducted a guerilla war against the French invader, had inspired the youth of Germany with hope and shame. The bonfires had already been piled and assembled, it required but a spark to set them alight. The picture of the once invincible army limping back in rags from Russia drove the youth of Germany into a frenzy of exultation. In a single night what had hitherto been but a secret underground movement broke into a wave of open resistance. However much Frederick William may have wished to hedge and temporise, he could not resist this typhoon of patriotic enthusiasm. He was swept off his feet.

Murat, with the remnants of the army, had been unable, after Yorck's defection, to retain East Prussia. On January 11, 1813, he withdrew his headquarters to Posen, where a few days later he was succeeded by the Viceroy Eugène. A line of defence was then established, running from Danzig, through Thorn, and along the Vistula. Behind this line Lagrange held the Oder with 10,000 men; and Grenier's army of 18,000 was hurrying up from Italy towards the north.

Alexander at that date disposed of some 110,000 men whom he had divided into four separate armies. The first, under Wittgenstein, after driving Murat out of East Prussia crossed the Vistula on January 13 and entered Pomerania. The second, under Tshitshagoff, was converging upon the fortress of Thorn. The third, under Kutusoff, was advancing on Plock; while the fourth, commanded by Miloradovitch, was seeking to roll up the French right wing.

Under this fourfold pressure the French armies were forced to retire to the Oder. The King of Prussia, in view of the fact

* "Drummers without drumsticks,
Cuirassiers dressed in women's clothes,
Knights without a sword,
Riders without horses,
Man, beast and cart—
Thus has God destroyed them!"

that Berlin was occupied by a French force under Augereau, escaped by night to Breslau. Already he had received from Alexander a letter assuring him that the one hope of Russia was to see Prussia restored "to her former splendour and her former power." He had not replied to this letter and had in fact assured Saint-Marsan, Napoleon's representative, that he would never enter into any agreement with the victorious Russians. At the same moment he sent Field Marshal Knesebeck to the Tsar's headquarters, carrying with him, not only a letter couched in mildly affectionate terms, but also a draft treaty of alliance. In this draft he offered to join the Russians against Napoleon on condition that he was guaranteed, not merely the possessions held by Prussia in 1806 (which it must be remembered included the Polish provinces and the town of Warsaw) but also further accessions of territory in northern Germany.

The Tsar reacted to this presumptuous suggestion with un-expected ruthlessness. He knew that Frederick William was not in a position to bargain, since on the one hand he was already irretrievably compromised by the Convention of Tauroggen, and on the other hand he could not resist the wave of popular excitement which had surged up among the Prussian people. Alexander therefore summoned Stein from Königsberg and sent him off post haste to Breslau. Stein, with his titanic, his adamantine, personality, was able in a few hours to frighten Frederick William out of his wits; he assured him (which was untrue) that the landowners of East Prussia had already sent a deputation to the Tsar demanding that Russia should assume the protection of their province; he assured him that any further hesitation might cost him his throne. In bewildered panic, on February 27, the King of Prussia agreed to the terms demanded of him. On the following day he joined Alexander at his head-quarters at Kalisch within the Polish frontier. The Treaty of Kalisch was signed and ratified on February 28, 1813.

The military clauses of this treaty provided that Russia should continue the war against Napoleon with an army of 150,000 men; Prussia for her part was to produce 80,000. These provi-sions were unambiguous and simple. The political clauses, however, were drafted with such imprecision, not to say evasiveness, that they formed the starting point of a long trail of uncertainty, misconception and distrust.

It is inevitable, in any alliance or coalition, formed for the immediate purpose of defeating a common enemy, that the several partners should hesitate to disclose their ultimate ambitions either precisely or in advance. The realisation of these objectives must obviously depend upon the nature of the final victory: if it be complete, then they may find that they have claimed too little; if it be incomplete, then they may find that they have claimed too much. Moreover, since even in the most favourable circumstances it is difficult enough to maintain unity of purpose, direction and sacrifice as between allies in war,—a natural tendency arises to postpone until victory has been won the discussion of issues which are certain to create controversy, to discourage other potential Allies, and to sow dissension. Yet the Emperor Alexander's refusal during 1813 and 1814 to disclose his real intentions exceeded the bounds of normal reticence and amounted almost to mystification. It is this mystification which runs like a thin wire (now muffled, now exposed) through the whole fabric of the Fourth Coalition.

It was known in Berlin, it was strongly suspected in Vienna, that the real aim of Alexander was to recreate a Kingdom of Poland by incorporating within it those provinces which Austria and Prussia had acquired as the result of the partitions of 1772, 1792 and 1795.[4] The Prussians, for their part, were not unprepared to accept this solution provided, as had been already hinted, that they obtained Saxony instead. The Austrians regarded any such combination with alarm. "If the Polish question," they warned Berlin, "remains unsettled, there is the danger that we may exchange the yoke of Napoleon for the yoke of Alexander." And since it was essential to secure the support of Austria for the new coalition, it was inevitable that the Polish question should, in the Treaty of Kalisch, be handled in the most enigmatic terms. Instead therefore of guaranteeing to Prussia her former frontiers, the treaty merely provided that she "should be restored to the material power which she possessed before the war of 1806." By stipulating at the same time that Prussia would receive a corridor linking her East Prussian provinces with Silesia it made it clear by implication that Prussia had agreed to abandon Warsaw to the Tsar of Russia.

Here was the hidden rift which almost split the Coalition of 1813-1814; it becomes necessary therefore to examine at the outset its origin and nature.

[4]

Exactly two years after the events which are described in this chapter (in January, that is, of 1815) Lord Castlereagh signed a secret treaty pledging Great Britain to go to war with Russia on account of Poland. It may seem incredible that any British Minister could have committed his country to hostilities against an ally to whom we were deeply indebted, and in a cause which, to the ordinary citizen, must have seemed questionable, unnecessary and remote. For twenty long years and more had the British people poured out their blood and money in order to liberate Europe from the tyranny of France; in 1814 their efforts were at last crowned with success; and it was then discovered that, so far from having created a free and stable Europe, they had incurred the danger of substituting for French domination the domination of Russia. It thus came about that the statesmen who, at the Congress of Vienna, planned the new European system, were less concerned with the danger of French militarism than with the menace of Russian expansion towards the west. And since the Russian problem centred upon the question of Poland, and since it is the latter question which will recur again and again in the pages which follow, it may be useful at this early stage to state its outlines in their simplest form.

Poland, it will be remembered, had been finally wiped off the map of Europe by the Third Partition of 1795. She had ceased, in any shape, to exist as an independent country. At Tilsit in 1807 Napoleon decided to recreate at least the nucleus of a Polish State under the title of the Duchy of Warsaw. Being anxious at the time to conciliate the Emperor Alexander he did not include within the boundaries of his new Duchy those areas of former Poland which Russia had obtained from the three partitions; the Duchy was formed from the Prussian, with the later addition of the Austrian, shares in the partitions. The area of the Duchy thus comprised some 2,750 square miles. The titular sovereignty was allotted to the King of Saxony, under the additional title of Grand Duke of Warsaw; in practice, however, Napoleon retained the administration and control entirely within his own hands.

When in 1812 the Emperor of the French embarked upon his Russian campaign he assured the Poles that he regarded it as his "second Polish war"; and it can be assumed that if, as he fully expected, he had forced Alexander to sue for peace, he would have insisted upon the recreation of pre-partition Poland and the withdrawal of Russia behind the Dwina and the Dnieper. The Poles of the little Grand Duchy of Warsaw were entranced by such a prospect; with tremendous efforts they raised an army of 80,000 men to assist Napoleon in his campaign; the remnants of this gallant force were still fighting on the side of the French at the battle of Leipzig in October 1813. Unfortunately for them it was not France but Russia who won the "Second Polish War"; and by December 1812 the armies of Alexander were in possession, not of Warsaw only, but of the whole of Poland.

When Alexander was a young man he had formed an intimate friendship with Prince Adam Czartoryski, a Polish youth of considerable intelligence, liberal sentiments and extreme beauty. On his accession he had appointed Czartoryski Foreign Minister and had made him the confidant of all his dreams of internal and external beneficence. He had promised him that, if ever the occasion offered, he would undo the great wrong done to Poland by the three partitions and would recreate a Polish State under his own protection and endow it with a liberal constitution. The opportunity had now come, not only to fulfil this promise, but to appear as the philosopher king, generous enough, and powerful enough, to put into actual practice the teachings of La Harpe.

He was aware none the less that in carrying out this plan he would be faced with grave difficulties both at home and abroad. Russian public opinion, after so great an ordeal and so vast a victory, would not have tolerated the cession (even to a satellite or protectorate) of territory which had been Russian territory, however ill-gotten, in 1811. The Russian governing classes were jealous of the Poles (whom they rightly regarded as being more intelligent than themselves) and did not like the idea of liberal institutions being accorded to Poland which it would be disturbing, dangerous and premature to accord to Russia herself.

However great might be the objections raised to his scheme by opinion in Russia, they were as nothing compared to the perturbation which any such idea was bound to arouse among her European neighbours. It was not to be expected that Austria or even Prussia would share the Tsar's desire to give practical expression to La Harpe's teaching or even begin to understand the sacred nature of the promises which, in his romantic youth, he had made to Czartoryski. Metternich and Hardenberg would examine the proposal in far more realistic terms. They would interpret it as a scheme whereby, under the guise of liberation and generosity, the Tsar was seeking to establish himself in the very midst of Central Europe and to extend Russian authority to within a few miles only of Berlin, Breslau and Vienna. And they would point out that, whereas Russia herself was not prepared to allot one inch of her own territory for the benefit of the new Kingdom of Poland, they themselves were being asked to surrender the vast and valuable provinces which they had acquired from the partitions. The only reply—and it was a disagreeable reply—which Alexander could make to such protests was that it was he, after all, who had defeated Napoleon and liberated Europe; that his armies were in possession of the whole of Poland,—Russian, Austrian and Prussian—and that, if they objected to his proposals, it was for them to turn him out by force.

It thus came about that the Tsar hesitated from month to month, from year to year, to define exactly what were his intentions in regard to Poland. And since a Polish settlement would inevitably involve some "compensations" at least to Austria and Prussia; and since these compensations would in their turn affect the whole future map of Germany and Italy; it is evident that the Tsar's mystifications regarding Poland, so disturbingly forecast by the vague terms of the Treaty of Kalisch, created a great unknown factor which, as will be seen, was constantly confusing and sapping the unity of the Coalition.

Meanwhile, however, under Stein's exorbitant pressure, Frederick William signed and ratified the Treaty of Kalisch on February 28, 1813. On March 16 following Prussia formally declared war on France. And on March 25 an appeal was launched, under the signature of Kutusoff, calling upon all Germans to rise against the oppressor.

The War of Liberation had begun.

3. The Intervention of Austria

THE PLAN for a spring campaign agreed to by the Russian and
Prussian generals at Kalisch in February 1813 might well have
proved successful had it been carried out with average co-ordination, courage and speed. The idea was that the allied armies,
under the supreme command of Kutusoff, should advance into
Germany in three main prongs. The right wing, numbering
some 50,000 men, under the command of Wittgenstein, Yorck
and Bülow, was to march upon Magdeburg by way of Berlin.
The left wing, numbering some 40,000 under the command of
Blücher, was to aim at Dresden. And Kutusoff himself, with

what was called the main army (although its numbers were no more than 35,000) was to follow in between.

They must have known that the Viceroy, Prince Eugène, was gathering together the scattered garrisons and detachments of the French armies in Germany with the intention of making a stand upon the Elbe. They must have known also that Napoleon in Paris was straining every effort to create a second *Grande Armée* which would advance into Germany the moment it could receive the necessary equipment. Their only hope therefore was decisively to defeat Eugene before Napoleon arrived.

Kutusoff was ailing, obstinate, and in principle opposed to all European ventures; he remained at Kalisch and refused to move. "We can cross the Elbe all right," he remarked, "but before long we shall recross it and with a bloody nose." It was only on March 7 that the main Russian army was set in motion and by March 18 it had got no further than Bunzlau in Silesia. It was there, on March 20, that Kutusoff died. His post as supreme commander was at first entrusted to Wittgenstein, and after the misfortunes which thereupon ensued, to Barclay de Tolly.

On April 16 Napoleon left Paris and on April 25 he joined the army at Erfurt. He had at his disposal a mixed force of 145,000 men, including 10,000 cavalry and 400 guns. Against this formidable army the Russians and the Prussians could scarcely muster more than 80,000. At 5 A.M. on May 3 Napoleon established contact with the allies in the neighbourhood of Lützen and a fierce fight ensued around the village of Gross-Gorschen. The allies were obliged, as Kutusoff had foreseen, to recross the Elbe and to abandon Dresden. Dissensions thereupon arose. The Prussians insisted that the armies should move northwards in order to defend Berlin; the Russians urged a withdrawal to Breslau. Frederick William was in despair. "This is Jena all over again," he stammered. "I see myself back in Memel." Alexander, on the other hand, displayed surprising calm. It was under his impulsion that it was agreed to leave the defence of Berlin to Bülow and to concentrate the bulk of the joint armies at Bautzen.

Napoleon remained at Dresden until May 17, reorganising his forces and accumulating reserves. On May 20 he moved upon Bautzen with 205,000 men. The allies were again defeated and again recriminations arose between them. The Russian Generals this time wished to retreat into Poland; the Prussians were anxious to defend Silesia. Again Alexander intervened and a compromise was reached under which the joint armies would fall back upon Pilsen.

Had Napoleon at this stage pursued the Russians and Prussians with his accustomed vigour there can be little doubt that he would have secured a victory more decisive even than Lützen or Bautzen and perhaps have brought the campaign to a conclusion. On June 1, however, he accepted Austria's good offices, and an armistice was signed at Pläswitz on June 4. This armistice was timed to last until July 10 and was subsequently extended for another four weeks.

It has remained a mystery why Napoleon consented to this armistice when, by a final effort, he could certainly have nipped the Fourth Coalition in the bud. Years afterwards at St. Helena he admitted that the Armistice of Pläswitz was the greatest error of his life. The explanation which he then gave is not convincing. "I saw the decisive hour drawing near," he said; "my star had waned; and I felt the reins slipping from my hands." Such a statement does not represent the actual mood or thought of Napoleon in the early summer of 1813.

His victories at Lützen and Bautzen had not in fact been overwhelming; the allies had been able to retire in good order and his own casualties had been heavier than theirs. He had been much hampered by a lack of cavalry and his newly as-sembled army, being largely composed of young recruits, had not proved itself either efficient or well disciplined. The high figure of stragglers and deserters which had marked the advance from Lützen to Bautzen did not argue well for their morale. He was much incommoded, and even alarmed, by the activities of German partisans upon his lines of communication and was obliged to recognise in the uprising of the German peoples a force which, in that it was irrational and therefore incalculable, defied immediate computation. He was rendered anxious moreover by the ambiguous and even menacing attitude of Austria, who was, he knew, placing her armies upon an immediate military footing. He hoped by diplomatic means to separate Russia from Prussia. This hope was not without practical foundation. The Prussian people, having recovered from the first rapture of liberation, were beginning to resent the exactions and manners of their liberators. "Better the French as enemies," ran the catch-word, "than the Russians as friends." And finally Napoleon's marshals and ministers, who wished to devote their later years to the enjoyment of the fortunes and honours which they had accumulated upon the battlefields of the Empire, were showing themselves increasingly recalcitrant, sullen and war-weary. It was the combination of these circumstances and considerations which in June 1813 induced Napoleon to consent to the disastrous armistice of Pläswitz. All of which amounts to saying that the ordeals of 1812 had for the moment (but only for the moment) robbed him of his accustomed temerity, self-confidence and resolve.

[2]

I intend in this narrative to introduce my main characters in the order of their appearance. The logical sequence of the story, beginning as it does on the Beresina and ending at Waterloo, extending as it does in ever widening ripples from east to west, falls naturally into four main Acts. In the first Act, namely, the tremendous drama or *desis*, of 1812, the centre of the stage is held by Alexander. The second Act, which extends from December 30, 1812, to June 4, 1813, from the Convention of Tauroggen to the Armistice of Pläswitz, is concerned with the sudden uprising of the Prussian and Germanic peoples, with the recreation of a second great army by Napoleon and with the victories which it achieved at Lützen and at Bautzen. The theme of the third Act is the intervention of Austria culminating in the battle of Leipzig in October 1813; the limelights during this Act converge upon Metternich. And in the long fourth Act, which covers the first and second abdications of Napoleon and the Congress of Vienna, two new characters hold the stage. The light sparkles upon the diamond facets of Talleyrand's brilliance; it bathes in a calm lustre the cool and simple imperturbability of Castlereagh. To these four Acts I shall add an epilogue. In this I shall show how Great Britain, as a god in the machine, having intervened in the *lusis* of the tragedy, thereafter, and by slow gradations, resumed her natural isolationism; and how, having by her intervention, tautened and solidified the Coalition, she caused it by her increasing abstentions to disintegrate.

The armistice of Pläswitz, in that it introduces an interval of ten weeks between Acts I and II and Acts III and IV, provides a useful interlude in which to consider the character of Metternich and the nature of Austrian policy; and to indicate the first tentative steps by which Great Britain (who until then had played but a maritime, peninsular or financial part in the coalition), came to assume an increasingly continental role and in the end to direct, perhaps even to dominate, the councils of the United Nations.

It is not easy to achieve an unbiassed estimate of Metternich.[1] To philosophic historians, such as Mr. Algernon Cecil, he appears as the wise and patient champion of the conservative principle; to the Whig historians he seems the very personification of reaction.

In trying to avoid these extremes of partiality or prejudice one is from the outset disconcerted by the horrible deterrent of Metternich's complacency and conceit. His own memoirs, the sententious letters which he addressed to Princess Lieven, disclose a degree of self-satisfaction which it is difficult either to forget or to forgive. He was profoundly convinced of the infallibility of his own judgment, of the unerring prescience which he had always shown; he was quite prepared to falsify facts and documents in order to substantiate this estimate of his powers of diagnosis or his gifts of foresight. "Error," he remarked in his old age to Monsieur Guizot, "has never approached my mind."

The irritation aroused in his contemporaries by this unutterable self-satisfaction was not diminished by Metternich's pose as a man of rank and fashion, as a potential artist or scientist, who had been forced by cruel circumstances to devote his amazing talents to the drab business of political affairs. He was by nature a lazy man, and his indolence jarred upon the nerves of those who held that even the most mobile intelligence must be fortified by the study of hard facts. Talleyrand complained of his "inconceivable superficiality"; Castlereagh regarded him as "a political harlequin." "He is," wrote Aberdeen, "I repeat to you, not a very clever man"; Count Bernstorff called him "subtle rather than vigilant"; Sainte Aulaire, when French Ambassador at Vienna, remarked that he "reserved to himself the privilege of never being wrong." "I never shared," wrote the Duke of Wellington, "the view that he was a great statesman; he was a society hero and nothing more": Fournier calls him, cruelly, "*ein Virtuose des Moments*"; and Edward Cooke, being a good English civil servant, reproved him for being "most intolerably loose and giddy with women." Professor Webster is even more lapidary in his condemnation: "A timid statesman," he writes, "though fertile in diplomatic expedients, he was an opportunist, pure and simple."

The distaste which Metternich aroused among his contemporaries was not softened by his extreme pomposity of manner. He was a handsome man, with his finely powdered hair, the uniform of a Knight of Malta with its black facings, the jewel of the Golden Fleece hanging at his neck. He enjoyed displaying his knowledge of foreign languages and would, in his harsh nasal voice, feel equally at home in German, French, English, Italian and even Russian. That is not a gift which enhances popularity. In addition he was intolerably prolix both in conversation and on paper. There were moments when even Princess Lieven found Metternich a bore. "Very long," she records of one of their later conversations, "very slow, very heavy."

Yet when all this is said, when all the contemporary dislike of him has been recorded, the fact remains that only a most exceptional man could have ruled Austria, and played so vast a part in European politics for a period of almost forty years. What, therefore, was the secret of Metternich's influence and power?

[3]

It is insufficient to contend, as some have contended, that Metternich owed his continuance in office to the personal friendship and loyalty of Francis I.[2] In his own memoirs Metternich has represented his sovereign as a man of infinite sagacity, rectitude and charm. This is an incorrect portrait. Francis was a lazy and somewhat puerile person. "When I see you enter my study," he once remarked to Cobenzl, "my heart sinks at the thought of all the business you bring with you." He was happier when engaged in his workshop stamping seals onto sealing wax or merely cooking toffee at the stove. It is certain that he found it a relief to place the affairs of state into the deft, competent and subservient hands of a permanent Minister. But this is not the only explanation. Throughout his life Metternich was exposed to bitter criticism and opposition within Austria itself. In his early years Stadion, in his later years Kolowrat, did all they possibly could to secure his downfall. Nor should it be forgotten that after the death of Francis he remained in power for a further thirteen years in spite of the consolidated opposition of the Archdukes and their adherents. Such tenacity must have been composed of sterner stuff.

Among the remarks (and they were numerous) which Metternich made about himself there is one which appears sincere enough, and which is difficult to reconcile with the charge of invariable opportunism. "I am bad at skirmishes," he said, "but I am good at campaigns." Flattered as he was by all the talk of a "Metternich system," he affirmed none the less that he had no system, but only certain fixed principles. It is in fact arguable that, although in the day to day conduct of affairs he displayed an opportunism which bounded upon levity, the main principles which guided his political course were unvarying and rigid. What were those principles?

In his attitude both to internal and to external affairs the whole of Metternich's political theory can be summarised in the one word "equilibrium." He interpreted that word in an almost mechanical sense, having a tendency to approach politics as he approached the astronomical clocks, the astrolabes and the other scientific instruments with which it was his hobby, in spare moments, to amuse himself. In internal affairs the pendulum had swung too far to the left and in the direction of chaos; repression was necessary to restore the balanced functioning of the machine. The only antidote to the disarrangements of revolution was the sacred word "stability." Similarly in international affairs the Balance of Power was an almost cosmic principle. Without internal and external equilibrium there could be no repose; and repose was essential to the normal happiness of man.

It was this belief in national and international balance which, while it led him to distrust all extremes, did create in him what Mr. E. L. Woodward has well called "his sensitiveness to the existence of general European interests." Metternich, sincerely and consistently, believed in the "Concert of Europe" as something transcending the particular interests of the individual European States. "Politics," he wrote in a revealing passage, "is the science of the vital interests of States, in its widest meaning. Since, however, an isolated State no longer exists and is found only in the annals of the heathen world . . . we must always view the *Society* of States as the essential condition of the modern world. The great axioms of political science proceed from the knowledge of the true political interests of *all* States; it is upon these general interests that rests the guarantee of their existence. The establishing of international relations on the basis of reciprocity under the guarantee of respect for acquired rights . . . constitutes in our time the essence of politics, of which diplomacy is merely the daily application. Between the two there is in my opinion the same difference as between science and art."

In the pursuance of his art Metternich's methods were flexible in the extreme; but he remained faithful to the principles of his science. His hatred of Jacobinism, his constant use of such phrases as "the revolutionary menace," certainly convinced his contemporaries and successors that he was a fanatical reactionary. "You do not," wrote Princess Lieven, "feel drawn to constitutions." That was an understatement of an undeniable fact. But Metternich did not regard himself as unprogressive. "I should," he once wrote, "have been born in 1900 and have had the twentieth century before me." We may smile at this anachronism; but is it in fact so very fantastic? Might not Metternich have understood even better than our own Liberals the true meaning and implications of the League of Nations? Might he not, with his acute sense of the solidarity of international interests, have preached, far in advance of his time, the limitations of State sovereignty?

It is this conviction, in which he never faltered, it is this sense of the community of European interests, which explains, not only his continuous control over the Austrian Empire, but the influence which he was able, for almost half a century, to exercise over the statesmen and rulers of his age.

[4]

In dealing with the delicate situation which confronted Austria in 1812 and 1813, Metternich possessed one advantage which was denied to the other leaders of the Coalition: he understood Napoleon. The picture which Sorel has painted of him as the wily diplomatist luring Napoleon to his doom and thereafter exacting vengeance upon Napoleon's unhappy son, is an exaggerated picture. Metternich never concealed the fascination which Napoleon's personality exercised upon him. "Conversation with him," he wrote, "has always had for me a charm difficult to define." "He would," he wrote again, "have played a prominent part at whatever epoch he had appeared." Metternich never denied his admiration for "the remarkable perspicacity and the great simplicity of the processes of Napoleon's mind." At the same time he cherished no illusion as to the suicidal nature of Napoleon's ambition. He was among the first, for instance, to realise that the Spanish expedition was a purely personal adventure and would, if it lasted, place an intolerable strain upon the patience of the French people. "It is no longer," he said, "the nation that fights." He foresaw the inevitable end, but wished to postpone Austria's intervention until the hour when all others would be exhausted and he could intervene, or mediate, with the maximum effect. He therefore played for time.

This, in fact, had always been his policy and method from the very day that he assumed office. On the morrow of Wagram he had advised the Emperor Francis that the aim of Austria should be "to tack, to efface ourselves, to come to terms with the victor. Only thus we may perhaps preserve our existence till the day of general deliverance." It was with this in mind that in 1810 he persuaded the Emperor Francis to sacrifice his own daughter on the altar of Napoleon's dynastic ambition. He was prepared to submit to almost any humiliation provided that he could maintain Austria intact until the moment of the final decision.

When the French invaded Russia in 1812 Metternich made a miscalculation. He did not believe that Napoleon would secure an overwhelming victory; still less did he foresee that Alexander would secure an overwhelming victory; his estimate was that Napoleon would achieve a partial victory. With this in mind he decided to insure himself with both sides. With Napoleon he made a limited liability treaty, under which Austria would supply a contingent of 30,000 who were to operate under the command of an Austrian general. At the same time he assured the Emperor Alexander that "Russia would find an active friend in the French camp without having to meet an enemy in war." And in fact the assistance given to Napoleon by Austria during the 1812 campaign was so tepid as to be hardly co-belligerent.

Already by October 1812 he realised that Napoleon would obtain no rapid decision in Russia and that the moment for Austria's intervention might not be far distant. He therefore disclosed to the Prussian Minister Hardenberg the general outlines of his plan for a "general pacification." France was to renounce her European conquests and retire to her "natural limits," meaning thereby the frontiers of the Pyrenees and the Rhine. The German States were to recover their independence under the joint protection of Austria and Prussia. Russia was to resume the position she had occupied before the Treaty of Tilsit. And Austria would annex Italian territory as far as the Mincio.

The disaster to Napoleon's armies in Russia filled Metternich with consternation. In place of the nicely balanced situation on which he had calculated, he was faced with a most unbalanced situation. The danger had arisen that Alexander would make a direct peace with Napoleon and that Austria might find herself ignored. In countering this danger Metternich acted with promptitude and skill. He sent Count Bubna to Napoleon and warned him that he should not count too much on the dynastic ties between France and Austria or upon the reputed rivalry between Austria and Prussia. He sent Count Stadion to the Tsar's headquarters to warn him that Napoleon was by no means vanquished and would be certain to raise a large new army and return to the attack. And he sent Baron Wessenberg to London (a capital which he had hitherto ignored) to suggest to the British Government that the moment for a "general continental peace" had now arrived. This latter mission was not successful. The British Government made it clear that they had no desire to make peace with Napoleon, until they had secured their own objectives in regard to Maritime Rights and the Low Countries and fulfilled their pledges to Spain, Portugal, Sicily and Sweden. They were shocked that Metternich should suggest a purely continental transaction; and they refused to accept Austrian mediation. "Nothing," wrote Lord Liverpool, "could be more abject than the councils of Vienna at this time": and even Castlereagh, who had at least some conception of the embarrassment of Austria's position, complained of Metternich's "spirit of submission" to France. They urged Austria to resume her historic role as "the ancient and natural Protector of the Germanic body." And Baron Wessenberg was attacked in the public prints, ran out of money, was left without instructions and information by his own Government, and was not received in London Society.

Metternich then decided to follow up these subsidiary missions by more direct action. His policy at the time was governed by the consideration that, although it might be possible to induce Napoleon to accept a "continental peace" (that is, a peace between France, Russia and Prussia and as such providing only for a settlement in Eastern, Central and Southern Europe), it would not be possible, especially after Lützen and Bautzen, to obtain a "maritime peace" (that is, a peace which would include British claims regarding Maritime Rights, the colonies, Spain, the Low Countries and Sicily). His aim therefore was completely to exclude Great Britain from the negotiations and thereby to isolate her from the Coalition.

With this in mind he visited the Tsar at his headquarters at Opocno and accompanied him to Reichenbach. It was there that he concluded with Russia and Prussia the Treaty of Reichenbach (June 24, 1813) under which he agreed to put four demands to Napoleon and to join in war against him if these demands were rejected. His four points were as follows: The dissolution of the Duchy of Warsaw, the enlargement of Prussia, the restitution to Austria of her former Illyrian provinces, and the re-establishment of the Hanseatic towns of Hamburg and Lübeck.

Fortified by this agreement he left immediately for Dresden where Napoleon had established his headquarters outside the city, in the neighbourhood of the Elsterwiese, and in the residence which the unfortunate Frederick Augustus had constructed for his beloved favourite, the Italian Camillo Marcolini.

The famous interview of June 26, 1813, which lasted for nine hours, began badly. Napoleon greeted Metternich with the words: "So you want war? Well, you shall have it. I annihilated the Prussian army at Lützen; I smashed the Russians at Bautzen; now you want to have your turn. Very well—we shall meet at Vienna." Metternich indicated that the issues of peace and war lay in the hands of the Emperor of the French. "Well, and what is it that you want?" snapped Napoleon. "That I should dishonour myself? Never! I know how to die; but never shall I cede one inch of territory. Your sovereigns, who were born upon the throne, can allow themselves to be beaten twenty times, and will always return to their capitals; I cannot do that; I am a self-made soldier." Metternich reminded him that Austria was offering France her mediation, not her neutrality. Russia and Prussia had accepted his mediation; they had agreed to the four points of Reichenbach; it was for Napoleon to do likewise and meanwhile an Austrian army fully mobilised and numbering 250,000 men was awaiting his decision. Napoleon, somewhat naturally, questioned the accuracy of these figures. Metternich countered by questioning the effectiveness of Napoleon's own troops. "I have seen your soldiers," he said to him. "They are no more than children. And when these infants have been wiped out, what will you have left?" It was this remark which provoked Napoleon's supreme outburst: he flung his hat into the corner and yelled at Metternich: "You are not a soldier," he yelled. "You know nothing of what goes on in a soldier's mind. I grew up upon the field of battle, and a man such as I am cares little for the life of a million men." Metternich did not offer to pick up the hat which remained in its corner; he leant against a little table which stood between the windows and said calmly to Napoleon, "If only the words that you have just uttered could echo from one end of France to the other!"

Napoleon at this pulled himself together and adopted a quieter tone; he began, as was his wont, to pace round the drawing room of Camillo Marcolini, talking to Metternich in insistent tones. On his second round he noticed his own hat in the corner and picked it up himself. He spoke more calmly. "I may lose my throne," he said, "but I shall bury the whole world in its ruins."

It was getting dark; it was already half past eight at night; Napoleon walked with Metternich to the door of the antechamber. He was by now calm, almost affectionate. He tapped the Austrian on the shoulder. "No," he said, "you will never make war against me." "Sire," Metternich replied (or says that he replied), "you are a lost man."

Outside, the Ministers and the Marshals crowded round Metternich. Berthier, the Prince of Neuchâtel, whispered to him: "Remember that Europe has need of peace. Above all, France—there is only one thing that she longs for, and that is peace."

Metternich, on returning to his Dresden hotel, sent an express to Prince Schwarzenberg, the Austrian commander in chief, asking how long it would take to put the army upon a complete war footing. The Prince replied immediately that if he could have another twenty days the forces already mobilised could be increased by 75,000. It thus became Metternich's first object to obtain from the French a four weeks' extension of the Armistice of Pläswitz. With this in mind he remained on three days at Dresden, conducting his negotiations through Maret, Duke of Bassano. Obtaining no satisfactory reply he ordered his carriages to be ready at 7 A.M. the next morning; a few minutes before that hour he received a note from Maret saying that Napoleon wished to see him before his departure. He found the Emperor of the French pacing up and down the gravelled paths of the Marcolini garden; together they entered the little study where Maret joined them. Napoleon asked Metternich what he desired. Metternich drew a piece of paper towards him and wrote down four conditions:

I—The Emperor of the French accepts the armed mediation of the Emperor of Austria.

II—Representatives of the belligerent Powers will on July 10 meet at Prague to confer with representatives of the mediating Powers.

III—August 10 is fixed as the time limit for these negotiations.

IV—Until that day all military operations will be suspended.

Napoleon accepted these four conditions. An hour later Metternich left Dresden to return to his Emperor at Gitschin in Bohemia.

[5]

It is unfortunate that the only account of the Marcolini interviews is that provided in Metternich's own memoirs. Writing after the event he was anxious to demonstrate, not only his own dexterity and courage, but the eagle vision with which he had foreseen, and prepared for, Napoleon's overthrow. It may well have been that he was impressed by what he saw of the condition of the new French army, even as he cannot have remained unaffected by the hints and prayers whispered to him by Napoleon's Marshals in the Marcolini anterooms. Yet it would not have been within his principles to desire anything so definite or so extreme as the complete downfall of the Napoleonic system, which after all stood for those elements of discipline and order which he much preferred either to the liberalism of Stein or the mysticism of the Emperor Alexander. What he would assuredly have preferred was a compromise solution under which France would have surrendered much, Russia gained but a little, Prussia have been restored to something approaching her former power, and Austria have established herself in northern Italy and Illyria. He may even have hoped at first that, in spite of Napoleon's implied rejection of the Reichenbach proposals, there might emerge from the Prague Conference some sort of "continental pacification." Such as would face the pugnacious British with a separate peace on the part of Russia, Prussia and Austria.

If so, his hopes were doomed to early disappointment. There were four circumstances which rendered the Prague Conference an unreality from the very day of its opening. In the first place, as Metternich might have realised, it is rare in history to find that any "armed mediation" secures peace; the mere fact that an army is waiting fully mobilised provokes the atmosphere and expectation, not of peace, but of war. In the second place, Caulaincourt, Napoleon's representative, being loyally anxious to save Napoleon against himself, and having no illusions either regarding the state of French opinion or the condition of the new French armies, privately urged the Allies to consent to no compromise solution. "Get us back to France," he whispered, "whether it be by peace or war, and you will earn the gratitude of thirty million Frenchmen." In the third place two British representatives, Lord Cathcart,[3] and Sir Charles Stewart,[4] had for some weeks been attached to Russian and Prussian head-quarters. They made it clear that Great Britain for her part would never subscribe to a peace in which her own interests and commitments were disregarded; and that no further subsidies would be forthcoming so long as she was excluded from the inner councils of the Allies. Their representations were strength-ened by the fact that while the Prague Conference was still in session, news arrived that at Vitoria on June 21 Lord Welling-ton had totally defeated the French armies, captured all their equipment, 143 guns and one million pounds in cash, and driven them back in confusion to the Pyrenees.[5] And in the fourth place Napoleon himself remained obdurate in his conviction that to surrender a single one of his conquests would be to sacrifice his throne.

And thus, on the night of August 12, 1813, the bonfires on the hills around Prague proclaimed to the world that the peace Conference had been disbanded; and that the armies of the Austrian Empire would now march against Napoleon together with their Prussian and their Russian allies. Metternich's daring, and it must be admitted brilliant, diplomatic offensive had collapsed.

4. The Frankfurt Proposals

[November-December 1813]

Military developments between August 12, 1813, and November 2
—The Battle of Leipzig, October 16-19—The Allied Sovereigns
enter Leipzig and on November 2 Napoleon withdraws his armies
across the Rhine—Dissensions within the Coalition—British
Maritime Rights—The complications introduced into the original
scheme by the advent of Austria—British policy as midway between that of Austria and Russia—The basis of British policy—
The Pitt memorandum to Vorontzov of 1804—Definition of
British rights and interests—The tendency of all peace-makers to
consider the future in terms of the past—The avoidance of
controversial issues—The danger of attributing false motives to
the statesmen of the past—Castlereagh's application of Pitt's
principles—His liabilities and his assets—His immediate and his
ultimate objectives—The Aberdeen mission of September 1813—
Aberdeen concludes a subsidy treaty with Metternich but is unable
to secure a general treaty—Dissension among the Allies on the
subject of invading France—Metternich's desire for a compromise peace—His meeting with Saint Aignan—The Frankfurt
proposals of November 8, 1813—Aberdeen's acceptance of these
—Castlereagh reaches the Continent.

THIS book is not a study of military events: it is an examination,
in terms of the past, of the factors which create dissension
between independent States temporarily bound together in a
coalition.

The political and diplomatic quarrels which all but shattered
the Grand Alliance of 1812-1815 were reflected in, and en-
venomed by, the disputes and jealousies which arose among
the several commanders in the field as well as by their constant
dissension regarding the strategic objects of the campaign.
Before considering the political difficulties which arose it is
necessary to record, as shortly as possible, the military events

which took place between the accession of Austria on August 12, 1813, and Napoleon's retreat across the Rhine on November 2.

The supreme command of the main allied armies had, after much bitterness, been entrusted nominally at least, to the Austrian commander in chief, Prince Karl von Schwarzenberg, a soldier of great personal integrity but one whose natural diffidence was increased by an almost pathological terror of Napoleon. The fact that the two Emperors and the King of Prussia were continuously present at Prince Schwarzenberg's headquarters did something at least to maintain the unity of allied strategy and to mitigate the independence, not to say the disobedience, of the Prussian, Russian and Austrian generals who commanded the several corps. Yet throughout the autumn campaign of 1813 the strategy of the allies was hampered by uncertainty of purpose and division of counsel. Had Napoleon possessed the self-reliance and rapidity of decision which had been his before the Russian campaign, he would have succeeded in separating the mixed forces arrayed against him and destroying them one by one. Fortunately the nervous diffidence which paralysed allied action was, for the moment, matched by a mood of sullen inertia on the part of Napoleon himself.

By the middle of August 1813 the armies of the Coalition— the Russians, Prussians, Austrians, Swedes and Mecklenburgers —numbered in all some 860,000 men. Against these Napoleon, by calling up all his available resources in France and in the Confederation of the Rhine, was able to muster an army of some 700,000. The forces of the Coalition were, under the plan drawn up at Reichenbach, divided into three groups: first the main army under Schwarzenberg based upon Bohemia; secondly an army of some 120,000 in Brandenburg under the Crown Prince Bernadotte; [1] and thirdly the army of Silesia, some 50,000 strong, under Prussian command. Instead of attacking the main army immediately, Napoleon in a fit of ill-temper lunged out into a diversion against Bernadotte. On August 21 Bülow defeated Oudinot at Gross Beeren and saved Berlin. On August 23 Blücher defeated MacDonald in Silesia. On August 26 and 27 Napoleon defeated the main Coalition army outside

Dresden. On August 30, however, this defeat was redeemed by the allied victory over Vandamme at Kulm. And on September 6, Marshal Ney was beaten at Dennewitz. By that date Napoleon had lost some 150,000 men; instead, however, of withdrawing before the allied armies could concentrate he hung on obstinately to Dresden and allowed Blücher to effect a crossing of the Elbe.

It was thus in the first week of October that Napoleon was obliged to withdraw to the neighbourhood of Leipzig. He had been able to concentrate there a force of 190,000 men with 734 guns; the allied armies converging from north and south upon the city numbered some 300,000 men with 1,335 guns. The battle of Leipzig opened on October 16: by the evening of that day the French, in spite of heavy losses, had gained the advantage. The morning of October 17 found Napoleon discouraged and indecisive. He sent a message through General Count Merfeldt to the Emperor of Austria asking for an armistice, and suggesting peace negotiations.

No reply was, for the moment at least, returned to these overtures; Napoleon decided to offer battle again upon the following day. On October 18 the French troops were driven back upon the city of Leipzig, their Saxon auxiliaries deserted to the allies, and by the evening Napoleon ordered a general retreat. There was only one bridge across the Pleisse and this became heavily congested during the night; disorder and confusion spread through the ranks and Napoleon himself was swept off his feet by the surge of soldiery. At daybreak upon October 19 the allies swarmed into the city and the bridge across the Pleisse was blown up. The Italian and German troops under Napoleon's command immediately deserted to the Allies; the French and Polish rear guards fought a gallant defence, but were obliged to surrender. Generals MacDonald, Bertrand, Lauriston and Reynier were taken prisoner; the French losses were estimated at 120,000 killed and wounded; victory was assured.

With the remnants of his army Napoleon retreated towards the Rhine. The Allies, owing to the exhaustion of their troops and disagreement among their generals, were unable either to intercept or adequately to pursue him. Brushing aside the Bavarians who, under General Wrede, sought to intercept him at Hanau, Napoleon reached Mainz on November 2 and at once crossed the Rhine. Of his second *Grande Armée*, only 70,000 men remained, of whom shortly afterwards some 30,000 died of typhus. The liberation of Germany was complete.

On October 20 the Allied Sovereigns entered the town of Leipzig in triumph. As they passed by the Hôtel de Prusse a pathetic and expectant figure was observed bowing amicably to them from the balcony. It was Frederick Augustus, King of Saxony. His greetings were not returned. On the following day he was curtly notified by the Emperor Alexander that he must consider himself a prisoner of war. He was transported to Berlin where he was booed by the populace. He was thereafter interned under allied supervision in the castle of Friedrichsfelde. His kingdom meanwhile was occupied and administered by a Russian general, Prince Repnin.

[2]

The basis of any Alliance, or Coalition, is an agreement between two or more sovereign States to subordinate their separate interests to a single purpose. In 1813, as in 1914 and 1939, that purpose was the defeat of a common enemy. So soon, however, as ultimate victory seems assured, the consciousness of separate interests tends to overshadow the sense of common purpose. The citizens of the several victorious countries seek rewards for their own sacrifices and compensations for their own suffering; they are apt to interpret these rewards and compensations in terms, not of international, but of national requirements. And the jealousies, rivalries and suspicions which in any protracted war arise between partners to an Alliance generate poisons which war-wearied arteries are too inelastic to eliminate.

Alliances, moreover, seldom assume their completed shape in the early stages of a conflict; there is generally an original nucleus of resistance around which the Coalition gradually forms. This process of development in its turn creates two causes of dissension. In the first place, the original partners, who stood alone when the danger was at its height, feel that it is they who merit priority of consideration: the later partners—whose assistance, although delayed, may have been decisive—feel that it was owing to their intervention that victory was won. In the second place, whereas the adjustment of war-aims as between the original partners may, owing to the presence of an immediate common danger, have proved comparatively simple, the arrival of new partners is bound to introduce fresh claims and further complications. And since the late arrivals usually feel less exhausted and more righteous than the original combatants, they are apt to press their claims with greater vigour than are those whose war-weariness has become acute.

The Coalition of 1813 furnishes a useful illustration of these natural processes. Great Britain, whose interests, as will be seen, were to a large extent detached from the interests of the other partners, had for more than twenty years stood alone against French domination when others collaborated or collapsed. In the Peninsular campaigns she had been the first to destroy the legend of Napoleon's invincibility. In 1812, as a result of the blind self-assurance of Napoleon, Russia had been forced into the conflict and had achieved unforeseen victory. When Prussia, owing to the pressure of German public opinion, joined the Alliance, it still seemed a comparatively simple thing to adjust the separate interests of the three partners to the common interest of the Coalition as a whole. The Emperor Alexander, as it then seemed, could liberate Poland, establish therein a "friendly government" and thereby render Poland a satellite kingdom subservient to the will of Russia. Prussia would be compensated for the loss of her Polish provinces by being allowed to annex Saxony; for that purpose it was necessary to create the fiction that the King of Saxony had behaved with such turpitude towards the common cause that he was unworthy of the slightest consideration. Great Britain could do what she liked with the Low Countries, Spain, Portugal, Sicily and the colonies and could preserve, if she insisted, her own strange theories regarding Maritime Rights.² And France, apart from the vexed question of Antwerp, would be restricted to her "natural" frontiers—namely, the Pyrenees, the Alps and the Rhine.

The common interest would thus be served by rendering France incapable of any further aggression. The separate interests of the three partners could also be satisfied: Russia and Prussia could obtain their desires in the east and north, whereas Great Britain would receive all the compensation that she could wish for in the west and upon the seven seas.

The intervention of Austria disturbed this simple pattern. Not only did it raise the intricate question of Italy and Illyria but it created a serious obstacle to the tacit arrangement come to at Kalisch between the Emperor Alexander and King Frederick William of Prussia regarding Poland and Saxony. On the one hand Austria was determined not to allow Russia, under the device of a free and independent Poland, to extend her frontier almost to the banks of the Oder. On the other hand she had no desire at all to see Prussia strengthened within the Germanic Body by the acquisition of the whole of Saxony. And since the Russo-Prussian design and the Austrian objections tended to cancel each other out, a situation was created in which Great Britain, by throwing her weight to one side or the other of the balance, could exercise an unexpectedly powerful influence.

What, therefore, in the autumn of 1813, was the policy, what were the desires, of the British Government and people?

[3]

"The English," snapped out Frederick the Great in the last year of his life, "have no system"; and it is indeed true that British policy prefers to be empirical. "It is not usual," wrote Palmerston in 1841, "for England to enter into engagements with reference to cases which have not actually arisen. . . . Parliament might probably not approve of an engagement which should bind England prospectively." "I have told Her Majesty," wrote Lord John Russell to Granville, ten years later, "that it is not the policy of this country to make engage-

ments except on a view of the circumstances of the moment."
Yet although our policy may seem elastic, there do exist certain
principles and interests which remain constant. Prominent among
those principles are (or were), the balance of power, the
independence of the Low Countries, and the free use of naval
supremacy.

In few cases, however, has British policy been defined with
such precision or foresight as in the formula which guided
Lord Castlereagh between 1813 and 1815. I use the word
"guided" advisedly, since the policy which Castlereagh pursued
with unruffled determination throughout those perplexing years
was in fact not original but had been bequeathed to him by Pitt.
The circumstances and nature of Pitt's definition are curious
and instructive; they merit examination.

In the year 1804, the Emperor Alexander, in one of his
moods of impulsive philanthropy, and under the influence of
Adam Czartoryski, sent Count Novosiltzov to London bringing
with him a scheme for the new Europe. Under this scheme
"feudalism" throughout the world was to be replaced by
"liberal" governments and the several Powers were to renounce
war as a means of policy. The British conception of Maritime
Rights was to be modified, the principle of neutrality firmly
recognised, and the whole new system was to be placed under
the joint guarantee of Great Britain and Russia. More practically, the King of Sardinia was to regain Piedmont, the Italian
republics were to be liberated from French rule; Switzerland
was to be re-established as a wholly self-governing Republic;
Holland to gain her independence, and the Germanies were to
be federated. The rights and interests of Austria and Prussia
were, in this document, completely ignored.

In normal circumstances Pitt, in accordance with the traditions
of British empiricism, would have returned but an evasive reply
to such proposals. Yet he was anxious at the time to entice Russia
into a new Coalition and he therefore decided to answer Alexander in detail. Since, however, he reposed but little confidence
in Count Novosiltzov, who was young and vain, he addressed
his reply, in the form of a "draft," to Count Vorontzov, the

Tsar's accredited Ambassador in London. The salient points in Pitt's "draft" were as follows.

He agreed entirely with the Tsar that it would be necessary to reduce France to her former limits, to liberate conquered territory, to create future barriers against French aggression, to form some system of collective security, and to re-establish the public law of Europe. He did not agree with the Tsar in thinking that the rights and interests of Prussia or Austria could be ignored; without their assistance the total defeat of Bonaparte would not be possible. Thus while he felt that in any case Holland should be liberated and enlarged, so as to include Antwerp and to form the necessary "barrier," he was not of opinion that the Italian republics could, after so long a period of subjugation, be usefully accorded independence. Such areas, together with Belgian and Luxemburg territory, should preferably be used as compensations and rewards whereby to induce Austria and Prussia to join the Coalition. Prussia, in other words, should be encouraged to expand towards the north and west, provided only that she did not encroach on Hanover, whereas Austria should be encouraged to seek compensations in the south. The elimination of Bonaparte should not be the avowed purpose of the new Coalition, but would be welcomed if the French themselves desired it. In return for agreement on these points Great Britain would be ready to place into the common pool many, if not all, of the colonial conquests which she had made at the expense of France and her satellites. And finally a general guarantee of their European possessions should be accorded to all the partners in the new Coalition.

At the time these proposals were rendered inoperative owing to the battle of Austerlitz and the new course adopted by Alexander himself after Tilsit. But Pitt's scheme, as will be seen, formed the very foundation of Castlereagh's policy and it was on the basis of the 1804 "draft" that he subsequently justified his actions to the House of Commons. It was from Pitt in fact that he derived four of his most constant conceptions of the new European order: i—The idea that Russia's expansion must be balanced by the strengthening of Austria and Prussia. ii—The idea that Prussia should increase the area of her influence in northern and western Germany. III—The idea that Austria should be encouraged by compensations in Italy, and IV—The idea that in return for the just equilibrium thus achieved Great Britain should restore some at least of the colonial territory which she had acquired.

It is significant also that Pitt, as Castlereagh after him, did not fully grasp the paradox which seems inseparable from all schemes of reconstruction following upon the defeat of an aggressor. He appeared on the one hand to have contemplated the utter overthrow of Napoleon and on the other the creation of safeguards which would scarcely be of the same character once Napoleon had been utterly overthrown. Much of the confusion of ideas which occurred in 1813-1814 was due to the fact that the Allies were never quite certain until the last moment whether their final objective was the complete elimination of Bonapartism, or whether, under certain safeguards, Napoleon should be allowed to retain his throne. When after much hesitation they decided to replace the Bourbons, this restoration in itself became one of their safeguards against a revival of Bonapartism; and they thus found themselves in the illogical position of having on the one hand to enforce guarantees against any renewal of French militarism and on the other hand to avoid rendering the Bourbon dynasty unacceptable to French opinion by the imposition of humiliating penalties or restrictions. It was upon this weak link in their logic that Talleyrand concentrated, as will be seen, with such extreme lucidity.

The compromise which was eventually reached was sensible and just. But the confusion of thought which blurred the councils of the coalition in 1813 and 1814 is illustrative of the temptation, or misfortune, which seems always to assail peace-makers after a victorious war against an aggressor. It is inevitable perhaps that they should envisage security in terms of safeguards, not against what may happen in the future, but against what has happened in the immediate past; and that they should design their precautions with reference to the war just terminated rather than with reference to the next war, which will be carried on with wholly different weapons, which will be conducted by totally different methods and which, in all probability, will not arise for another thirty years.

If, moreover, we are to derive any instruction from the European crisis which was inaugurated by the French Revolution and which culminated in the defeat of Bonapartism, it is useful to dismiss from our minds the assumption that the diplomatists who framed the final settlement at Vienna were more selfish, stupid or reactionary than the ordinary run of men. Such an assumption might tempt us to believe that future negotiators will be more enlightened, progressive, prescient, unselfish and alert. The problem of preserving the unity of a mixed coalition, the problem of adjusting national interests to international needs, are constantly recurring problems which at times transcend the capacity of human intelligence. They are problems which in modern times, when public opinion is scarcely less ignorant and certainly more assertive, will become even more difficult. It was inevitable that the statesmen of 1813-1814 should have hesitated to imperil a loose Alliance by raising prematurely ultimate issues of a highly controversial nature. It was not that they failed to foresee these difficulties; it was rather that, while Napoleon was still unconquered, they desired to evade disputes between themselves. And although the great protagonists of that age (Alexander and Talleyrand, Metternich and Castlereagh) were obliged to consider the rights and interests of their own countries, yet they were fully aware that more important than any such sectional desires was a general European interest, namely an assurance of peace, an acquired sense of security and a passionate need of civil repose.

[4]

In carrying out the precepts of his tremendous predecessor, Castlereagh was well aware of the difficulties which he would be forced to confront: the cool pertinacity with which he applied Pitt's guiding theories to the diplomatic situation of 1813-1814 compels our admiration.

He was aware that Metternich, in his momentary role of continental mediator, preferred in his heart of hearts the discipline and order of the Napoleonic system to the liberalism of the British, the sentimental intuitions of Alexander, or the rabid German nationalism of the *Tugendbund* and Stein. He was aware that the Austrian Minister feared the consequences of a complete overthrow of Bonapartism and would prefer a negotiated peace, such as would maintain the continental balance of power, and leave Great Britain unsatisfied and possibly alone. He was particularly alarmed by the evident intention of Metternich to exclude Great Britain from the inner councils of the Coalition and to present if possible a plan agreed to by himself, the Tsar and Frederick William, the acceptance of which would restrict British influence, the rejection of which might lead to Britain's exclusion. "Engagements of secrecy against us," he warned Cathcart after Reichenbach, "are of bad precedent and must not be."

Yet how, in the autumn of 1813, could he assert against Metternich Britain's demand for an equal voice in Coalition policy? British liabilities were many, the assets few. It was true that through all those years Britain had stood alone against Napoleon, yet it was unlikely that this gigantic fact would arouse any deep emotional response in a man who remembered Austerlitz and Wagram and who was responsible for mating the Corsican ogre to a daughter of the House of Hapsburg. It was true that Great Britain enjoyed command of the seas, but to a foreigner of a wholly continental habit of thought this would appear not so much as a proof of power but as a memory, in terms of Maritime Rights, of the abuse of power. These rights Castlereagh was determined at all costs to maintain. "England," he wrote to Cathcart on July 14, 1813, "can be driven out of a Congress: but not out of her Maritime Rights." It was true that in Spain Wellington's armies had inflicted defeat after defeat upon the French; but to an Austrian this campaign (at least until the decisive battle of Vitoria) must have seemed but a subsidiary enterprise.

Two assets only did Castlereagh possess which might be

expected to exercise upon the mind of Metternich a persuasive influence. The first was the large colonial Empire which Britain had won from Napoleon and his satellites and which, within limits, gave Castlereagh certain bargaining assets. The second—and it was the more important of the two—was money. Without subsidies even Austria could not hope to continue the war. It was to the banker of Europe, rather than to an equal fellow combatant that Metternich might be forced to pay attention. To oppose Metternich would have entailed the dislocation of the whole Coalition and the certainty of a separate peace: to conciliate him might entail concessions and compensations of which the sturdy British public might not (and did not) approve.

Castlereagh's ultimate objective was to co-ordinate the several separate treaties already existing between the old and new partners to the Alliance into a single comprehensive instrument binding all alike. His immediate objective was to win Austria to Britain's side.

It may seem strange that the British Foreign Secretary, being aware of the delicacy of the situation, should have chosen as his emissary Lord Aberdeen—a young man of twenty-nine, ignorant of continental conditions, and known only to his contemporaries as a traveller in the Levant, and as one of the earliest of our philhellenes.

Lord Aberdeen was a precocious young man. Having endured a harsh and unloved childhood, he had as a boy been brought up in the family of Pitt. At the age of eighteen he had undertaken his first continental journey and had dined several times at Malmaison, where Napoleon had captivated him by his "beauty" and the winning charm of his smile. From there he had journeyed to the Near East, had supped with Ali Pasha at Janina, and at Athens had identified and excavated the Pnyx. At the age of twenty-three he had been offered and refused the Sicilian Embassy; at the age of twenty-four he had been made a Knight of the Thistle; at the age of twenty-five he had refused the Embassy at St. Petersburg. It was only under great pressure that in 1813 he accepted the Embassy at Vienna, which at that date entailed joining the Emperor Francis and Metternich at their headquarters at Toeplitz.

Travelling by Gothenberg and Stralsund he reached Berlin on August 24, at a moment when Napoleon was at the very gates of the city. "It put me in mind," he wrote, "of the state of Athens on the approach of Philip to Chaeronea." From there, by difficult stages, he posted to Toeplitz where he arrived on September 2.

He was appalled by the "mutual discontent and ill-will existing in the different armies." He found the Emperor Francis "awkward and rather foolish" but this immediate impression was modified when he discovered later that the Emperor was well versed in the Latin poets and that his knowledge of Italian literature was unsurpassed.

The impression which the young thane himself created was not, at first, a good one. "I find him very shy," wrote Gentz,[3] "embarrassed and embarrassing, morose, sticky, ice-cold, and, as it seemed to me, not fully master of the French language." Three days later, on September 5, Aberdeen met Metternich himself. He fell an immediate victim to the Austrian's abundant charm. "Do not," he wrote bumptiously to Castlereagh on September 12, "think Metternich such a formidable personage. Depend upon it, I have the most substantial reasons for knowing that he is heart and soul with us; but, my dear Castlereagh, with all your wisdom, judgment, and experience . . . I think you have so much of the Englishman as not quite to be aware of the real value of foreign modes of acting."

It was no very difficult task for Aberdeen to obtain from the Austrian Minister a treaty under which, in return for a subsidy of one million pounds, Austria agreed not to make peace with Napoleon except by common accord. In securing his second objective, namely the consent of Metternich to a general treaty binding all the allies, he was met with polite evasions. Aberdeen went so far as to exceed his instructions and to assure Metternich in writing that Great Britain would have no objection to Murat[4] retaining the throne of Naples. Even this concession, which proved of subsequent embarrassment to Castlereagh, did not produce the general treaty which the British Cabinet so much desired. With the victory of Leipzig the British public jumped to the conclusion that peace was now a matter of weeks only, perhaps even of days. "I have great comfort," wrote Lady Burghersh to her mother on October 27, "that it is totally impossible there can be another battle." If British interests were not entirely to be ignored, it was evident that some ambassador of greater weight and experience than Aberdeen should be sent to allied headquarters. Alexander's emissary, Count Pozzo di Borgo,[5] had already been despatched to London to represent that a situation in which the three British Ambassadors—Aberdeen, Cathcart and Charles Stewart—all contradicted each other was not one which would be allowed to continue. Castlereagh, somewhat unwillingly, agreed to go himself. He left London on December 28, 1813.

[5]

It was indeed high time that some responsible British Minister should be present on the Continent, since the irresponsibility of Lord Aberdeen had permitted Metternich to rush the Coalition into what might have proved a compromise, and therefore inconclusive, peace. When, on November 2, Napoleon had withdrawn his armies across the Rhine the Coalition forces had moved slowly up and occupied the east bank of the river, while the statesmen and diplomatists had gathered together at Frankfurt. The Russian troops and generals were not unnaturally anxious to return to their now distant home. Although Blücher and Gneisenau wished to invade France and secure the downfall of Napoleon, Frederick William was himself hesitant and afraid. Bernadotte of Sweden, being impatient to obtain Norway, advised against any crossing of the Rhine frontier. And while Alexander was determined to avenge the burning of Moscow by the occupation of Paris, Metternich, having regained in Italy what he had lost in the old Austrian Netherlands, was anxious only for a suspension of hostilities and the conclusion with Napoleon of a continental peace.

He was aided in this scheme by a chance event which occurred in the first weeks of November. The French Minister at Weimar who had been captured by the Russians, and released owing to Metternich's intervention, arrived in Frankfurt. He was the Baron de Saint Aignan, a brother-in-law of Caulaincourt. Metternich decided to make use of this intermediary whom fate had flung across his path.

On November 8 he informed Saint Aignan that he was now willing to take up the overtures which Napoleon, after the first day of the Battle of Leipzig, had made to the Emperor Francis, through Count Merfeldt. He indicated to him, as a possible basis for peace negotiations, that if France would retire within her "natural" frontiers (which would give her Belgium, but not Holland) he had reason to suppose that Great Britain would be "reasonable" about Maritime Rights. Saint Aignan, when putting these terms in writing, twisted this assurance into a formula to the effect that "Great Britain was ready to recognise the liberty of commerce and navigation which France had the right to claim." Aberdeen, while making verbal reservations regarding this formula, did not reject it completely. Nor does he seem to have raised in any form the vital question of Antwerp or the subsidiary questions of Sicily and Norway. In informing Castlereagh of what had passed he adopted the futile expedient of assuring him that he had made it clear that any assent he may himself have indicated was "perfectly unofficial." Aberdeen's part in this transaction was rendered all the more indefensible owing to the fact that he insisted, not merely that Saint Aignan should not be allowed to see either of the two Emperors, but that the whole negotiation should be concealed both from Cathcart and Charles Stewart. And the latter, when he heard of the negotiations from the Prussians, was so incensed that he threatened, not unnaturally, to resign.

Lord Stanmore, in his biography of his father, contends that Lord Aberdeen showed great acumen on this occasion. "In this transaction," he writes, "Lord Aberdeen again gave proof of that calm soberness of judgment and moderation which so eminently distinguished him." To his credit it must be admitted that, having in Metternich's company driven across the battlefield of Leipzig, he had been so appalled by the horrors which obtruded on his gaze that he had come to the conclusion that any peace, even a compromise peace, would be better than a continuation of war. But he must have known that his action was contrary to his instructions; he must have known that he was agreeing to principles which the Cabinet at home would most unwillingly accept; and he certainly knew that British opinion was by then determined that no peace should be negotiated which would leave Napoleon on the throne of France. The fact that he kept Lord Cathcart and Sir Charles Stewart in ignorance of his concessions can only suggest that he was seeking, as young diplomatists so often seek, to score a personal success behind the backs of his more experienced colleagues.

Had Napoleon immediately and unconditionally accepted the Frankfurt proposals he might have retained his throne and secured a peace such as Metternich at least desired. Fortunately the reply which he sent through Maret, Duke of Bassano, on November 18 was ambiguous; he merely acknowledged the communication and suggested a conference. A few days later Maret was succeeded in the post of French Foreign Minister by Caulaincourt, who was known to be in favour of peace. In a note of December 5, Caulaincourt accepted the Frankfurt proposals as a basis for negotiation. It was then too late. Not only were the British Cabinet determined at any cost to secure that Antwerp should be freed from French control, but the Emperor Alexander, under the influence of Stein, had refused to accept the Frankfurt suggestions. Once again both Metternich and Napoleon had been defeated by the latter's confidence in the resilience of his own genius, by the belief that his star, so dimmed in Russia, would rise again.

It was at this moment that Castlereagh, after stopping a few days in Holland, reached the new Allied headquarters at Basle.

5. The Advent of Castlereagh

[January-March 1814]

Castlereagh reaches Basle, January 18, 1814—His conversations with Metternich—His Cabinet Memorandum of December 26, 1813, as a definition of British War aims—His relations with the Cabinet, the Opposition and the Prince Regent—Summary of his aims—Their adjustment to continental conditions—He visits Alexander at Langres on January 23—Dissensions at Headquarters—He insists on maintenance of Maritime Rights—The Conference of Châtillon opens in February 1814—Nature of that Conference and the interaction of military and political events—Aims of the several plenipotentiaries—Caulaincourt's policy at Châtillon—He is willing to accept the "ancient limits" but Napoleon refuses—The Conference adjourned between February 10 and 17—The "crisis of Troyes"—Austria threatens to make a separate peace—The effect of Napoleon's victories at Montmirail and Montereau—Castlereagh assuages the general panic—Châtillon negotiations resumed—Napoleon's separate overtures to the Emperor of Austria—The allied advance resumed on March 1 —The last stages of the Conference—The Treaty of Chaumont of March 9, 1814—The Grand Alliance is at last formed.

LORD CASTLEREAGH, as we have seen, left London on December 28, 1813. His only ministerial colleague was Frederick Robinson, subsequently Lord Goderich, and at that time Treasurer to the Navy. Lady Castlereagh accompanied the party as far as The Hague where, much to her indignation, she was deposited pending further developments. The Foreign Minister had brought with him his private secretary, Joseph Planta, and two Foreign Office clerks. The whole party occupied four travelling carriages and the expedition from first to last cost the British tax-payer no more than £10,546.

Their ship (the *Erebus*—Captain Forbes) was much delayed at Harwich owing to a thick fog; the prelude to the great frost of 1813-1814 which attained such intensity that sheep were roasted upon the surface of the River Thames. During his few days at The Hague Castlereagh was able to arrange in principle for the marriage of the Hereditary Prince of Orange to Princess Charlotte of Wales, a marriage which was to cement our close relations with the new Kingdom of Holland. He at the same time induced the Dutch to leave their interests entirely in British hands.

Thus fortified, Castlereagh pursued his cold and difficult journey to Basle. He travelled without stopping, sleeping in his carriage on the way and spending only one night at an inn. His route ran through Münster, Paderborn and Cassel to Frankfurt. "My dearest Em," he wrote to his wife from the latter city on January 15, 1814, "German dirt is beyond the worst parts of Scotland, and nothing after you leave Holland to amuse in the costume of the people." "Robinson and I," he wrote again, "have hardly seen any object other than the four glasses of the carriage covered with frost which no sun could dissolve, so that we were in fact imprisoned in an ice house for days and nights from which we were occasionally removed into a dirty room with a black stove smelling of tobacco smoke or something worse."

He was dressed in red breeches and jockey boots which gave to the amused eyes of foreign observers the impression of some military disguise. But he stood the rigours of that journey with considerable fortitude. Lady Burghersh, meeting him a few days later, found him handsome and unwontedly gay. "As brown as a berry," she records, "with a fur cap with a gold band." He reached Basle on January 10, 1814.

By that date the allied armies, having, much to the Emperor Alexander's mortification, violated the neutrality of Switzerland, had crossed the Rhine and advanced into French territory. The Tsar himself established his headquarters at Langres. Metternich, however, awaited Castlereagh's arrival at Basle and so did Stein. The Austrian Minister lost no time in suggesting to Castlereagh that the Emperor Alexander's departure for Langres was intended as a personal insult to the Prince Regent; fortunately the Tsar had left behind him a letter apologising for his absence and urging Castlereagh to visit him without delay and meanwhile to come to no definite conclusions. And Stein spared no pains in advising Castlereagh not to fall a dupe to the reactionary wiles of the Austrian intriguer.

Metternich himself found Castlereagh "imperfectly informed of the situation on the Continent" but claimed that within a few hours he had understood the whole position and that "a complete identity of views" had been established. During the week that he remained at Basle, Castlereagh's conversations with Metternich were both intimate and prolonged. The latter was delighted by the unexpected reasonableness of the British Minister. He could not, he wrote, speak too highly of his "amenity, wisdom and moderation."

What justification had Metternich for these emotions of delighted relief? He had considerable justification.

[2]

Before leaving England Castlereagh had, on December 26, 1813, drawn up his own instructions in the shape of *A Memorandum of Cabinet*. This paper represented the results of ministerial conferences over the past six weeks. While still in London, moreover, he had expounded his general ideas to the Russian and Austrian Ambassadors (Count Lieven and Baron von Wessenberg) as well as to Baron von Jacobi, the representative of the Prussian Government. He had also attempted to elicit from them a statement of the views and intentions of their respective Courts; but since these views had expanded since the Frankfurt proposals, the information which he could obtain from them was neither authoritative nor up to date.

Castlereagh had been accorded by the Cabinet a remarkably free hand. Lord Liverpool was not particularly interested in foreign policy except in so far as it might affect votes; he was apt at moments to regard Castlereagh rather as leader of the House of Commons than as Minister for Foreign Affairs and to attach to parliamentary opinion an importance which the latter neither appreciated nor desired. The other Ministers, having expended their energies on the prosecution of the war, were not inspired by any passionate interest in, or enthusiasm for, the problems of European reconstruction. Castlereagh's main critic in the Cabinet was Vansittart, the Chancellor of the Exchequer, who, being by nature a defeatist, was apt at awkward moments to develop tendencies towards appeasement. His main ally was Lord Bathurst, who was always equable, conciliatory and wise. Nor had he, at that date, much to fear from the Opposition. In the House of Commons, Whitbread and Tierney, although formidable debaters, were too ignorant of foreign conditions to drive home any incisive attack; in the House of Peers, Lords Grey and Holland had been discredited by the reliance they had placed upon the alarmist reports sent to them by Sir Robert Wilson[1]—a Whig partisan who had acted as military attaché, or, as the phrase then ran, military correspondent, with the Russian and Austrian armies. Wilson's presages of discomfiture and defeat had been stultified by the victories of Vitoria and Leipzig. The isolationist views which were later developed by the rising commercial classes, who were more interested in imperial trade and expansion than they were in continental commitments, did not affect Castlereagh to the same degree as they subsequently affected Canning; and although Wilberforce and "the Saints" brought powerful pressures to bear upon him in regard to the slave trade he was able, by sympathy and attention, to curb their natural impatience. Finally, he was fortunate in his relations with the Prince Regent who, in spite of many voluble indiscretions, brought to foreign affairs a more balanced judgment than that which marked his handling of domestic issues. It may be said therefore than few British Foreign Ministers can have entered upon international discussions with a greater latitude of action or with more confidence that their decisions would be supported by the Government at home.

Castlereagh's main purposes on leaving for the Continent, and as expressed in his Cabinet Memorandum of December 26, 1813, can be summarised as follows:

I—*Maritime Rights*. He was to secure that the unfortunate admissions of Aberdeen in Frankfurt should be recognised as having been made without authority and that the Allies should agree that such questions should not be discussed at any Conference.

II—*A General Alliance*. He was to establish "a clear and definite understanding with the Allies, not only on all matters of common interest, but on such points as are likely to be discussed with the enemy, so that the several Allied Powers may in their negotiations with France, act in perfect concert and together maintain one common interest."

To achieve this "common interest" Great Britain would be prepared to surrender some of her colonial conquests, but only if and when the following safeguards were obtained:

(*a*) The absolute exclusion of France from any naval establishment on the Scheldt, especially at Antwerp.

(*b*) The guarantee of the security of Holland by giving her a "barrier" in the Belgian Netherlands which should include Antwerp.

(*c*) The complete independence of Spain and Portugal and the guarantee of their territory by the continental Powers against any attack by France.

(*d*) It was "highly desirable," although not an absolute condition, that the States of Italy should be restored and that the King of Sardinia should obtain, not only Piedmont, but also Genoa and Savoy. If Murat remained in Naples, then Tuscany and Elba should go to the Sicilian Bourbons as compensation.

(*e*) The Grand Alliance should be continued after peace had been signed and future security against French aggression should be guaranteed by "a certain extent of stipulated succours."

III—*The Dynastic Question*. It was assumed in London at the time that Austria at least would insist upon Napoleon retaining his throne. Provided that France were restricted to her "ancient" as opposed to her "natural" limits then Great Britain would consent to this, however unpopular it might be with British public opinion.

IV—*Colonial Concessions*. If these purposes were secured, then Great Britain, "being desirous of providing for her own security by a common arrangement rather than by an exclusive accumulation of strength and resources," would be ready to make certain colonial "compensations." She would wish to keep the Cape of Good Hope which she had taken from Holland but would be prepared to pay

Holland in compensation the sum of two million pounds—this sum to be spent on the construction of Dutch fortresses on the new French frontier. She would also, for strategic reasons, wish to retain Malta, Mauritius, the Bourbon and Saintes Islands and Guadeloupe (which for some extraordinary reason she had promised to Bernadotte). She would also retain Heligoland which she had taken from Denmark. All other colonies, however, which she had acquired from Napoleon and his satellites, including the Dutch East Indies, were to be restored. These were major concessions. It was estimated at the time that the colonies captured from France in the West Indies alone were worth £31,048,000, those from Holland £39,157,000 and those from Denmark £5,014,440.

It is curious to note that at this date Castlereagh, in suggesting these vast colonial concessions, added no rider regarding the abolition of the slave trade. Wilberforce, when later he heard of this omission, wrote to Lord Liverpool describing it as "absolutely irreligious and immoral."

These proposals, when read to his colleagues in the Cabinet Room in Downing Street, seemed wise, moderate and unselfish. Great Britain regarded herself, not only as the original and leading antagonist of Bonapartism, but as the lynch pin of any continental Coalition. The fact that we had stood alone during all those dangerous years, the fact that after Trafalgar Napoleon had been unable seriously to dispute our maritime supremacy, induced parliamentary and public opinion to imagine that we had acquired some arbitral position in world affairs. They did not fully understand that our European allies thought mainly in terms of continental armies, an area of effort in which, in spite of Wellington's peninsular victories, we played at the time but a subsidiary role. It did not occur to the British Cabinet that it might seem exaggerated on our part to demand a Grand Alliance and a "common interest" (which implied an immediate settlement of the two problems of Poland and Saxony) in return for the cession of distant colonies of which men like Metternich or Alexander had scarcely heard. What possible importance could Sumatra or Martinique possess in comparison with Thorn or Cracow? The speed with which Castlereagh adjusted the maritime to the continental scale of values is one of his major claims to the title of a sound diplomatist.

Such were the aims which Castlereagh had in mind when he embarked upon his ice-bound journey to Basle and Langres. After a few hours' conversation with Metternich he realised that things were not exactly what they had seemed to be in London. He had shared the general opinion at home that Napoleon was already beaten and that peace could almost immediately be concluded: Metternich assured him that many arduous battles lay ahead. He had assumed that it would not be an insuperable task to agree as between the Four Allies upon "one common interest"; Metternich made it clear to him that the main difficulty would prove, not the decision regarding France's future frontiers, but the decision regarding Poland. It may be doubted whether at the time even Metternich foresaw that this terrible and incessant problem would require a further eighteen months to solve. He discovered that neither Metternich nor the Emperor Francis was, as he had expected, really anxious to see Napoleon maintained upon the throne, and that they would prefer a regency under Marie Louise. He learnt to his astonishment that the Emperor Alexander had some wild idea of giving the throne of France to Bernadotte. Yet he was glad and surprised to find that Metternich did not desire the restoration to Austria of her former Netherlands dominions, and that he had already refused Alexander's suggestion that Austria should exchange her Polish provinces in Galicia for Alsace-Lorraine. He was delighted to discover that Metternich was not at all interested in Maritime Rights and seemed quite prepared to support the British view that the Kingdom of Holland should be buttressed by a barrier at Antwerp. Metternich for his part was much relieved to discover that Castlereagh, in spite of his supposed English liberalism, was not particularly struck by Stein's ideal of a liberal and unitary Germany and that the English Minister's conception of "a just equilibrium" accorded very much with his own theories of the balance of power. More specifically Metternich welcomed Castlereagh's ready acceptance of his own theory of the danger which Europe would now have to meet in the imperialistic tendencies of the Russian colossus and of his contention that Prussia should be compensated, not with the whole Kingdom of Saxony, but by concessions in the west such as would enable her to keep a watch upon the Rhine. The importance of the Basle meeting was not so much that any definite agreement was reached between the two Ministers; it was rather that an identity of thought and feeling was established between Metternich and Castlereagh which lasted, without serious derangement, until the latter's death.

It was in such a mood of relieved solidarity that, on January 23, they started off together to visit the Emperor of Russia at his headquarters at Langres. Castlereagh, as Aberdeen before him, was appalled by the jealousies and dissensions which he found to exist between the military leaders of the Allies. Even more than before he became convinced that the whole Coalition might still disintegrate unless welded together by some firm and unequivocal Act of General Alliance. He found, however, that neither Austria nor Russia were willing to enter into any such compact until a settlement of the Polish question had been reached; and that the Tsar was determined to maintain his sphinx-like attitude upon this subject until the final victory over Napoleon had been secured. It was in vain that Castlereagh, in the hope of breaking this vicious circle, indicated that Great Britain must refuse to surrender any of her colonial conquests until a firm Allied agreement had been reached such as would secure "that having reduced France by their union, they were not likely to re-establish her authority by differences among themselves."

Yet although these vital points were left unsettled, agreement was reached on certain minor issues. Castlereagh made it clear that although Great Britain might be willing to make peace with Napoleon, yet this must depend upon the wishes of the French people themselves. He indicated also that if Napoleon were dethroned the only possible alternative which would be acceptable to the British Government and people was the restoration of the Bourbons. It was without much difficulty, moreover, that he secured Alexander's agreement to restrict France to her "ancient" rather than to her "natural" limits,[2] and to constitute the Kingdom of Holland "with an increase of territory and a suitable frontier." It was also agreed that the question of Maritime Rights should in future be excluded from all discussions and that eventually a Congress, to be attended by the three Sovereigns, should be held at Vienna to settle such questions as might remain over for discussion once peace had been signed with France. The results of these somewhat tentative discussions at Basle and Langres were embodied in a document dated January 29, 1814, and entitled The Langres Protocol.

Meanwhile Caulaincourt from Lunéville had been writing to Metternich to urge that peace negotiations should at once be opened. Napoleon had now accepted the Frankfurt proposals, and so had Lord Aberdeen; what possible reason could there exist for further delay? The Emperor Alexander, who was still determined to dictate peace from Paris, contended that in any circumstances it should be made clear that the Allies would be unwilling to permit France to discuss any territorial settlements outside her own "ancient limits." Lord Castlereagh feared that such insistence would bear in French eyes "too much the character of a blind and dishonourable capitulation." Provided he could obtain Antwerp and exclude Maritime Rights from all international discussion, he had no desire at all to impose on France the humiliation of unconditional surrender. Napoleon at Elba asserted that it was Castlereagh and Castlereagh alone who had prevented peace being concluded on the basis of the Frankfurt proposals. This was only half true, since Alexander was himself determined at that date to enter Paris as a conqueror. Yet it was agreed, none the less, that peace discussions might be opened at Châtillon-sur-Seine. Realising that these negotiations would prove inconclusive, Castlereagh decided that he would not himself be a plenipotentiary; he instructed the three Ambassadors, Lord Aberdeen, Lord Cathcart, and Sir Charles Stewart, to represent Great Britain. They were to form what Castlereagh in his stilted style called "a Commission composed of His Majesty's diplomatic Servants." Meanwhile he remained fairly contented with the results of the conversations at Basle and Langres. "We may now," he wrote home, "be considered as practically delivered from the embarrassments of the Frankfurt negotiations."

And in fact, although he had not obtained his General Alliance, he had saved Maritime Rights without having in return to commit himself finally to the surrender of a single colony. He had obtained the restriction of France to her "ancient limits" and had, to all appearances, eliminated from the succession to Napoleon's throne both Marie Louise and Bernadotte. He had reason, for the moment at least, to be content with his achievements.

[3]

The Conference of Châtillon furnishes a classic example of the impossibility of conducting diplomatic negotiations during the actual progress of a military campaign. In the course of those six weeks the dissensions between the Allies reached their first supreme climax and achieved a solution which was at least temporarily effective. It is necessary therefore to examine in some detail the development of the Conference of Châtillon and the interaction of military and political hopes and fears by which it was rendered abortive.

In order better to grasp the course of this complicated negotiation it will be useful to consider at the outset the following comparative tables of military and diplomatic dates:

Military Events	*Diplomatic Events*
Feb. 1. Allied victory at La Rothière.	Feb. 5. Châtillon Conference opens.
Feb. 11. French victory at Montmirail.	Feb. 7. Allies offer "ancient limits."
Feb. 18. French victory at Montereau.	Feb. 9. Caulaincourt accepts this.
French occupy Troyes.	Napoleon refuses.
Feb. 22. Allies retreat towards Langres.	Feb. 10-17. Conference suspended.
	"Crisis of Troyes."

Military Events	Diplomatic Events
Mar. 1. Allies resume advance.	Feb. 21. Napoleon makes direct overtures to the Emperor Francis without result. He insists on "natural frontiers."
Mar. 9. Blücher defeats French at Laon.	
Mar. 12. Wellington enters Bordeaux.	
Mar. 18. Allies advance on Paris.	Mar. 10. Caulaincourt offers the renunciation of all French sovereignty beyond "frontiers of France."
(Mar. 31. Capitulation of Paris.)	
(Apr. 11. Abdication of Napoleon.)	
	Mar. 15. Caulaincourt offers to abandon everything except Lucca and Neuchâtel.
	Mar. 18. Allies reject this offer.
	Mar. 19. Châtillon Conference dissolves.

Viewed in this summarised, and much over-simplified, form, the Conference of Châtillon falls into four distinct phases, each phase being dominated by a victory or a defeat in the field. During the first period, from February 5 to 10, the proceedings were dominated by the allied victory at La Rothière. Thus whereas Caulaincourt, who desired to save his master from the consequences of his own obstinacy, wished to make peace on almost any terms, the Russians and the Prussians believed that victory was already theirs and had no desire that the Conference should reach any definite conclusions. The second period is marked by the suspension of the Conference between February 10 and 17, and by the discussions which took place at Troyes between the principal Allies. It was only Napoleon's two victories at Montmirail and Montereau which induced Alexander to consider the continuance of peace negotiations. These victories had in their turn increased Napoleon's self-assurance and thus when the Conference entered its third stage he was unwilling to allow Caulaincourt any latitude for concessions. The fourth and final stage was inaugurated by Blücher's victory at Laon on March 9. From then on Caulaincourt made desperate efforts to save Napoleon from complete disaster, whereas the Allies, realising that total victory was now assured, had by that date determined to dictate the terms of peace in Paris.

Such, in its simplest outline, was the shape of the Châtillon Conference. Yet the flux and reflux of those six anxious weeks cannot properly be understood unless we also examine the motives which animated the protagonists. Napoleon fully realised that to sacrifice all the conquests won by the Revolution and himself would entail the loss of his throne; he saw that the phrase "ancient limits" would suggest another phrase to the French people—the phrase "ancient dynasty." He believed however that his supreme military genius would still enable him to triumph over the overwhelming forces of the Coalition, the war-weariness of the French people, and the lassitude and suspected disloyalty of his own Marshals. Caulaincourt on the other hand was well aware that the Allies, in spite of their timidity and dissensions, would triumph in the end; his only desire was to achieve as rapidly as possible some form of peace which would enable his beloved master to retain his throne. The Emperor Alexander remained determined, in spite of the disaffection of his armies and the open protests of his generals, to avenge the capture of Moscow by the capture of Paris. Metternich, with his temperamental hatred of all extremes, was seeking to achieve a compromise peace which, while safeguarding the balance of power, would not expose Europe either to the extension of Russian influence or to the chaos that might follow on the collapse of the Bonapartist system. Hardenberg and Humboldt were inclined towards a peace of negotiation but were hampered, partly by Frederick William's subservience to Alexander, and partly by the determination of Blücher and his generals to achieve a purely military decision. And Castlereagh, while inclined to share Metternich's apprehensions, and while humanely anxious to avoid all unnecessary bloodshed, was alive to the fact that he could subscribe to no terms which did not meet the desires of the British Cabinet and Parliament and was aware that British public opinion, having been conditioned by twenty years of animosity, would much resent any peace which left the Corsican usurper on his throne.

Behind these immediate differences of opinion there lay the eternal conflict of policy between the Austrians and the Russians. Apart from disagreement on strategic matters, apart from conflicting views regarding the future of France and Western Europe, there remained the insoluble Polish problem. In Alexander's passionate mind that problem formed itself into the question: "Am I, the conqueror of Napoleon, to be denied my life-long dream of undoing the great wrong of 1795 and rebuilding under my protection a prosperous and independent Poland?" To Metternich's cool calculation the question was: "What will happen to the balance of power if, having rid Europe of the domination of Napoleon, we replace the western menace by an eastern menace, and establish Russian influence a few miles only from the banks of the Oder?" So profound a conflict of war-aims was not easily to be reconciled: the task which confronted Castlereagh in that month of February 1814 was difficult indeed.

[4]

Caulaincourt has been criticised for missing two opportunities of making peace at Châtillon; the first opportunity is said to have occurred on February 7 and the second on February 17. If we examine the circumstances we find that Caulaincourt was not himself to blame.

He arrived at Châtillon on January 21, accompanied by De La Besnadière, seven secretaries and twenty-two servants, and established himself in the elegant house of M. Etienne. He was obliged to wait eight days before the other plenipotentiaries arrived. The first formal meeting of the Conference was held in the Hôtel de Montmaur at 1 P.M. on February 5; it lasted only twenty minutes and was not auspicious. Caulaincourt was informed by the Allies that in no circumstances could Maritime Rights be discussed at the Conference since any such discussion would "be contrary to the usages hitherto observed in transactions of the present nature." He did not complain of this exclusion and in fact accepted it as inevitable. What distressed him was the tone adopted by the allied representatives. "Compared to the English," he records, "who are men of honour, frank in the defence of their own interests, but straight—the other plenipotentiaries seemed to embody passion, bitterness and resentment." Count Razumovski, the Russian plenipotentiary, was particularly insulting and sought to impress Caulaincourt with the might and majesty of the Coalition. "I am well aware of it," replied the French delegate with dignity, "I am well aware that France has the honour of being alone."

The second meeting of the Conference took place two days later on February 7. Caulaincourt can hardly have expected that the Allies would renew the favourable offer they had made at Frankfurt. Since then three things had happened. The French had been obliged to evacuate Holland; Murat had openly abandoned the cause of Napoleon; and the Allies had invaded France. He was none the less shocked by the abrupt manner in which he was informed that as a basis of any peace conversations France must at once agree to be reduced to her "ancient limits." "He could not," records an eye-witness, "repress a movement of impatience and bitterness." He asked whether if this condition were accepted, hostilities would cease immediately; he was accorded no definite reply. Although he had in theory been given full powers by Napoleon he well knew that his Emperor would not accept such a condition as an absolute preliminary to any further negotiations. He was obliged therefore to ask for further instructions. "Only your Majesty," he wrote, "can decide whether I should sign."

This communication reached Napoleon at Nogent on the night of February 7-8. Rumigny, who was present when Napoleon opened Caulaincourt's letter, records that his rage was "supernatural";—"his cries were those of a trapped lion." At one moment it appeared that the Emperor had decided to accept the allied offer; but when Maret in the early morning brought for his signature the letter of acceptance, he was poring over his maps; he had received information which indicated that Blücher had exposed his flank. "Do not let us rush anything," he said;

"there will always be time for us to sign a peace such as they now propose." The offer was rejected.

Caulaincourt, whose desire for negotiation was urgent and anguishing, found himself in an intolerable position. "I was," he records, "in a fever of despair; death was in my heart. . . . I confess that when I found myself face to face with some of the plenipotentiaries I had emotions which were akin to those of madness." In desperation therefore he addressed on February 9 a letter to Metternich stating his willingness to accept the "ancient limits." When Napoleon heard of this he was enraged. Meanwhile, under Alexander's orders, the Conference had been suspended and the scene now shifts from Châtillon to the Tsar's headquarters at Troyes.

Alexander, supported by the Prussian generals, was at this date under the impression that Napoleon had been decisively beaten at La Rothière and that the road to Paris lay open to the Allies. This view was not shared by the cautious Schwarzenberg, who pointed out that whereas the armies of the Coalition were rapidly disintegrating, Napoleon was even now receiving reinforcements from the south. Hardenberg, Metternich and Castlereagh all contended that if the Allies could now obtain peace on the basis of the "ancient limits" it was wrong for them to risk further casualties, and possible defeats, by prolonging the war. Alexander replied through Nesselrode that he would not accept "a majority vote." Metternich countered by saying that neither would his master accept such "tyrannical" methods on the part of the Russian Emperor, and by threatening to withdraw the Austrian armies from the field and to make a separate peace. In conjunction with Hardenberg and Castlereagh he then drew up a "protocol," which was in fact an ultimatum, suggesting that Napoleon should be offered an immediate armistice, on condition he surrendered the fortresses of Antwerp, Mainz, Mantua, Bergen-op-Zoom, Hüningen and Besançon, and that peace negotiations should then be opened on the basis of the "ancient limits." The implication was that if Alexander refused to accept this protocol the three Allies, or at least Austria and Great Britain, would disrupt the Coalition, withdraw their forces, and make separate overtures.

It was Castlereagh who was charged by his colleagues to convey to the Emperor Alexander this unwelcome declaration. He argued that the Tsar's determination to dictate peace from Paris "was full of hazard, at direct variance with the principles upon which the Confederacy had been cemented . . . and that it might lead to disgrace and disunion." Alexander replied by hinting (as he had learnt from Lieven) that Castlereagh was not accurately representing the views of the Prince Regent, of the Cabinet or of British public opinion. And Frederick William meanwhile informed his Ministers that whatever happened he would not permit an open breach with the Russians. It seemed therefore that the Coalition was in fact in danger of disintegrating.

It was then that the news of Napoleon's victories at Mont-mirail and Montereau reached Troyes. Something like panic supervened. "We are uncertain," wrote Lady Burghersh, "dilatory and (*entre nous*) frightened." "The Tsar," recorded Hardenberg in his diary, "has gone to pieces and the King [Frederick William] talks all the time like Cassandra." Aberdeen, writing from Châtillon on February 28, expressed the fear lest the delegation might be captured by the local population who were forming armed bands. Prince Schwarzenberg advised the allied sovereigns to ask for an armistice and urged a general retreat. Metternich himself was alarmed. Castlereagh alone appears to have kept his head. "I cannot express to you," he wrote to Metternich, "how much I regret the proposition of armistice. . . . An offer so inconsistent with the proceedings here and of so little dignity in itself cannot fail to invite the enemy to assume a tone of authority. . . . If we act with military and political prudence how can France resist a just peace demanded by 600,000 warriors? Let her if she dare: and the day that you can declare that fact to the French nation rest assured that Bonaparte is subdued." "Nothing," he wrote to London, "keeps either power firm but the consciousness that without Great Britain the peace cannot be made." And meanwhile, in the hope of restoring shattered confidence he suggested that a military committee should be appointed to set down on paper the existing and potential resources of the Coalition. The "crisis of Troyes" suddenly dissolved; the panic subsided: and Alexander consented that the Conference of Châtillon should be resumed.

[5]

It was then that Caulaincourt's second opportunity arrived . . . the opportunity of February 17. By that date, however, Napoleon was so elated by his victories that he was talking of having "annihilated his enemies" and of "being at the gates of Munich within a few weeks." "Providence," he wrote to Caulaincourt on February 17, "has blessed our armies; sign nothing without my orders since I alone know the situation." In vain did Caulaincourt protest against this optimism. "I see the dangers," he wrote despairingly, "which threaten France and Your Majesty's throne and I entreat you to prevent them. We must make sacrifices, and we must make them in time." "Besides," remarked Napoleon to Rumigny, "I do not read Caulaincourt's letters; tell him that they tire and bore me beyond limit."

On February 21, none the less, Napoleon from Nogent-sur-Seine addressed a letter to the Emperor Francis offering a separate peace with Austria. This letter, in spite of the fact that it began, "Sir, my brother and very dear father-in-law," was not tactfully worded. "I have," it began, "destroyed the Prussian and the Russian armies." "I urge Your Imperial Majesty," it continued, "to make peace with me on the basis of the Frankfurt proposals. . . . There is not a Frenchman who would not rather die than accept conditions which would erase France from the map of Europe and render her people the slaves of England. . . . What interest could Your Imperial Majesty have in placing the Belgians under the yoke of a Protestant Prince one of whose sons will become the King of England?" The reference to Russia was even more disobliging. "Your Imperial Majesty," wrote Napoleon, "could put an end to the sufferings of a nation exposed, not to ordinary ills, but to the crimes of these Tartars of the desert, who scarcely deserve the name of human beings."

This letter produced no effect: the discussions at Châtillon proceeded as before.

By March 1 Schwarzenberg declared that the allies were prepared to resume the advance; on March 9 Blücher defeated the French at Laon; on March 15 Caulaincourt was at last empowered to put definite proposals before the Conference, in which he offered to abandon all territory except Lucca and Neuchâtel, but made no mention of Belgium. Three days later the Allies rejected this proposal and declared the Conference terminated. The march on Paris had begun.[8]

Yet the panic which had stricken allied headquarters at Troyes during that week of February had one important result. The dissensions which had then arisen had proved a shock even to the most quarrelsome. Metternich had been appalled. "You have no idea," he wrote to Stadion, "what sufferings the people at headquarters impose upon us! I cannot stand it much longer and the Emperor is already ill. They are all insane and should be confined in asylums." Castlereagh, who had behaved throughout with admirable fortitude, realised that his moment had come. The Grand Alliance, which he had for so long striven to achieve, was signed on a card table at Chaumont on March 1, 1814, and published on March 9. Its terms were simple and conclusive. Under the first article the Four Powers pledged themselves to continue the war until their objects were attained. These objects were then defined as an enlarged and independent Holland, a confederated Germany, an independent Switzerland, a free Spain under a Bourbon dynasty, and the restitution of the Italian States. In return for this Castlereagh promised that Great Britain's contribution in men or money would be double that of any continental Power. It was agreed that the Quadruple Alliance thus constituted should last for twenty years after the conclusion of hostilities. And the four Great Powers (since this expression now entered diplomatic vocabulary) were to assist each other in the event of any attempt upon the part of France to disturb the arrangements come to at the forthcoming peace.

The Treaty of Chaumont was Castlereagh's first great diplomatic achievement. "My treaty," he called it thereafter; and writing to Hamilton of the Foreign Office on March 10, he expressed the hope that it would "put an end to doubts as to the claim we have to an opinion in continental matters." It will have been noted, however, that the problem of Poland was still unsolved. There were those who believed (and Alexander himself may have been one of them) that a Poland reconstituted under the Russian aegis would in fact be able to maintain her political and military independence. There were others who shared Metternich's apprehension that Russia would be obliged by circumstances to secure the future Kingdom of Poland that maintained a "friendly," or in other words a subservient, attitude towards her enormous neighbour. The consequences of such an extension of Russian power into the very heart of central Europe were incalculable and alarming. Napoleon, when at Elba, also foresaw these consequences. In conversation with Colonel Neil Campbell on October 31, 1814, he expressed himself as follows: "If the Russians succeed in uniting the Poles heartily in a common interest, the whole of Europe ought to dread them. It will be impossible to foresee or to limit the consequences. Hordes of Cossacks and barbarians, having seen the riches of more civilised countries, will be eager to return. They will overrun Europe, and some great change will probably result from it, as has been the cause in former times from the incursions of barbarians."

6. The First Peace of Paris

[May 30, 1814]

The final defeat of Napoleon and the capitulation of Paris—A phase of diplomatic confusion—Talleyrand receives the Tsar in the Rue St. Florentin—Castlereagh remains at Dijon—His views on the Bourbon restoration—The visit of Baron de Vitrolles— Public opinion at home—Bordeaux proclaims the Bourbons— The situation in Paris—Napoleon at Fontainebleau—The defection of Marmont—The negotiation of the Treaty of Fontainebleau—The question of Elba—Terms of the Treaty of Fontainebleau—Napoleon's attempted suicide—He leaves for Elba—The negotiation of the First Peace of Paris—Prince Hardenberg's scheme for a general settlement—The Tsar refuses to consider it—The question of the colonies—The slave trade—Reparations —Works of art—Signature of the treaty—Its main terms— Consideration of their apparent leniency.

THE TREATY OF CHAUMONT was published on March 9, 1814. On the same day Blücher captured Laon and Napoleon withdrew behind the Aisne. Although his position was by then desperate he acted during those remaining three weeks with astounding skill and energy. "I am still the man," he wrote on March 14, "that I was at Wagram and Austerlitz." This view was confirmed by contemporary observers. Writing to Edward Cooke on March 22 Sir Charles Stewart referred to the "masterly military movements he has of late made." "He has never," wrote Sir Charles, "shown himself greater." The Duke of Wellington discussing in later years Napoleon's strategy during these essential weeks, expressed himself as follows: "Excellent —quite excellent. The study of it has given me a greater idea of his genius than any other. Had he continued that system a little while longer, it is my opinion that he would have saved Paris. But he wanted patience. . . . He did not see the necessity of adhering to a defensive warfare." From Rheims on March 17 Napoleon issued a statement intended to counter the effect of the Treaty of Chaumont. He offered to surrender all his conquests "beyond the French borders"; he offered to evacuate Holland and to establish Belgium as an independent Kingdom under a French prince; he made no definite promises regarding the left bank of the Rhine. If the Allies withdrew from French territory and undertook to restore the French colonies he would accept peace on these terms. No reply was returned to this pronouncement. On the following day, March 18, Napoleon established contact with Schwarzenberg's main armies but withdrew without fighting in the direction of St. Dizier. His aim was to make a feint across the Marne in the hope of threatening the Allied lines of communication and drawing them away from Paris. He contended in later years that if he had gained "but three days' march" he could have joined up with his armies in the south and driven the Allies from France. Unfortunately he confided his plans to Marie Louise in a letter which was captured by Tettenborn's Cossacks on March 22 and sent to headquarters. A council of war was held on March 24 by the roadside on the outskirts of Vitry. Clausewitz records that, when others hesitated, it was the Emperor Alexander who insisted that they should ignore the threat to their communications and march straight on Paris.[1] By the afternoon of March 30 the allied armies had reached the outskirts of the city; the capitulation of Paris was signed at 2 A.M. on March 31, 1814. Napoleon received the news at Juvisy and retired to Essonnes and then to Fontainebleau.

[2]

On looking back upon the occurrences of the eventful fortnight between March 21, 1814, and April 13, between the capitulation of Paris and the ratification by Napoleon of the Treaty of Fontainebleau, we are apt to assume a greater degree of allied unity than in fact existed. We take it almost for granted that the Coalition were united in desiring the dethronement of Napoleon and the restoration of the Bourbons and that they executed this joint purpose with celerity and skill. These are incorrect assumptions. In all alliances or coalitions formed for military purposes there is, as has been said, a disposition to postpone or to evade diplomatic differences which are liable to raise controversial issues and thereby to impair the unity of decision required in military operations. In the event of sudden victory a phase of diplomatic confusion is bound to follow; events then proceed, not according to some pre-arranged plan, but owing to the intervention of such secondary elements as improvisation, unexpected opportunity, chance or the presence at the opportune moment of some individual (whether important or unimportant) who possesses a definite and lucid scheme. It was the interposition of these secondary elements which sent Napoleon to Elba and brought Louis XVIII back to the Tuileries.

Talleyrand [2] had remained in Paris. He was the one man who, in the succeeding uncertainty, was coldly determined on the overthrow of the Bonaparte dynasty and the restoration of the Bourbons.

As a member of the Council of Regency Talleyrand ought to have accompanied the Empress Marie Louise when, under Napoleon's orders, she fled from the capital to Blois. He evaded this duty by an ingenious stratagem. He arranged that a friend of his, Monsieur de Rémusat, a captain in the National Guard, should intercept his carriage at the octroi on the road to Blois and order his return to Paris. He was thus in his house in the Rue St. Florentin when the allies entered. Early in the morning of March 31, while he was still dressing, he was visited there by Count Nesselrode, Minister of the Emperor Alexander and an old acquaintance. Count Nesselrode had been warned that it would be unsafe for Alexander to establish himself at the Elysée since that palace was said to have been mined; Talleyrand at once offered the Tsar the hospitality of his own house in the Rue St. Florentin. He then proceeded to draft with Nesselrode a proclamation to the French people.

While this was being drafted the Emperor Alexander, accompanied by the obedient and unnoticed Frederick William, had entered the capital. Preceded by the enormous Cossacks of the Imperial guard, flanked by his ministers and generals, the uniforms of the allied military attachés adding splashes of blue and scarlet to the jingling procession, the Agamemnon of Kings rode slowly through the streets. In gaping astonishment the citizens of Paris gazed upon their conqueror. His enormous feet were thrust into stirrups of wrought gold; his waist was tightly restricted by a wide black belt; huge shining epaulettes concealed the fact that his shoulders were sloping and slightly bowed; above the high gold collar, below the vast green hat worn sideways under its cascade of cock feathers, they saw the face of a pale benignant calf. To those who doffed their hats at his passage, he responded with the wave of a dimpled hand: with a smile from a subtly curling lip.

He reached the doorway in the narrow Rue St. Florentin. "Monsieur de Talleyrand," he said on dismounting, "I have decided to stay in your house since you possess my confidence and that of my allies. We do not wish to settle anything until we have heard your views. You know France, her needs and her desires. Say what we should do, and we shall do it." Once again Talleyrand found himself in a key position at a critical moment. Seven years ago Napoleon, in the presence of the whole court, had called him "a piece of dung in a silk stocking." The hour of retribution had arrived.

On the following day, April 1, Talleyrand, in his capacity as Vice-Grand Elector, summoned a meeting of the Senate under his own chairmanship. Only 64 out of the 140 Senators attended. He persuaded them to appoint a Provisional Government consisting of himself, Dalberg, Jaucourt, Beurnonville and Montesquieu. On the following day, April 2, the Senate proclaimed the deposition of Napoleon and invited Louis XVIII to return to France.

The Provisional Government installed themselves on the ground floor of the Rue St. Florentin while the Emperor Alexander occupied the first floor above. The Emperor Francis, feeling that it would be indelicate to enter his son-in-law's capital as a conqueror, stayed behind at the Hôtel Dampierre at Dijon, and Metternich and Castlereagh remained with him.

King Frederick William scarcely counted. Childish, solemn and unhappy, the King of Prussia took little part in politics but spent his afternoons in Paris sadly tobogganing down the slides of the Montagnes Russes. The question whether the Bourbons should or should not be restored to the throne of France therefore rested, during those crucial days between April 1 and April 6, with the Tsar of Russia alone.

Sir Charles Stewart, who had accompanied the Tsar into Paris, much deplored the advantage which the absence of Metternich and Castlereagh gave to Russian policy. "It is deeply to be regretted," he wrote to Liverpool on April 4, "that His Majesty's Secretary of State for Foreign Affairs, by accidental occurrences, has been thrown out of the way of affording that incalculable benefit which his presence could not fail of producing here at this moment."

[3]

Alexander had no very definite prejudices or desires in regard to the future French dynasty. His mind flitted from one bright idea to the other. He had no sympathy for the Bourbons, whom he regarded as outworn, incompetent and vastly conceited. At one moment he had favoured the candidature of Bernadotte; at another his mind veered towards the nomination of the King of Rome with the title of Napoleon II, and under the Regency of his mother, the Empress Marie Louise. The Duc d'Orleans also appealed to him as a possible candidate; he even thought of Eugène Beauharnais. In the face of Talleyrand's hints and suggestions, he avoided committing himself, alleging that he desired only to consult the wishes of the French people and that these wishes were as yet obscure.

He had lost, during the previous three weeks, all personal contact with Francis I, with Metternich and with Castlereagh. They had remained in the rear of the armies and had in fact been driven, with undignified haste, from pillar to post owing to the brilliant lunges of Napoleon's final campaign. The Baron de Vitrolles, the deserving but self-appointed agent of the royalist cause, has left in his memoirs a vivid picture of these flittings. He describes Castlereagh, in a white cape, eating a hurried luncheon in the courtyard of the Château de Vandœuvre. Castlereagh had propped his luncheon upon the rumble of his travelling carriage and stood on tiptoe to enjoy the salmi of partridge and the champagne which had been prepared. Vitrolles found him non-committal, handsome, very cold. Eventually the party reached Dijon and there for ten days they remained.

Castlereagh himself was not sorry to be at Dijon. "This is a delightful town," he wrote to his wife on March 30. "It is the only one I have seen where the people look clean and good-humoured." It was not, however, the amenities of Dijon that restrained him. He did not wish to be immediately identified either with the terms of Napoleon's abdication or with those of a Bourbon restoration. He pleaded that the roads were still too unsafe to permit of his coming to Paris, and he was much annoyed when Lady Burghersh, by dashing alone to Paris to rejoin her beloved husband, rendered this excuse an obvious prevarication. What were the reasons for this deliberate, and possibly dangerous, abstention?

Once again we can trace to the doctrine of Pitt the clue to Castlereagh's hesitation. His master had always declared that it would be a mistake for Great Britain or any other Power to impose the Bourbons on France unless and until the French people had themselves manifested "a strong and prevailing disposition" for their former dynasty. It was with this in mind that Castlereagh, when consulted by Wellington regarding a request that the Bourbon princes might be attached to the British army, had replied that he must remain opposed "to any step which should, even in appearance, mix our system with that of the Bourbons." He shared the Tsar's doubts regarding the competence of Louis XVIII and his family; he shared Metternich's suspicions that the French army, and a large section of the French public, remained loyal to Bonaparte; he may have felt, in his heart of hearts, that a more stable system could be secured if Napoleon, or at least some Bonaparte regency, retained control. And thus when Baron de Vitrolles joined them, he was at first received both by Metternich and Castlereagh "with imperturbable silence."

One feels sorry for Vitrolles. His passion for the Bourbons was unclouded by any knowledge of their faults. His confidence in his own importance and abilities was apparent from the setting of his long thin lips and the fixed stare of his protruding eyes; it was only by chance that he played, at a crucial moment, a dramatic part; and he showed much persistence, some courage, and no little initiative, in performing services which, as he recorded later, "it was easier to forget than to reward."

It is probable that by the time he reached Dijon Castlereagh had realised that, after the experience of the Châtillon Conference, any peace which left Napoleon himself upon the throne would prove unstable. In any case it is clear that he did not wish Great Britain to be directly or primarily identified with the restoration of the Bourbons. His aim, as he wrote in his clumsy style to Liverpool on March 22, was "to bring Great Britain forward in whatever may regard the interior of France rather as the ally and auxiliary of the continental Powers than as charging herself in chief and making herself responsible for what cannot be conducted under the superintendence of her own Government." Thus when Vitrolles left in order to visit Monsieur at Nancy, Castlereagh's last words to him were "Let those act who are stronger than we are and more free to make decisions."

Two circumstances then arose which led him to adopt a more decisive attitude. The Prince Regent, the Cabinet and British public opinion were already manifesting extreme hostility to any maintenance of the Bonapartist system and a marked preference for the restoration of France's ancient dynasty. "You can scarcely have an idea," Liverpool had written as early as February 12, "how *insane* people are in this country on the subject of any peace with Bonaparte." "The Methodists and the women," noted Stratford Canning, "are particularly warlike." It was not, however, until March 22 that definite instructions were issued to Castlereagh that on no account should any peace be made with the Corsican usurper. And by that time other important developments had occurred.

On March 26 the news reached Dijon that Bordeaux had openly declared for the Bourbons and that the white cockade was being worn. On March 28, at a dinner which he gave to Metternich, Stadion, Hardenberg, Razumovski and Munster, and in the presence of the representatives of Holland, Bavaria and Spain, Castlereagh himself toasted the restoration and the person of Louis XVIII.

It is not clear why, even before the capitulation of Paris, Castlereagh and Metternich should have permitted and led so public a demonstration. They were not the men to be afflicted with impetuosity, or to be influenced by the solvents of a dinner-party. Their reasons were both positive and negative. They had each come to see that any peace with Napoleon, or even a Bona-partist regency, was by then an impossibility. It may well have been that, in committing themselves to the Restoration, they were anxious to forestall any attempt on the part of the absent Tsar to establish a republic in France or to hand the French throne to Bernadotte or Eugène Beauharnais. And it is curious to reflect that the arrival at a moment of indecision of so foolish, although well-meaning, a man as Vitrolles may have tipped their judgment.

Meanwhile Paris itself, from all accounts, remained sullen and unexpressive. The allied troops, on entering the capital, had put on white brassards for the sole purpose of mutual identi-fication; the Parisian populace took these to be the Bourbon symbol, but responded half-heartedly. On the night of March 31 the Vicomte Sosthène de la Rochefoucauld had engaged workmen to pull down the statue of Napoleon from the Colonne Vendôme. They burst open the door of the column and climbed the stair; the winged victory in Napoleon's hand had already been dislodged when further proceedings were stopped by some officers of the Semenow Regiment and the demonstration proved a fiasco. The Comte de Moubreuil for his part drove round Paris with the Legion of Honour tied to his horses' tails. Dis-concerted as he was by these rumours and counter-rumours, anxious as he was to avoid assuming any leading part in these transactions, Castlereagh did not enter Paris until April 10; and by that date a decision had already been reached.

[4]

Napoleon arrived at the palace at Fontainebleau at 6 A.M. on March 31, and established himself in the small apartments on the first storey leading out of the Gallery of François Ier. The faithful Caulaincourt, having secured interviews both with the Emperor Alexander and with Schwarzenberg, rejoined his master late on April 2. Napoleon that afternoon had been reviewing at Essonnes the VIth corps of Marshal Marmont;[8] he was unaware that the Marshal was already in communication with Schwarzenberg and had already offered to desert to the side of the allies. He still believed that with Marmont's 20,000 men at his disposal he could drive the allies from Paris, link up with the armies of the south, and re-establish the situation. It was on April 3 that he heard that the Senate on the previous night had decreed his deposition. He at once held a council with Berthier, MacDonald, Ney, Lefebvre and Oudinot. He disclosed his plan to them but gathered from their embarrassed silence that they were opposed to the renewal of the campaign. On April 4 therefore he despatched Caulaincourt and Ney to Paris with a written offer of his abdication in favour of his son, the King of Rome. On their way through Essonnes they visited Marmont who was much embarrassed by their arrival; he confessed that he had already agreed with Schwarzenberg to desert Napoleon and to place his corps at the disposal of the Allies; he pretended however that Napoleon's offer of abdication changed the whole position and agreed to accompany them to see Schwarzenberg at his headquarters at Petit Bourg. After a few private words with Schwarzenberg Marmont assured them that all was satisfactorily explained and that he would come on with them to Paris. They reached the Rue St. Florentin in the early hours of April 5 and were at once received by Alexander. At that hour, in the room below, Talleyrand was closeted with Baron de Vitrolles to whom he was about to deliver a letter inviting Monsieur,[4] the brother of Louis XVIII, to make a formal entry into Paris. Their conversation was interrupted by the sound of spurs upon the parquet flooring and an aide-de-camp entered to inform Talleyrand that Napoleon's emissaries had arrived with new proposals and were discussing them with the Tsar upon the floor above. Talleyrand quietly replaced in his pocket the letter to Monsieur which he had almost handed to Vitrolles. "This is an *incident*," he said. "We must see how it turns out. For the moment you must not leave Paris. The Emperor Alexander does unexpected things; he is not for nothing the son of Paul I."

Talleyrand was justified in his apprehensions. At the second interview which Caulaincourt, MacDonald and Ney had with the Tsar in the early hours of April 5, Alexander showed signs of being ready to accept Napoleon's suggestions. He was touched by the plight of his great friend of Tilsit days; he was anxious to avoid all further bloodshed; he was above all conscious that the military position of the Allies was not unassailable. At that moment, however, an aide-de-camp entered and spoke to the Tsar in Russian. Caulaincourt understood what he was saying; the aide-de-camp had informed his master that Marmont's entire corps had marched from Essonnes to Versailles and placed themselves at the disposal of the Allied Sovereigns. Caulaincourt was appalled by this act of treachery. "We are lost," he whispered to MacDonald, "he knows everything." Making some excuse, Alexander left the room. He hurried downstairs to talk with Talleyrand. With icy force the latter denounced Napoleon's offer as a mere manoeuvre; whatever form of regency were established the influence of Napoleon would remain dominating, sinister and decisive; the only hope of repose for France was the restoration of the Bourbon dynasty.

The Tsar returned to Caulaincourt and informed him that Napoleon must abdicate without conditions. "We shall not deprive him of all hope of existence," he said. "We shall give him a kingdom of his own." "What sort of kingdom," asked Caulaincourt, "and where?" Corsica was suggested, but that was impossible since it was a department of France. Sardinia was suggested, but that also was impossible since it belonged to the House of Savoy. Corfu was suggested, but Alexander regarded that island as too close to the Balkans and the Eastern Question. And thus, between noon and 2 P.M. on April 5 they decided on Elba. Caulaincourt returned dejectedly to Fontainebleau, where he arrived at 1 A.M. on April 6. The Emperor was asleep and, entering his bedroom, Caulaincourt roused him by shaking him deferentially by the shoulder. He gave him the news. Napoleon received it with calm bitterness; the defection of Marmont, he said, had robbed him of a great victory; he sent for Ney who shook his head sadly and said that the army was tired out." At 6 A.M. Napoleon sent for them again. Could Marie Louise be allowed to join him instantly? Would she be able to persuade her father to accord him Tuscany? And why Elba of all places? He sat down heavily at the table and signed his unconditional abdication.[5]

On that day, April 6, in Paris the Senate under Talleyrand's direction had passed the new Constitution or Charter. The second article of this document ran as follows: "The French people freely call to the throne of France Louis-Stanislas-Xavier of France, brother of the last King—and after him the other members of the House of Bourbon in the old order." The fate of the Bonaparte dynasty was sealed.

Again Caulaincourt returned to Paris, and again he saw the Tsar. The latter, as always, was gentle and considerate. It was impossible to grant Napoleon Tuscany; even as it was, it would be difficult enough to induce Metternich and Castlereagh to endorse the promise of Elba. The Empress would be amply provided for. All possible consideration within reason would be shown to the Emperor and his family. Caulaincourt spent the rest of the night drafting the terms of the arrangement. Throughout April 8 and April 9 he remained in constant negotiation with Alexander and Nesselrode. He had a private meeting with Talleyrand at the house of his sister-in-law. He found him obdurate. There were objections to Elba; there were objections even to Napoleon's annuity being defrayed from French funds.

On the next day, April 10, both Castlereagh and Metternich arrived in Paris. The former, Caulaincourt records, was "obliging, positive and frank. He kept his word to me in everything." The latter was less conciliatory. They both raised objections to the choice of Elba. Castlereagh would have preferred, in Lord Liverpool's words, "some less objectionable station." He was prepared even to consider that Napoleon should be granted asylum in Great Britain, where Fort St. George had already been suggested. It is doubtful whether this suggestion would have been approved by the Cabinet. A subsequent proposal that the fallen Emperor should be interned at Gibraltar was attacked by *The Times* newspaper in trenchant terms. "We should be really sorry," wrote *The Times*, "if any British possession were polluted by such a wretch. He would be a disgrace to Botany Bay." Fouché for his part urged that the ex-Emperor should be deported to the United States. Metternich contended that to send Napoleon to Elba would be to invite another war within two years. He even objected to the proposal that the Empress Marie Louise should be accorded the Duchy of Parma. At 3 P.M. a final meeting took place in Alexander's room. The terms of the Treaty of Abdication were finally agreed to. They then descended to the lower floor where Talleyrand and the Provisional Government were assembled. Talleyrand gave his accession to the Treaty (subsequently called the Treaty of Fontainebleau) and Caulaincourt in return handed them Napoleon's Act of Abdication. Talleyrand took the occasion to suggest to Caulaincourt and MacDonald that they might now take office under the Bourbon dynasty. They refused this offer abruptly. "The Prince of Benevento," records Caulaincourt, "was incapable of changing colour or of turning pale, but his face swelled out, as if stuffed with rage and about to explode." A further delay was caused by the difficulty of determining the order in which the several plenipotentiaries should affix their names; it was in the end decided that separate documents should be prepared for each. It was not therefore till the early morning of April 12 that the treaty, although dated April 11, was finally signed. Caulaincourt returned with it that afternoon to Fontainebleau in order to obtain Napoleon's ratification.

[5]

The Treaty of Fontainebleau, officially entitled "A Treaty between the Allied Powers and His Majesty the Emperor Napoleon," was not an ungenerous document. By article 1 Napoleon renounced for himself, his successors and descendants, as well as for all the members of his family, "all right of sovereignty and dominion, as well over the French Empire and the Kingdom of Italy, as over any other country." By article 11 he and the Empress Marie Louise were permitted to retain their rank and title during their lifetime. His mother, brothers, sisters, nephews and nieces could continue to call themselves Princes of the Bonaparte family. By article 111 the Island of Elba was to form a separate principality to be possessed by him "in full sovereignty and property." He was to be given an annual revenue of two million francs from French funds. By article 1v the Duchy of Parma and Guastalla was to be granted in perpetuity to the Empress Marie Louise with reversion to the King of Rome. By article v the Powers undertook to induce the Barbary pirates to respect the flag of Elba. Articles v1 and vii made provision for annuities to be paid to members of Napoleon's family including an annual pension of one million francs to the Empress Josephine. Under article viii it was provided that Eugène Beauharnais, Viceroy of Italy, should be accorded "a suitable establishment out of France." The remaining articles dealt with debts, pensions, the return of the State diamonds and the number of French soldiers which Napoleon might take with him to Elba as a body guard. Under article xvi a ship was to be placed at Napoleon's disposal to take him to Elba, the vessel thereafter to remain his property. It was in this brig, the *Inconstant*, that he eventually escaped. This treaty was signed by Metternich, Stadion, Razoumovski, Nesselrode, Hardenberg, Ney and Caulaincourt. It was not signed by

Castlereagh; he merely acceded, on April 27, to those parts of it which concerned the grant of sovereignty over Elba and the Duchy of Parma.

On reaching Fontainebleau on the afternoon of April 12 Caulaincourt found Napoleon in a state of abstracted depression. "Life has become unbearable for me," he said. "I have lived too long." That night the fallen Emperor attempted to commit suicide. Ever since the Russian campaign he had worn round his neck a little envelope of black taffeta containing a mixture of opium, belladonna and hellebore.[6] At 3 A.M. he summoned Caulaincourt to his bedside and handed him a letter of farewell to the Empress Marie Louise. Observing that his master was unwell Caulaincourt offered to summon the doctor. Napoleon prevented him and confessed that he had taken poison. Spasms then supervened followed by violent nausea. Caulaincourt dragged the Emperor to the window and he seemed for a moment to revive. "How difficult," he gasped, "it is to die." Dr. Yvan arrived and Napoleon begged him to administer a further dose. "I am not a murderer," replied the doctor, realising that the nausea had relieved his stomach of the poison. Napoleon then fell into a coma; by 11 A.M. the next morning he had recovered and was able to walk for a time in the garden. His spirits instantly revived. He was cheered by receiving a letter from the Empress promising to join him in Elba. The prospects were not too desperate. He would settle down quietly upon his island; he would lead a domestic life; he would write his memoirs.

He returned to the Palace and ratified the Treaty of Fontainebleau.

On April 16 the allied Commissioners who were to conduct him to the frontier and to protect him against "insult or attack" arrived at Fontainebleau. They were General Schouvaloff, General Köller and Colonel Neil Campbell. At noon on April 20 the Imperial Guard were paraded in the Cour du Cheval Blanc. Napoleon made them a short address, embraced their commander, General Petit, and buried his face in their standard.

He then entered his carriage and drove off at a gallop towards the coast.

The convoy consisted of fourteen carriages with an escort of sixty-two lancers: they travelled via Briare, Nevers and Roanne. On reaching Provence there were demonstrations of hostility on the part of the populace. At Avignon an attempt was made to stop his carriage; when he arrived at Orgon he found the inhabitants engaged in hanging him in effigy; when they heard that Bonaparte himself was among them they attacked his carriage with sticks and stones. He was rescued with difficulty by the allied Commissioners and for the next stage of the journey he disguised himself as a postilion, riding ahead of his own carriage dressed in a blue livery with a small round hat upon his head. The next day he was unable to ride and took his place in Count Schouvaloff's carriage disguised in an Austrian uniform. He cowered back in the recesses of the carriage, "exhibiting," as Colonel Campbell records, "more timidity than one would have expected from a man of his calibre."

On the evening of April 27 they reached Fréjus and spent the night at the inn. Napoleon was unwilling to take passage in the French frigate since, knowing his unpopularity with his own navy, he feared that he might be exposed to insult. He therefore embarked, at sunset on April 28, in H.M.S. *Undaunted* (Captain Usher) and set sail for Elba. He landed at Porto Ferrajo at 2 P.M. on May 4, 1814.

[6]

Having disposed of Napoleon and his family, it remained for the Allies to conclude peace with Bourbon France. In view of the fact that Louis XVIII had already accepted the principle of the "ancient limits" this task appeared at first to present no great difficulty. Castlereagh himself was optimistic enough to imagine that a general settlement could be reached by May 15. Austria and Prussia, however, were unwilling to conclude a treaty with France until some agreement had been reached as between the Allies regarding the future of Poland and the disposal of other territories outside the new French borders. They foresaw that once Great Britain had obtained her desires in regard to Antwerp, the Belgian frontier, Holland and the colonies, she might disinterest herself in the settlement of other European questions. They foresaw also that once a treaty of peace had been signed with France it would be difficult in practice to exclude her from all discussions regarding the future balance of power. Talleyrand for his part was anxious to play for time. On the one hand he hoped that with the arrival of Louis XVIII in Paris the Allies might be gradually induced to abate their extreme insistence upon the frontiers of 1792. On the other hand he was aware that his own influence with the royalist party was much hampered by his previous record and relied upon the intelligence and tolerance of Louis XVIII to strengthen his position.

On April 29 Prince Hardenberg for Prussia brought the issue to a head by presenting a definite scheme for a general settlement. Under this scheme all Saxony and the left bank of the Rhine should be given to Prussia; Austria would obtain the Tyrol together with compensations in Italy; Russia was to obtain the main portion of the Duchy of Warsaw, but the districts of Tarnopol and Cracow were to remain Austrian; a German federal constitution was to be drafted and minor territorial compensations to be given to Bavaria, Baden and Piedmont.

The Tsar, as might have been expected, refused even to consider so extreme a proposal. He insisted that in any case his future Kingdom of Poland must include the Prussian fortress of Thorn. He contended that peace should be made with France before any of these matters came up for discussion between the Allies. Metternich did not accord to Hardenberg the support which was expected, since a dispute had in the interval arisen between Prussia and Austria regarding the former's occupation of the fortress of Mainz. On May 21 another attempt was made to reach a general settlement in Paris but this also broke down in face of the Tsar's evasive obstinacy. The Allies were obliged therefore to concentrate upon concluding a treaty of peace with

France irrespective of other and more remote difficulties between themselves.

A Conference of the four Allied Powers was established on May 9. In colonial matters Great Britain displayed a lenient attitude. "I still feel doubts," Castlereagh had written to Liverpool on April 10, "about the acquisition of so many Dutch colonies. I am sure our reputation on the Continent as a feature of strength, power and confidence is of more real value to us than any acquisition thus made." But when Talleyrand sought to claim Tobago, and still more when he hesitated to make any declaration regarding the abolition of the slave trade, Castlereagh displayed sudden firmness. He threatened, unless his wishes were met, to transfer the negotiations to London. Talleyrand gave way.

Two other questions caused some difficulty. Napoleon had financed his campaign by his own conquests; the Napoleonic wars had cost Great Britain some seven hundred million pounds in cash. "It will be hard," wrote Edward Cooke, "if France is to pay nothing for the destruction of Europe and we are to pay all for saving it." The Prussians were even more insistent in their demands for reparation; they asked that Prussia should be repaid the sums which Napoleon had extracted from her in 1812. The French delegate replied that sooner than pay over these monies Louis XVIII "would submit to be arrested and kept a prisoner in his palace." This argument appears to have much affected the Allied plenipotentiaries who did not possess that acute financial acumen which was manifested by the Reparation Commission of 1918. They decided that the new France should start with a clean balance sheet; they did not even demand, as they had every right to demand, the repayment of sums spent on the maintenance of French prisoners of war, of whom 70,000 had been supported for years in England alone.

A second difficulty arose in connection with the works of art which Napoleon had looted from foreign cities in the course of his wars. The French had always expected that these would have to be surrendered and had resorted to the somewhat childish expedient of hiding the originals in the cellars while displaying in the galleries of the Louvre copies which they hoped would escape detection. Lord Aberdeen, who, unlike Castlereagh, was interested in works of art, pleaded that they should remain in Paris since to transport them to their home towns might damage their texture. More potent was the argument that the loss of these superb trophies might have an unsettling effect upon the Parisians. And thus, for the moment at least, the works of art were allowed to remain.

The treaty as finally negotiated became known as the First Peace of Paris; it was signed on May 30, 1814. Under this treaty France renounced all her claims over Holland, Belgium, Germany, Italy, Switzerland and Malta. She ceded to Britain the colonies of Tobago, Santa Lucia and Ile de France, and to Spain the Spanish portion of San Domingo. Her own frontiers were reduced to those which she had held on November 1, 1792, with the following significant additions. On the Rhine, the *thalweg* or centre stream was fixed as the boundary. In the Department of Mont Blanc she received Chambéry and Annecy. Certain enclaves, such as Avignon and Montbéliard, were included in French territory: France thereby gained some 150 square miles, with a population of 450,000, as an addition to her "ancient limits." A secret article provided for the independence of the German States and their union in some form of federation. Another secret article provided that "the relations from whence a system of real and permanent balance of power is to be derived shall be regulated at the Congress upon principles determined by the Allied Powers amongst themselves."

This was a diplomatic formula for stating that the Polish question had been shelved and that when eventually it came up for discussion France would not be permitted to intervene. It was an optimistic formula.

The terms of the First Peace of Paris may seem to us today amazingly lenient. Their generosity, however, was not sentimental, but politic. What the Allies desired above everything was security and repose. They well knew that the loss of the Napoleonic conquests would in itself prove a severe shock to French public opinion. They realised fully that any further amputations could only weaken the position of the Bourbons and lead to a revival of Bonapartism. That they should have exacted no indemnities or reparations from France may to our minds appear fantastic altruism; Lord Castlereagh, although an admirable diplomatist, was not a financier; he preferred to cut his losses, and there are many economists today who would contend that in so doing he displayed wisdom. Nor is there any cause for undue self-righteousness on our part regarding our lack of colonial acquisitiveness. Imperialism in those days had only just begun to be economic; Castlereagh, unlike Canning, thought more of naval stations adapted to sailing ships than he thought either of raw materials or markets. He was unaware of the immense riches of the Dutch East Indies which he so amicably surrendered. And even had he foreseen their commercial potentialities he would none the less have rated these as of less value than the repute of his country and the confidence which her moderation would inspire abroad.

7. London Interlude

[June 1814]

The Tsar's miscalculation of his own position—By seeking to follow simultaneously two alternative policies he failed in both—He failed to secure agreement upon his Polish policy before signing peace with France—His overtures to the Polish émigrés—Kosciuszko—His difficulties with Russian public opinion—He also failed to get France and Great Britain on his side—His dislike of Louis XVIII—The Compiègne interview—The visit of the Grand Duchess Catherine to London and her provocative conduct—Alexander and Frederick William land at Dover—The antipathy between the Tsar and the Prince Regent—The London festivities and the incidents which occurred at the King's Theatre and the Guildhall banquet—Effect of the Tsar's conduct upon the Ministers and the leaders of the Opposition—Metternich profits by the ill-feeling aroused—Meagre results of the London visit—Its effect upon public and political feeling in Great Britain.

THE TSAR of Russia never recovered (perhaps because he had abused) the dominant position which was his at the moment of Napoleon's abdication. He failed to realise that good diplomacy must be based on confidence; and that confidence can only be created by consistency and truthfulness. He believed that he alone among monarchs was the interpreter and champion of the principles of Christian liberalism. Affected as he was by the plaudits of the multitude as by the flattery of those who, like Madame de Staël, regarded him as the phoenix of the century, he imagined that the rocks of national interest could in some way be melted by the alchemy of his twisted smile or be dissolved by the unguents of his volatile benignity. Even as Woodrow Wilson in 1918, he had convinced himself that the momentary enthusiasm of the people reflected the true spirit of the future; that borne upon the tide of popular approval he

could float affably down the ages radiating virtue and dispensing
beneficence; and that to him alone had been granted some
special dispensation of Providence, some pre-ordained revelation,
denied to all other men, and thereby sanctifying disloyalty.

Had his character been as firm as his intelligence was rapid,
had his protestations of saintliness not been marred by the personal habits of a voluptuary, had he been able to adjust the
requirements of his own Empire to that spirit of self-sacrifice
which he demanded of others, then indeed he might have
become the representative and even the leader of those hidden
forces which stirred in the first four decades of the nineteenth
century. So soon, however, as the glamour of those startling
spring weeks had begun to fade, it was recognised that the Tsar's
personality was too disintegrated to carry conviction. The incon-
sistencies of his nature became nakedly apparent and men ceased
even trying to reconcile the parricide with the saint, the neurotic
with the hero, the autocrat with the liberator, the prophet with
the man of pleasure, the trickster with the evangelist. To few
men, not even to Woodrow Wilson, has such an opportunity
been accorded; vanity, idleness, indulgence, and a strain of
almost childish duplicity came to blur his vision. As the years
passed he sought to hide himself from his own inconstancy in a
cloud of mysticism, until in the end the cloud thickened into
depressive mania and bowed his shoulders and dimmed his
kindly eyes.

Two alternative policies were open to Alexander during the
important interlude between the abdication of Napoleon and the
opening of the Congress of Vienna. In attempting both, he
bungled both.

He might, on the one hand, have refused, with Prussian
support, to sign a Treaty of Peace with Bourbon France until
his own Polish scheme had, at least in principle, been accepted
by his allies. He might, on the other hand, have sought to profit
by the interval to bring Great Britain and France over to his
side and thus form a solid block wherewith to counter Metternich's antagonism. As it was, he committed the strategic error
of failing to concentrate against his major enemy and of dis-

sipating his forces in incidental skirmishes and manoeuvres. He pressed his Polish thrust to the point where it aroused the disquiet of Castlereagh and Talleyrand although hesitating, while his authority was still dominant, to press it home. And concurrently he drove Louis XVIII, the Prince Regent, Talleyrand and Castlereagh into the camp of Metternich by insulting each of them in turn and by seeking in his folly to flirt with the Opposition both in France and England.

As a result of these ill-considered stratagems he was eventually faced, as we shall see, with a secret anti-Russian alliance between Austria, Great Britain and France. The errors which, by their accumulation, brought about his final defeat were not only diplomatic but temperamental. And since the Tsar's mishandling of the situation is most illustrative of the disasters which ensue when temperament is allowed to affect diplomacy, the somewhat grotesque incidents of this interlude between Paris and Vienna need to be examined in some detail.

[2]

The Tsar must have been well aware, as his ministers and opponents were well aware, that by concluding peace with Bourbon France while the Polish question was still unsettled he was exposing himself to two disadvantages. Once France had ceased to be an enemy it was obvious that she would strive to be recognised as an equal partner among the United Nations, and it was probable that in order to acquire such a position she would at first assume the leadership of the small or unsatisfied Powers. At the same time she would tend inevitably to exploit for her own advantage the differences between the major Powers and would be obliged, sooner or later, to adhere either to the Russian or the Austrian camp.

It was obvious also that once Great Britain had achieved her desires in regard to Antwerp, Maritime Rights and the colonies, she would have no further motive to appease Russia and might tend, in the general interests of the balance of power, to support Austria in her opposition to Russian ambitions.

How came it therefore that the Emperor Alexander, during the important weeks which followed upon the abdication of Napoleon, failed to profit by the occasion offered? Why did he not induce Hardenberg to modify his extreme proposals of April 29 and join with him in presenting Great Britain and Austria with some reasonable suggestion which it would at the time have been difficult for them to reject? How came it, in other words, that at so early a stage Alexander should have discarded his trump cards and have played his remaining cards petulantly and in the wrong order?

There is evidence to show that his first intention was not to leave Paris until he had obtained in principle some agreement to his Polish scheme. Both La Harpe and Adam Czartoryski had joined him at headquarters. The latter, writing to Novosiltsov on May 20, that is ten days before the signature of the Peace of Paris, was triumphantly confident that no peace would be signed without a Polish settlement. "Austria," he wrote, "is protesting loudly, and claiming Cracow. As a result all negotiations for a general peace have been suspended."

The Tsar moreover went out of his way during those few weeks to conciliate such Polish émigrés as were on French soil. The officers of Poniatowski's corps, which had served so brilliantly under Napoleon, were cordially forgiven. The whole corps was reviewed by Alexander on the plain of St. Denis and he assured them that they might return to their country taking with them their arms, their uniforms and their standards. He went further. The national hero, Tadeusz Kosciuszko,[1] was at that time living in retirement at Berville in the neighbourhood of Fontainebleau. The Tsar treated him with every consideration and sent a Russian guard of honour to present arms to him outside his cottage. Kosciuszko replied by addressing a memorial to the Emperor in which he demanded the complete independence of Poland, a constitution on the British model, and an undertaking that all serfs would be emancipated within ten years. This was asking much. Alexander replied that "with the assistance of the Almighty" he hoped to "realise the regeneration

of the brave and honourable country to which you belong."
"I trust," he added, "that I shall have your help." Kosciuszko
was not convinced. At a ball in Paris given by the Countess
Jablonowska he was asked whether he intended to return to
Poland. "Only," he answered in a loud voice, "if Poland be
really free." Alexander, as was intended, overheard this remark. "Gentlemen," he replied in resounding tones, "we must
so arrange matters that this brave man can return to his fatherland." But Kosciuszko remained unconvinced. Even when the
Grand Duke Constantine, that insane hyena, escorted him to
the front door holding a huge candelabrum to guide his footsteps he still remained suspicious of Russian sincerity. Instead
of returning to Poland, the victor of Raclawice retired to
Solothurn.

There is no reason to suppose that the Tsar was at this date
indulging in any hypocritical manoeuvres. To General Sokol-
nicski, who had greeted him as the liberator of Poland, he
replied sadly: "I am not a charlatan; I shall only expect your
gratitude when I have deserved it. I have many difficulties to
face." To La Harpe he said: "I intend to give them back as
much of their country as is practically possible. I shall give them
a constitution which I shall myself develop as time goes on."
Such protestations were undoubtedly sincere. But, as he said,
there were grave difficulties. It was not merely the opposition
of Metternich which he had to surmount; his Polish schemes
were also regarded with acute distaste by large sections of
Russian opinion. The governing classes were enraged that their
sentimental Emperor should have claimed no compensations for
the ordeals which Holy Russia had endured and no rewards for
the overwhelming victories which her arms had won. It seemed
to them an act of insanity on his part to abandon all annexations
and indemnities and to create upon the very borders of Russia
an autonomous State enjoying political and social institutions
which were denied to the Russian people themselves. It was
whispered even that Nesselrode, the Tsar's chief Minister,
shared these doubts. And however sincerely Alexander may

have agreed with the views of La Harpe, he was fully aware that if a palace revolution occurred it would not be La Harpe who would be murdered but himself.

[3]

It may have been considerations such as these which induced the Emperor Alexander to postpone a final solution of the Polish problem until he had been able to return in triumph to his own capital and to convince his people of the wisdom, as well as the justice, of his scheme. Considering the then inflamed condition of Russian nationalism this may have been a prudent act of procrastination. But nothing except temperamental levity can explain the second diplomatic error which he then committed. For instead of employing the interlude to conciliate the rulers of France and England he did everything possible to outrage their susceptibilities. He alienated Louis XVIII [2] and the Prince Regent; he alienated Talleyrand.

It is not always possible to deduce from documents, or even from contemporary gossip, the immense part played by human vanity in international affairs. The Tsar may have persuaded himself that the provocative attitude which he adopted towards both Louis le Désiré and the First Gentleman of Europe was due to the fact that the former was an undesired invalid and the second not a gentleman. He may have been convinced that both Louis XVIII and the Prince Regent were relics of a former age and bore no serious relation to the bright new gospel of which he was himself the evangelist. But in fact the attitude which he assumed both in Paris and in London was governed by personal pique; nor did he realise that to insult a Head of the State, however unpopular he might be, was to insult the State itself.

The origin of the mood of injured vanity which at this stage assailed the Tsar can be traced to the afternoon of April 21 and to the hall of Grillon's hotel in Albemarle Street. Louis XVIII had been detained at Hartwell in Buckinghamshire by an exceptionally severe attack of gout; when he was at last able to move, he drove in triumph to London on his way to Dover and the Tuileries. He was met by the Prince Regent and a cavalcade of gentlemen and officers on the outskirts of the capital and escorted to his hotel. In replying to the Prince Regent's congratulations he used the following unfortunate phrase: "It is to the counsels of Your Royal Highness, to this glorious country, and to the steadfastness of its inhabitants, that I attribute, after the will of Providence, the re-establishment of my House upon the throne of its ancestors."

This phrase appeared next morning in *The Times* newspaper and was quickly conveyed to Alexander. The conqueror of Napoleon, the Agamemnon of Kings, read it with intense and ill-concealed indignation. The distaste which he had always felt for the House of Bourbon was deepened by this invidious compliment; it thereafter extended to the person of the Prince Regent and his Ministers.

On April 29 Louis XVIII arrived at Compiègne and on the following day he received the Emperor Alexander in private audience. The interview was not a success. The Tsar had prefaced his visit by a memorial in which he urged the restored monarch to exercise moderation in his government of the French people and to "husband the memory of twenty-five years of glory." Louis had not welcomed this advice. He adopted towards the Tsar a gracious rather than a grateful manner. He did not rise from his seat but merely waved the Tsar into a chair beside him. After a few conventional phrases had been interchanged he suggested that the Emperor might wish to retire to his room. A procession was formed and Alexander was conducted through the suite of apartments allotted to the Comte d'Artois, through the suite of apartments allotted to the Duc de Berri, and finally through the suite of apartments allotted to the Duchesse d'Angoulême. When at last, by a dark and ill-lit passage, the Tsar reached his own rooms he was outraged by their unimportance. He informed Czernicheff, who had accompanied him as adjutant, that in no circumstances would he remain that night at Compiègne; he would return to Paris the moment dinner had been served. Nor did the meal, when it took place, assuage his indignation. Louis XVIII entered the dining room before him, and when the attendants hesitated with the dishes, the restored monarch called to them, in the high-pitched voice which he adopted when he intended to be rude, "Me first!" Driving back to Paris that night the Tsar voiced his outraged feelings. "Louis XIV," he expostulated, "at the height of his power would not have received me differently at Versailles. One would actually think that it was he who had come to place *me* on *my* throne!" His reaction was immediate. He drove to Rambouillet to pay his respects to Marie Louise; he drove to Malmaison to visit the Empress Josephine; he drove to the Hôtel Cerutti to pay a formal call on Queen Hortense. And when, but a few weeks later, Josephine died of pneumonia, he sent a regiment of Russian guards to honour her funeral. The Bourbons were offended by this demonstration of Bonapartism. And Talleyrand, in spite of the large sums of money which he had received from Alexander's privy purse, decided that the Tsar could never become a stable component in any European pattern.

[4]

The scene now shifts to the Pulteney Hotel at No. 105 Piccadilly and to the person of the Grand Duchess Catherine, sister of the Tsar and widow of Prince George of Oldenburg.

The Grand Duchess had always exercised upon her brother a disturbing influence; to him she was the "delicious lunatic" who both stimulated and justified his disregard for the processes of reason. While flattering his vanity, while abetting his lusts, while pandering to the religious jargon which was already affecting the shape of his thoughts, she deliberately allowed her Slav love of mischief to titillate the jealousies and rancours of his unstable temperament. "She had," records Princess Lieven, "an excessive thirst for authority and a very high opinion of herself which perhaps exceeded her deserts. . . . Her mind was cultivated, brilliant and daring; her character resolute and imperious; she startled and astonished the English more than she pleased them." Although an ugly little woman with a squat

Kalmuk nose, she made up for this deficiency by the vivacity of her manner, the sparkle of her eyes, and the luxuriant beauty of her hair. In addition she was a most restless person; at one moment she hoped to marry the Emperor of Austria: "He may be dirty," she wrote, "but I can wash him": at another moment she became enamoured of the Archduke Charles; she rejected with contempt the advances of the Dukes of Kent and Sussex; and finally she fell in love with the Crown Prince of Würtemberg, married him, and died.

The Grand Duchess Catherine arrived at Sheerness in the *Jason* frigate on March 31; she was met on arrival by the Russian Ambassador and by Princess Lieven (at that time only Countess). The latter found her "greedy of everything, especially of people": they took a dislike to each other from the start. The Lievens had engaged for their Emperor's sister the whole of the Pulteney Hotel in Piccadilly, at the cost of 210 guineas a week. In writing to her brother the Grand Duchess referred to it as "a furnished mansion, the finest in the town, where we are now lodged." She urged him, when he himself came to London, not to accept the hospitality of one of the Royal Palaces, but to share her apartments at the Pulteney. This in itself caused great inconvenience and offence.

Shortly after reaching her hotel the Grand Duchess received a visit from the Prince Regent. He arrived while she was still changing from her travelling clothes and she met him half way down the staircase in a state of flustered irritation. "Your Grand Duchess," muttered the Prince Regent to Princess Lieven when he left, "is not good-looking." "Your Prince," remarked the Grand Duchess when the Ambassadress returned upstairs, "is ill bred."

An official dinner at Carlton House was even more inauspicious. The Grand Duchess, in the days since her arrival, had taken pains to solicit and respond to the plaudits of the London crowds; she had received the leaders of the Opposition; she had announced her intention of visiting the Princess of Wales, and was only deterred from so doing by a threat on the part of Lieven that if she did so he would resign his post. She went out of her way to seek the intimacy of the Princess Charlotte and it was commonly believed that it was owing to her influence that the heiress to the throne of Britain defied the wishes of her father and his Government and refused to marry the Hereditary Prince of Orange. In her letters to her brother in Paris she painted a favourable, if not glowing, picture of this princess. She applauded her plump figure and her "great intelligent eyes of pale blue" which had at times "the fixed look of the House of Brunswick." She found "much wit and doggedness in her nature"; the Princess Charlotte seemed to her to possess "a will of bronze in the least things, a searching reasoning power, and manners so odd that they take your breath away. . . . She looks like a boy, or rather like a young rascal, dressed as a girl."

Such indiscretions and such intimacies were not a happy prelude to a dinner at Carlton House. Princess Lieven was in despair. The Grand Duchess threw an initial chill over the party by insisting that the band should be sent away since music made her vomit. In the ensuing hush the Prince Regent sought to brighten things by asking the Grand Duchess why she still wore mourning for her late husband and by suggesting that in a woman of her obvious charms widowhood could never be prolonged. "She answered," records Princess Lieven, "by an astonished silence and looks full of haughtiness. It was a lamentable beginning."

The Prince Regent, as the dinner proceeded, sought to exercise all his charm. He was not successful. "Handsome as he is," wrote the Grand Duchess to her brother, "he is a man visibly used up by dissipation and disgusting rather. His much boasted affability is the most licentious, I may even say obscene, strain I have ever listened to. You know I am far from being puritanical or prudish; but I avow that with him and his brother I have not only to get stiffly on my stiffs, but not to know what to do with eyes and ears. A brazen way of looking where eyes should not go."

The climax was reached towards the end of that unfortunate dinner. The Grand Duchess took occasion to reprove the Prince Regent for the strict discipline which he exercised over the

Princess Charlotte and for the seclusion which he imposed upon her. "When she is married, madam," the Prince Regent answered unwarily, "she will do as her husband pleases: for the present she does as I wish." Smiling innocently the Grand Duchess answered, "Your Highness is right. Between wife and husband there can only be one will." "This is intolerable," whispered the purple Regent in an aside to Princess Lieven. "From that evening," records the latter, "she and the Regent hated each other mutually, and the feeling remained to the end."

[5]

The original intention had been that the Tsar should come alone. Castlereagh thought this an invidious proposal and urged the Prince Regent to "dilute the libation to Russia" by also inviting the Emperor Francis and King Frederick William of Prussia. "The Tsar," he wrote, "has the greatest merit and must be held high but he ought to be grouped and not made the sole feature for admiration." The Austrian Emperor, who loathed all public ceremonies and who knew that he was unpopular in England, refused the invitation and sent Metternich in his place. The King of Prussia accepted, bringing with him both Hardenberg and Blücher. The two sovereigns, with the accompanying Ministers and Generals, reached Dover at 6.30 P.M. on Monday, June 6. The King of Prussia spent the night at the York Hotel: the Emperor of Russia who "appeared somewhat indisposed by the common affects of a sea voyage in windy weather" accepted the hospitality of Mr. Fector, a local resident.

A tremendous reception had been prepared for them in London. The Prince Regent rode out to Shooter's Hill to meet his illustrious visitors; the Old Kent Road was blocked by waiting carriages and thronged with thousands of expectant citizens anxious to applaud the Russian liberator. They were disappointed. The Emperor Alexander slipped past them unnoticed in Prince Lieven's carriage. He reached the Pulteney Hotel at 2.30 in the afternoon of Tuesday, June 7, and was gaily greeted by his sister as he entered the lounge. They passed upstairs together to their private apartments.

Meanwhile the rumour that the Tsar had already arrived spread rapidly through London. A vast crowd gathered in Piccadilly and the Tsar, when he appeared upon the balcony, was hailed with rapturous acclaim. The Prince Regent had by then returned to Carlton House and sent a message to Alexander announcing his intention to visit him immediately. They waited for hours in the upstairs room. The Tsar could not conceal his impatience and the Grand Duchess did her best to inflame his irritation. "That is what the man is like," she hissed to her brother, while Princess Lieven listened in dismay. At 4.30, while the crowds below increased their tumult, a message was brought to the Tsar from Carlton House. "His Royal Highness," he read, "has been threatened with annoyance in the street if he shows himself; it is therefore impossible for him to come and see the Emperor." This was a humiliating admission. The Tsar again entered Prince Lieven's carriage and drove to Carlton House. He found the Prince Regent, as was not unnatural, embarrassed and tetchy. It would all have been so simple if the Tsar had agreed to go to St. James' Palace instead of to a public hotel; the Regent could then have driven to visit him through the comparative privacy of the Mall. "A poor Prince," remarked Alexander to Prince Lieven as they drove back together to the Pulteney. "But one," Prince Lieven answered (or at least his wife says that he answered), "who helped you to win a glorious war and a peace to match." Such was the only private interview which took place between Alexander and the Prince Regent.

Thereafter ensued an almost unbroken round of public and private festivity. In the mornings, such was the utter simplicity of his manners, the Tsar could be seen before breakfast, walking with his sister in Hyde Park or Kensington Gardens. He would return to his hotel followed by an admiring crowd. "On ascending the steps of his hotel," we read in *The Times* newspaper, "His Imperial Majesty turned round to the people and most condescendingly took off his hat." Together the brother and sister visited Westminster, St. Paul's, Greenwich and the Royal Exchange; from there "they repaired with equal curiosity to visit the British Museum." They breakfasted at the Star and Garter and drove on to Hampton Court and Frogmore; they went to the races at Ascot; they were present at a Quaker meeting; and on Sunday they attended divine service in the Russian Chapel in Welbeck Street.

Every night there were banquets, balls, and gala performances at the several theatres. An address was presented to the Tsar by the Mayor and Corporation of London to which he replied in the German language. At night the streets of London were illuminated. The screen at Carlton House was lit by flares of scarlet and topaz interspersed between palm trees in tubs; in front of Lord Castlereagh's house at No. 18 St. James' Square there was an immense transparency representing a large dove with a branch of olive in its mouth. There were Courts, levées and drawing rooms twice a week. Banquets were offered by the Goldsmiths' Company and the Merchant Tailors; Lord Liverpool and Lord Castlereagh provided state dinners; and there were balls given by the Salisburys, the Hertfords and the Cholmondeleys. The Tsar also accepted hospitality from leaders of the Opposition such as Lord Grey and the Duke of Devonshire; the Prince Regent did not attend these functions.

The antipathy between the Tsar and the Prince Regent did not diminish as the days wore on. The Regent kept his guest waiting for a whole hour on the occasion of a review in Hyde Park; the Tsar countered by arriving for dinner at Carlton House at 11 P.M. excusing himself by saying that he had been detained by a long audience which he had accorded to Lord Grey. On the night of Saturday, June 11, there was a gala performance at the King's Theatre. The Prince Regent and his guests were entertained with Pacitta's opera *Aristodemo*, followed by a "Scotch Divertissement" as well as by the ballet *Le Calife Voleur*. In the interval a special hymn of welcome was sung from the stage by Madame Grassini and Signora Tramizzami. It was on this occasion that a further unfortunate incident occurred. The Princess of Wales entered her box noisily in the middle of the performance and curtseyed to the Emperor Alexander and King Frederick William. They rose in the royal box to return her salute; at which the assembled company burst into tumultuous applause. On Tuesday, June 14, the Tsar and his sister left London for Oxford. "The Emperor and his sister," records *The Times*, "drove to Merton College which, though mouldering in many parts from the effects of centuries, contains apartments commodious and excellent." It had been the Prince Regent's hope and intention that the Emperor should be detained at Oxford on the occasion of Lady Jersey's ball. The Tsar in order to spite him drove through the night from Oxford and appeared at Lady Jersey's house at 2.30 A.M.; he danced till six.

The climax of this damaging visit was reached on the occasion of the Guildhall banquet on Saturday, June 18. The Emperor Alexander, dressed in scarlet and gold, drove down to the City in the Prince Regent's state coach drawn by the Hanoverian creams. His sister the Grand Duchess insisted upon accompanying him, although it had been pointed out to her that it was not customary for ladies to be present on such occasions. A special anteroom had been constructed for the assembly of the royal guests and hung with scarlet silk. The royal party, having been mustered by the Court Chamberlain, passed into the Guildhall through an aisle of waiting guests towards the dais. The King of Prussia gave his arm to the Grand Duchess Catherine; the Emperor Alexander gave his arm to the Duchess of York; the Prince Regent, giving his arm to Princess Lieven, followed behind. On passing up the aisle the Tsar caught sight of the two leaders of the Opposition, Lords Grey and Holland. He stopped to address to them a few amicable words. The Prince Regent, in the face of the assembled company, had to pause and wait. During the banquet which followed he maintained, as Princess Lieven records, a "haughty silence" towards Alexander and his sister. "All agree," wrote Creevey, "that Prinny will die or go mad; he is worn out with fuss, fatigue and *rage*."

It was a tremendous banquet. It cost twenty thousand pounds. The seven hundred guests could feast their eyes upon the top table on the dais and observe the heroes of the hour—Platoff and Blücher, Yorck and Bülow, Metternich and Hardenberg. "The dinner," records the *Annual Register*, "was as sumptuous as expense or skill could make it." There was a large baron of beef surmounted by the royal standard and attended by the serjeant carvers and the principal cooks. There was a fine turtle "very handsomely presented by Samuel Turner Esquire, a West Indian merchant." There was gold plate and many toasts and special songs recited by the artists of the Italian Opera. The Grand Duchess at this repeated her remark that music always gave her nausea and asked the singers to stop; it was only with difficulty that they persuaded her to agree sulkily that "God Save the King" might be played after the royal toast. Her conduct on this occasion excited much resentment. The Emperor Alexander, who was becoming increasingly deaf, did not understand the embarrassed mutterings which went on around him. Even the mild Lord Liverpool was incensed. "When folks don't know how to behave," he said to Princess Lieven, "they would do better to stay at home and your Duchess has chosen against all usage to go to men's dinners."

It was not only the members of the Government who were shocked by the impertinence of the Grand Duchess and her brother. The leaders of the Opposition had also been embarrassed by the demonstrations which the Tsar was continually making in their favour. So far from being impressed by Alexander, Lord Grey described him to Creevey as "a vain silly fellow." It was all very well, they felt, for British politicians to say unkind things about the Prince Regent; but for a foreigner to insult him publicly was an affront to the State. Something of this feeling seems to have affected the public as a whole; as the visit drew to its unhappy close it was observed that the London crowds no longer greeted Alexander with their former rapture; their loudest plaudits were reserved for Blücher the Prussian and for Platoff, the flamboyant Cossack leader. And it was thus

with a sense of anticlimax and chilled sympathies that, on
Monday, June 27, the Emperor Alexander embarked again at
Dover.

[6]

Castlereagh, in his optimism, had imagined when in Paris
that all major outstanding questions would be easily settled
during the London visit and that the ensuing Congress at Vienna
would only last four weeks. Metternich shared this view. They
did not foresee what havoc would be caused to their arrangements by the social festivities arranged for the visiting monarchs or by the mood of mischievous ill-temper in which the
Emperor Alexander, goaded by his sister, had indulged. Metternich was not sorry to see a gulf widening between the British
and the Russian Cabinets. He had himself been at pains during
the visit to avoid all contact with the Opposition leaders and to
behave with the utmost tact. He made fun of Alexander when
talking to the Prince Regent, and of the Prince Regent when
talking to Alexander; he fanned the embers of their smoulder-
ing antipathy with little soft asides. There was no prospect in
such circumstances of doing any profitable business in London.
Castlereagh endeavoured to obtain a firm agreement that the
Congress should open at Vienna not later than August 15; the
Tsar insisted that this would not give him time to return to Russia and sound his own public opinion; the formal opening of the
Congress was therefore postponed until October 1, although it
was agreed that the Ministers of the three Great Powers should
meet together before that day. It was also agreed that no
definitive action should in the meanwhile be taken in any of the
areas at present in the occupation of Russia and Prussia. This
was an important reservation since Russia at the time was in
occupation of almost the whole of Poland and Saxony, whereas
the Prussians were established on the left bank of the Rhine
and held the fortress of Mainz. And finally each Power undertook to maintain 75,000 troops on a mobilised basis pending the
conclusion of a final peace. That, apart from a general agreement that Holland might obtain Antwerp and Great Britain the

Cape of Good Hope, was all that Castlereagh could secure. A whole month had been wasted by these acrimonious festivities. The British public, feeling instinctively that Alexander, by his frivolous petulance, had misjudged their enthusiasm and slighted their susceptibilities, ceased from that moment to regard Russia as the hope of the new world. Whereas both the Government and the Opposition came to the conclusion that the Emperor Alexander was lacking in any dependable sense of proportion and that the future security of the British Empire, or in other words the balance of power, must be based upon the more calculable interests of the older Europe.

8. The Congress Assembles

[September 1814]

Castlereagh's early conception of the balance of power—The attitude of Russia compels him to adopt "fresh considerations"—The menacing secretiveness of Russian policy and the activity and intrigues of Russian agents abroad—Castlereagh's first idea of an alignment with Prussia and Austria is complicated by Prussia's subservience to Russia and Austria's suspicions of Prussia—The conception of "a just equilibrium" as a system advantageous, not to Great Britain only, but to Europe as a whole—Castlereagh realises that such a system can no longer be based upon the assumption of an independent Poland and that Russian expansion westwards must be controlled—His correspondence with Hardenberg—His visit to Paris—His arrival in Vienna—Castlereagh's personality and his prestige—The three other British Plenipotentiaries—Lord Cathcart—Lord Clancarty—Sir Charles Stewart—The British Delegation—The French Delegation—The Russian Delegation—The Austrian Delegation—The Prussian Delegation—Minor Delegations—Nuisances and eccentrics.

CASTLEREAGH, with his aloof brain, was not the man to be perturbed by the vanities which the London interlude had disclosed. If they affected him at all, it was with contemptuous relief that the infatuation for Russia which had at first inflamed left-wing opinion should so rapidly have been chilled by the Tsar's self-dramatisation and unreliability. The British Minister's aim, as always, was both general and particular. He wished to safeguard the general security of Europe by creating a balance of power such as would render it impossible for any single nation to contemplate a successful war. He also wished to safeguard the particular security of Great Britain by placing Antwerp and the Scheldt in friendly hands and by defending the independence of the Low Countries against any threat of renewed French aggression.

He appears at first to have taken an optimistic view of the ease with which the Congress would be able to conduct its labours. "The Emperor," he wrote to Wellington on August 7, "arrives [at Vienna] on September 27 and we should have time to discuss the more difficult matters previous to the assembly of Congress on October 1, having previously methodized the less complicated parts of the arrangement." The process of "methodizing" will be described in the next chapter; it proved far more difficult than that.

Nor was this his only disappointment. He had hoped at first that "at the end of so long a struggle, the several Powers might have enjoyed some repose, without forming calculations that always augment the risks of war." He had been forced to admit however that "the tone and conduct of Russia have disappointed this hope and forced upon us fresh considerations."

It was indeed true that Russia, having endured harsh suffering and achieved magnificent triumphs, was assuming an attitude of arrogant secretiveness which caused dismay to her partners in the Quadruple Alliance. The impetuosity of the Slav temperament was, in the person of the All-Russian Autocrat, exaggerated to the point of mental instability. "The great oddness of the Emperor," wrote Lord Walpole from St. Petersburg on August 9, 1814, "was suspected in very early age; and medical men now here were brought over on that account." The Russian generals and diplomatists moreover, having convinced themselves that Russian arms alone had liberated Europe from an odious tyranny, being intoxicated by the military prestige which Russia had unexpectedly acquired, began on every occasion and in every country to indulge in self-assertiveness and intrigue. "Well, so far as that goes," boasted a Russian general when discussing the impending Congress, "one does not need to worry much about negotiations when one has 600,000 men under arms." At the same time from the remotest corners of Europe, Asia, Africa and even America reports began to pour in regarding the presence of mysterious Russian agents and the activities of energetic and overbearing Russian diplomatists. "I know not," wrote Sir Henry Wellesley to Castlereagh from

Madrid in October 1814, "whether M. Tatisheff acts upon instructions from his Court, but, if he does, it seems to be the object of the Emperor of Russia to establish a predominant influence throughout Europe, and particularly in those Courts where Great Britain, by the assistance which she afforded to them during the war, has acquired a just influence." Such reports were too numerous, too frequent and withal too consistent, to be ignored; if the balance of power were to be preserved some "fresh considerations" would certainly become essential.

From an interesting letter written by Castlereagh to Wellington on October 25, 1814, it is possible to retrace the phases of thought through which he passed. His first hope and desire had been that each Power, having obtained what was essential to its own security, would settle down to a period of repose without conflict with any of its neighbours. This hope was dissipated by Russia's attitude in regard to Poland; an attitude which was at one and the same time intransigent and enigmatic. Some more definite alignment was evidently necessary if Russian imperialism were to be curtailed. What form should such an alignment assume?

It is clear that the combination which Castlereagh, in the true Pitt tradition, would himself have preferred was one between Austria, Prussia and Great Britain, assisted by the Low Countries and the smaller German States, and constituting "an intermediary system between France and Russia." So far from sharing Talleyrand's fear that a strong Prussia established in the Rhineland might constitute, not a present safeguard, but a future menace, he was convinced that Prussia was the only available Power capable of countering France's inevitable desire to regain possession of Antwerp. In which illusion he was surrendering to the all too common error of estimating the factors of future stability in terms of those factors which had caused and influenced the recently concluded war.

This combination was, however, rendered impossible by the subservience which Prussia persisted in displaying towards Russia and by the extreme and justifiable alarm with which

Metternich regarded any undue increase of Prussian power within the Germanic body. Thus gradually, and against his will, Castlereagh was thrown back upon an alliance with our former enemy against our major ally; and found himself obliged to seek his required balance in a combination of France, Austria and Great Britain against Russia and Prussia.

[2]

His original idea, the pattern which first formed in his mind, was somewhat ingenuous. It seemed to him that the centre of the whole problem, and perhaps its clue, was Poland. It was obvious that if a strong and absolutely independent Poland could be created, then so far from extending Russian power towards the west, one might be able to remove it further to the east. But if Poland were to be truly independent and not a mere satellite of Russia, then she must be powerful; and if she were to be powerful then she must obtain an area of territory and an amount of population infinitely larger than that comprised within Napoleon's Duchy of Warsaw. This would mean that Russia, Prussia and Austria would each have to surrender to the new Poland the vast provinces which they had taken from her under the three partitions of the eighteenth century. And this in its turn would entail important "compensations" at least to Austria and Prussia. The resultant adjustments would, however, themselves prove beneficial. By compensating Prussia in Saxony and the Rhineland one would render her a strong Germanic Power and an assistant against any future French aggression. Austria, for her part, would find her compensation in Italy and the Illyrian provinces. By this means a perfect balance could be achieved. The reconstituted Poland would form a useful buffer between Russia and the West: Austria and Prussia would become of almost equal weight in central Europe; a close, and if possible a dynastic connection between Great Britain and the Netherlands would safeguard the estuary of the Scheldt; and a pacified and pacific France, joined by family ties both to Spain and the Two Sicilies, would provide a further counterpoise. A balanced Europe would thereby be created in which Great Britain, using her mastery of the seas for the benefit of all, could exercise the almost effortless function of preserving both her own security and the peace of the world.

Castlereagh's ideal of a just equilibrium was not understood by his contemporaries, and even today there are many people who imagine that the balance of power, instead of being one of the most stable guarantees of peace, is in some unexplained manner the cause of wars. The policy of the just equilibrium has moreover been prejudiced in continental and American eyes by the fact that of all policies it is the one most advantageous to the British Commonwealth and Empire. Having obtained all the possessions which she could possibly desire or assimilate, wishing only to enjoy in tranquillity the position of privilege which she had won through many centuries of violent effort, having through satiety acquired the temperament of a civilian sedative race, it was only natural that the England of the nineteenth century should see in the balance of power the ideal policy by which, with the minimum of effort, she could retain her rich possessions and enjoy her ease. The fact that she shrouded this policy in an aura of self-righteousness, that she draped its extremely realistic advantages in the vestments of superior virtue, tempted foreign observers to regard it with suspicion and to blind themselves to the fact that, apart from being advantageous to Great Britain it was also advantageous to the world at large. The century of British supremacy which stretched from 1814 to 1914 was a period which conferred immense benefits of peace and prosperity not only upon the British Commonwealth and Empire, but upon the whole community of nations. And the reasons are obvious. Having nothing to win and much to lose Great Britain became an essentially conservative, and therefore peace-loving, nation; she was strong enough to discourage aggression in others and vulnerable enough not to practice aggression herself; and dreading above all things the domination of the Continent by a single militarist Power she identified herself throughout the nineteenth century with the interests of small nations and the encouragement of liberal institutions. It is thus a mistake to regard the balance of power as some iniquitous plotting of forces; it was rather the achievement of such a distribution of strength as would render aggression by any single country a policy of the greatest uncertainty and danger.

Castlereagh believed at first that, with the downfall of the Napoleonic system, such a balance could readily be achieved. He soon realised however that so far from Poland proving the solution of the problem it was bound to become the focus of all difficulties. It became evident that neither Russia, Prussia nor Austria would surrender enough Polish territory to render the new Poland large enough or strong enough to maintain her own independence; and it was also evident that, whatever professions might be made by the Emperor Alexander, Poland would in fact become a dependency of Russia and that the frontier between Poland and Europe would in the end become the western frontier of the Russian Empire. So far therefore from Poland becoming a valuable buffer State able to restrain Russian influence in central Europe, it would be little more than a Russian province and as such extend the Russian frontier to within striking distance of Vienna and Berlin. Castlereagh's early pattern of the balance of power was thereby dislocated: he saw at once that "fresh considerations" must arise.

In his conversations in London with Metternich and Hardenberg, Castlereagh had outlined his original conception of the future equilibrium. He soon realised that Metternich, while appearing with his usual obliquity to agree to this suggested pattern, was in fact determined not to give to a reconstituted Poland those provinces which, under the partitions, Austria had obtained. It was also evident that the Austrians looked with suspicion upon any compensations which might unduly increase the weight of Prussia within the Germanic body. The attitude of Prussia was even less co-operative. On the one hand there was the sullen, stupid, sentimental subservience of King Frederick William to his "divine friend" Alexander. On the other hand there was the undisguised greed manifested by the Prussian General Staff.

On August 8 Castlereagh sought to extract from Hardenberg some definite statement of Prussian intentions. He drew attention to the menacing attitude being adopted by Russia. She was creating a strong Polish army under her own command: she was massing troops in north-eastern Europe. Hardenberg's reply was not encouraging. It suggested that the Prussian Government interpreted the balance of power, not as some general European interest, but in terms of the extension of Prussia's frontiers at the expense of her neighbours. While admitting the disturbing implications of Russian expansion, Hardenberg appeared more concerned with Bavaria's apparent desire to obtain the fortress of Mainz and Austria's evident ambition to secure for herself a slice of Saxony. He urged that the only possible solution was to give Prussia the whole of Saxony, to share out the Rhineland between Prussia and Austria, and to induce the new Kingdom of the Netherlands to enter the German Confederation as a member of the Burgundian Circle. This latter suggestion aroused Castlereagh's special distaste.

Rumours had meanwhile been filtering through to London that under Talleyrand's influence Louis XVIII was contemplating the repair and improvement of his personal relations with the Emperor Alexander. Such rumours were not without foundation. In an unctuous letter which Talleyrand sent to the Tsar on June 13 he had ventured to address his Imperial Majesty as "the hero of my fancy, and dare I add, of my heart." If Bourbon France, that still uncertain quantity, were to throw her weight on Russia's side, then the desired balance would become even more uneven. Castlereagh decided therefore that it would be a good thing to accept Talleyrand's invitation and to visit Paris on his way to Vienna. Before doing so he consulted the Duke of Wellington who replied with lapidary good-sense. "The situation of affairs," wrote the Duke, "will naturally constitute England and France as arbitrators at the Congress, if these Powers *understand* each other. . . . But I think your object would be defeated, and England would lose her high character and station, if Prince Talleyrand's line is adopted which appears to me tantamount to the declaration by the two Powers that they will be arbitrators of all the differences which may arise. We must not forget that only a few months ago it was wished to exclude the interference and influence of France from the Congress entirely."

It was indeed evident that Great Britain and France, having for quite different reasons no special demands of their own to make to the Congress, and desiring jointly a general balance of power, would be in a position of mediatory advantage in regard to the other Powers whose ambitions were bound to conflict. But it was also evident that were Great Britain too openly to make common cause with France she would not only be violating the secret clause of the Peace of Paris (under which the issues arising among the victorious Powers should be settled as between themselves alone) but might provoke a counter-combination of her former allies.

Castlereagh left England on August 16 and after a short stay in Brussels and Antwerp reached Paris on August 24. In his conversations with Louis XVIII and Talleyrand a similarity of views was established. Castlereagh found indeed that the French monarch and his Minister were embarrassingly friendly. He felt it necessary "rather to repress the exuberance of this sentiment and to prevent its assuming a shape which by exciting jealousy in other States might impair our respective means of being really useful." Talleyrand was too intelligent not to realise the need of such discretion. But the fact remains that the understanding established during that two days' visit not merely prevented Talleyrand from placing himself at the disposal of Russia, but created between him and Castlereagh a basis of co-operation which was to have a determinant effect during the supreme crisis of the Vienna Congress.

[3]

Leaving Paris on August 27 Castlereagh, accompanied by Lady Castlereagh and her sister, travelled by slow stages to Vienna where he arrived on September 13. He first established himself in a modest flat giving onto the street known as Im Auge Gottes. This proved too small for their expanding social requirements and they subsequently transferred themselves to a more important apartment, containing twenty-two rooms and situated in No. 30 Minoritenplatz. Castlereagh possessed a solitary soul and derived but little pleasure from the amenities of society. He had little gift for intimacy and the only two people whom he really loved, his wife and his half-brother Charles Stewart, never shared with him the lonelier recesses of his mind. The former, with her blousy sprightliness, with her wide-eyed uncomprehending self-satisfaction, was too unintelligent to understand the inner mysteries of Castlereagh's nature.[1] The latter, being a conceited man, was too insensitive. The social shyness which had tormented Castlereagh since his boyhood in County Down had induced him to hide himself behind a screen of glacial good manners. Handsome and seemingly imperturbable, his sober apparel contrasting with the gold lace and decorations of the foreign potentates and plenitotentiaries, he would in his uncertain French exchange conventional but icy compliments with those who addressed him. Even to his own compatriots he appeared incomprehensibly aloof. "He can neither feel nor feign," said Canning. "So opposed," wrote the Duke of Buckingham, "was his nature to display." Only those who watched him fingering tenderly the flowers in the North Cray garden or playing with children realised the gentler delicacies of his temperament. To the foreigners who flocked to Vienna he was an enigmatic figure. They were impressed by the patrician dignity of his demeanour; they were amused by his almost bourgeois domesticity. They would recount to each other how on Sunday mornings Lord Castlereagh, his wife and sister-in-law, his colleagues, his staff and his domestics, would all gather in the drawing-room at the Minoritenplatz and sing Church of England hymns to the harmonium. From their curricles and coaches they would observe him strolling through the streets of Vienna arm in arm with Lady Castlereagh, gaping at the shop windows like a provincial upon a holiday. They would titter together when they heard that Lord and Lady

Castlereagh took dancing lessons in the morning and when they observed how sadly each of them had profited by such instructions. Yet under all their giggling they were both impressed and disconcerted. Here was a man of astounding distinction who was not, in their sense, a man of the world. Here was a man possessed of exceeding power, who did not use his power to achieve what seemed obvious successes. Here was a man whose values and methods were different from theirs; a man who, in the glittering kaleidoscope of the Vienna Congress, remained always central, immutable, colourless and dominant. His prestige was immense.

Even Gentz, reflecting upon England's position at the Congress, discarded for the moment the poisons of his vivid pen. "England," he wrote, "appeared at Vienna with all the glamour which she owed to her immense successes, to the eminent part which she had played in the Coalition, to her limitless influence, to a solid basis of prosperity and power such as no other country has acquired in our days—in fact to the respect and fear which she inspired and which affected her relations with all the other Governments. Profiting by this, England could have imposed her will upon Europe. England renounced this noble privilege. Lord Castlereagh took up a neutral attitude which was often surprising; being in the position to become the arbiter of Europe, he only afforded her weak and partial assistance. This without question was the main cause of the unsatisfactory results of the Congress."

Gentz failed to understand how any country, possessed of dominant power, could fail to use it for her own purposes; he could not understand that England was unwilling to assume any undue responsibility for Europe and desired only that the continental nations should settle their own affairs reasonably as between themselves; he grossly underestimated or ignored the immense influence for peace which Castlereagh did in fact exercise at Vienna; nor did he admit that, but for Castlereagh's resolution, there would have been war again upon the continent of Europe. Yet even in Gentz's criticism one can detect a note of puzzled admiration.

[4]

There were three other British plenipotentiaries in addition
to the Foreign Secretary. Castlereagh did not regard them as
possessing an authority in any way equal to his own. "You will
find the others," he wrote to Wellington on December 17,
"useful in matters referred to subordinate commissions . . .
but they take no part in transactions between Cabinet and
Cabinet." There was in the first place Lord Cathcart, our ambassador at St. Petersburg and first British Commissioner with
the Russian armies. Lord Cathcart's repute has suffered from
the abuse showered on him by his subordinate Sir Robert Wilson
who, in his disloyal and emotional manner, corresponded with
the leaders of the Opposition deriding his chief's abilities and
incidentally providing the Whig politicians with much wholly
incorrect information. Lord Cathcart seems, however, to have
been a slow-witted man. "He never begins to think," wrote
Sir Charles Stewart, "until other people have finished." His
value to Castlereagh was that he possessed much knowledge of
Russian conditions and was able to exercise a certain influence
upon the Tsar.

The third plenipotentiary was Lord Clancarty, who had done
much useful diplomatic work in the Netherlands, and whose
zeal, ability and uprightness earned a high tribute from Talleyrand. And the fourth was Sir Charles Stewart, Castlereagh's
own half-brother, a dashing soldier, whose credit was diminished
by the ostentation of his person and the violence of his manner.
Lord Stewart (as he subsequently became before succeeding his
brother as third Marquis of Londonderry) was regarded by the
Congress as a wholly ridiculous figure and was made much mock
of under the title of "Lord Pumpernickel." The Weimar
publisher, Carl Bertuch, in his diary of the Congress displays
unwonted animus against the person of Charles Stewart. *"Ein
insolenter Patron,"* he calls him, *"ohne Conduite."* Even his
compatriots were puzzled by the influence which Stewart exercised upon his brother. "Castlereagh," wrote John Croker, "had

a real respect for Charles' understanding and a high opinion of his good sense and discretion. This seems incomprehensible to us, who know the two men; but the fact was so." And Croker's opinion was confirmed by the Duke of Wellington.

The Foreign Office delegation was, as always, understaffed. Lord Castlereagh had brought with him the Under Secretary, Edward Cooke, who adopted towards the Congress the detached and ironical attitude of the chronic invalid. Joseph Planta, the devoted private secretary, did all he could to relieve both those above him and those below him of their incessant labours. The clerical work was executed by only ten young men from the Foreign Office who, considering that they had to do all the translating and to copy in long hand Castlereagh's voluminous and contorted despatches, can have found little time for any personal enjoyments. And a cohort of King's Messengers, whose duties during those times were always hard and often perilous, hurried backwards and forwards with incessant delays and mis-adventures between London and Vienna. However otiose may have been the occupations of the minor delegations, the staff which Lord Castlereagh brought to Vienna were constantly and intolerably overworked.

The foreign delegations were more lavishly equipped. Talleyrand had secured a large house, the Kaunitz Palace, in the Johannesgasse, not far from the cathedral, where his niece, the Comtesse Edmond de Périgord, then aged twenty-one years, acted as hostess. As second plenipotentiary he had brought with him the Duc de Dalberg, a man who had much first-hand knowl-edge of German questions, but whose value was diminished by his obstinacy and indiscretion. His two other plenipotentiaries had been carefully selected. They were the Marquis de la Tour du Pin and Count Alexis de Noailles, who as a former aide-de-camp to the Comte d'Artois was in the confidence of the extreme royalists. For more serious business he had the help of Count de La Besnadière, an official of the French Foreign Office and a man of great intelligence and industry. They were assisted by a numerous and elegant staff.

The Emperor Alexander had appointed as his plenipotentiaries Count Andréas Razumovski, Count Stackelberg, and Count Nesselrode, his Foreign Minister. The latter, according to Aberdeen, was "not quite clever enough for the Emperor." They were assisted by a horde of heterogeneous specialists. There was the Alsatian Baron Anstett, who served on the Statistical Committee. La Harpe himself was present for counsel on Swiss problems. There was the Corsican Count Pozzo di Borgo and the Corfiote Count Capo d'Istria. Freiherr vom und zum Stein advised him in German matters, and Prince Adam Czartoryski on Polish affairs. The arrogant and outspoken intransigence of the former stimulated and depressed the Emperor's nerves. Stein had a way of exposing to the Tsar in harsh and very forcible language the inconsistency between his liberal professions and his actual conduct. Patiently the Tsar would reply to these reproofs: "*Oh ja!*" Stein would shout back at him, and again "*Oh ja!*" With Czartoryski the Tsar's old relations of affectionate intimacy had been clouded, partly by the renewal of the former connection between Czartoryski and the unhappy Empress (in regard to which the Tsar was becoming increasingly less complacent) and partly by the discovery that behind his back his Polish friend had been corresponding with the Whig leaders in London. The Tsar's intention none the less was to be his own first plenipotentiary and to treat with the Foreign Ministers as an equal. His several foreign advisers, while their presence aroused considerable indignation among the Russian staff, were never accorded his entire confidence. Nobody within the Russian delegation knew exactly where he stood. The Tsar moved in a theocratic aura.

Metternich also had decided to have no rival near him. He admitted as second Plenipotentiary the reliable and harmless Baron von Wessenburg. Baron Binder helped him with Italian questions, State Councillor Hudelist was a useful member of the statistical committee, and Count Radetzky became his expert on military and strategic matters. As his personal secretary, and as Secretary General of the Congress, he had the support of Friedrich von Gentz. As his public relations officers he employed Herr Pilat, the editor of the *Oesterreichische Beobachter*.

For Prussia appeared Prince Hardenberg,[2] assisted, since he was almost totally deaf, by Baron Wilhelm von Humboldt. General von dem Knesebeck served as military adviser; among a large staff of experts the most outstanding was Johann Gottfried (or as he sometimes called himself, John Godfrey) Hoffman—who came by sheer efficiency to dominate the Statistical Committee.

The minor delegations were too numerous to mention. Count Münster, the representative of Hanover, bore a special relation to Lord Castlereagh and an even more special relation to the Prince Regent. There were some thirty-two minor German royalties, most of whom had brought with them their wives, their mistresses and their Secretaries of State. The King of Saxony, being in disgrace, was not invited to the Congress; his interests were unofficially defended by Count Friedrich von der Schulenberg. For Naples there were two delegations, one of them charged with the interests of Murat, and the other with those of the legitimate Bourbon dynasty. The Pope was represented by Cardinal Consalvi, the Sultan of Turkey by Mavrojeni Pasha. Several unofficial deputations had also arrived in Vienna; the Jews of Frankfurt had despatched special representatives to watch the general interests of Jewry; there was a deputation from the German Catholics; Herr Cotta of Augsburg was there on behalf of the publishing trade.

The Vienna Congress, like all international gatherings, possessed its nuisances and its eccentrics. The most tiresome of all the plenipotentiaries was Don Pedro Gomez Labrador, the representative of Spain. He was determined not to play "the part of the marionette" and he sought with almost inconceivable maladroitness to imitate the technique of Talleyrand. Even the Duke of Wellington, who had much experience of the Spanish temperament, called him "*la plus mauvaise tête* that I have ever met." And in fact Labrador throughout behaved with a wrongheadedness which drove both Castlereagh and Talleyrand to despair. The Congress was also enlivened by the eccentric presence of Sir Sidney Smith who, while purporting to hold a watching brief for the royal House of Vasa, was in fact more interested in inducing the Congress to take concerted measures against the Barbary corsairs. The antics of Sir Sidney, his ingenious vanity, the startling appearance which he presented with his yellow Swedish ribbon and disordered hair, much embarrassed the official British delegation, but inspired the foreigners with almost affectionate amusement. The hero of Acre—"that mere vaporizer" as Croker called him—made them laugh.

The affluence of so many otiose visitors to Vienna created serious problems of housing, maintenance and expense. In order to distract their attention from the actual futility of their presence a vast programme of entertainment was devised. This programme, while it threw a heavy burden upon the Austrian exchequer and thereby rendered the Congress increasingly unpopular with the Austrian public, has left behind it the legend that the Congress—"that base pageant" as Byron called it— devoted its whole time to social festivity. At any international gathering it is bound to happen that some of the attendant staffs find time hang heavy on their hands, whereas others are demonstrably overworked. The proportion established at Vienna between the employed and the unemployed was an ill-balanced proportion; the repute of the Congress has suffered accordingly.

Moreover, the presence in Vienna of so numerous and heterogeneous a collection of delegations—frequently self-appointed— while it increased the opportunity for intrigue rendered organisation a matter of extreme complexity. The Great Powers, who were ultimately responsible for the conduct and success of the Congress, strove by every means to placate, to ignore, to discipline and to circumvent the frustrated plenipotentiaries who buzzed around them. The problems of procedure and organisation which their presence created were urgent and almost desperate. And since it was in dealing with these problems that the main alignment of the Congress first took shape they will be examined in some detail in the chapter which follows.

9. The Problem of Procedure

[October 1814]

The initial mistake—The Four Allies had agreed by secret treaty to keep the direction of affairs in their own hands—At the same time they had invited every Power to send representatives to Vienna—The resentment aroused by this misunderstanding is exploited by Talleyrand—An agreed plan of procedure had not been thought out in advance by the conveners of the Congress—The distinction between the Big Powers and the Small Powers not accepted—The Big Four had no logical or legal basis for claiming the supreme direction—They strive, prior to Talleyrand's arrival, to reach an agreed basis and finally adopt a compromise which is embodied in a protocol—Talleyrand, when shown this protocol on September 30, refuses to accept it—The scene which ensued—The protocol is abandoned and purely empirical methods are resorted to—The appointment of the ten committees—The importance of the Statistical Committee—Talleyrand obtains admission to this Committee and eventually to the Big Four—Thereafter it becomes the Council of Five and in fact directs the Congress and prepares the Final Act.

THE FIRST two problems which face any international conference are "Who is to issue the invitations?" and "Who is to be invited?" The first question had been determined by Article XXXII of the Peace of Paris which provided that the Congress should be held in Vienna. This meant that it would be the Emperor of Austria who would convene the Congress and act as host. It also meant that the Austrian Foreign Minister would act as President. In the same Article XXXII it was also, and most imprudently, laid down that invitations would be issued to "all the Powers engaged on either side in the present war." Under the first Secret Article of the same treaty, however, France had been obliged to agree that the disposal of the territories which she had surrendered, as well as "the relations from which a system of real and permanent balance of power in Europe is to be derived," should be decided by the four Great Powers of the Quadruple Alliance (Russia, Austria, Prussia and Great Britain) strictly between themselves. The fact that this secret article had not been communicated to the minor Powers, or the *Sous-Alliés* as they were called, created misunderstanding from the outset. Every country, whether belligerent or neutral, whether enemy or allied, whether great or small, responded to the invitation and sent expensive delegations to Vienna under the impression that they would be granted the opportunity to establish their respective claims or at least to contribute their influence and opinions to the new European order. The four Great Powers, on the other hand, were bound to each other to keep the direction of affairs entirely in their own hands and to decide all important matters as between themselves. It is not surprising therefore that the smaller Powers should have felt that they had been invited to Vienna under false pretences; and that the organisation of the Congress should from the start have led to embittered dispute.

In every conference the problem of organisation, the actual plan of procedure, acquires a significance which is often under-estimated. However much the conveners of a conference may twist or turn or prevaricate, they cannot prevent this problem from imposing itself at the very outset of their deliberations. The dissensions which it is bound to create cause the several parties to a conference to adopt a certain alignment; and it often occurs that groups of Powers, who might hesitate to display their divergence when matters of major policy are under consideration, show symptoms of disintegration when questions of procedure are discussed. It has been found, for instance, that an ally or satellite, pledged to the support of a Great Power on the main lines of policy, will exploit a point of procedure or organisation in order either to manifest his independence or to enhance the price of his servility. It thus arises that the initial problem of organisation, unless carefully prepared before the conference assembles, is apt to become a disintegrating problem.

The Conference of Algeciras, for instance, was actually brought to a final climax on a minor point in the following day's agenda: on March 3, 1906, a vote on procedure was taken which placed Germany and her supporters in a minority of ten to three. At the Paris Conference of 1919 the difficulty of reconciling President Wilson's egalitarian doctrines, and his theory of open covenants openly arrived at, with the efficient conduct of business and the actual proportions of responsibility, led the five Great Powers to have recourse to subterfuges and delays which not only impeded the work of the Conference but created an atmosphere, on the one side of dissimulation, and on the other of distrust.

Yet in no international negotiation of which we possess full records did the problem of organisation or the actual details of procedure acquire so great a significance as at the Congress of Vienna. For it was in the fissure which this problem created in the frontage of the Quadruple Alliance that Talleyrand inserted his little wedge. And the effects of this insertion were so important to the subsequent development of the Congress that it is necessary, and not uninteresting, to examine how this crack or fissure occurred.

Metternich, after the London interlude, had returned to Vienna on July 18. After giving general instructions for the proper reception of the impending visitors, he retired to the little health resort of Baden a few miles only to the south of the capital. Castlereagh reached Vienna on September 13 and two days later an informal meeting was held between the plenipotentiaries of the four Allies, namely Metternich, Hardenberg, Castlereagh and Nesselrode. It was followed by four more formal conferences at which the problem of procedure was discussed. The Emperor Alexander, King Frederick William and Talleyrand did not arrive until September 23. And, as has been said, the formal opening of the whole Congress had been publicly announced for October 1.

None of the Big Four seems to have realised in advance to what an extent the problem of organisation and procedure would create opportunities for dissension and intrigue. "Not even the English," Talleyrand wrote to Louis XVIII, "whom I thought more methodical than the others, have done any preparatory work on this subject." On their arrival at Vienna the Big Four realised to their horror, and to Talleyrand's delight, that they had allowed themselves little more than a fortnight in which to solve this initial complexity. The proposals and counter-proposals which in the resultant flurry they exchanged were controversial, intricate, illogical and confused.

It must be remembered that at that date the distinction between Great Powers and Small Powers—a distinction which even to this day is invidious and delicate—did not exist. It was born during that hurried fortnight between September 13 and October 1, 1814. The assumption until then had been that all sovereign and independent States were in theory equal, whatever might be their responsibilities or physical strength. This was the first difficulty.

The second difficulty (as has been said above) was that, although the four members of the Quadruple Alliance had under a secret article of the Peace of Paris reserved for themselves the decision in all important matters, this reservation had not been communicated to, or accepted by, the other Powers represented at the Congress or even the Powers who had signed the Paris treaty. For although Talleyrand himself had been shown, and had been forced to accept the Secret Article, the representatives of Spain, Portugal and Sweden, who had also acceded to the Treaty, were in no sense bound by that article. There existed therefore no legal, contractual, logical or moral basis upon which the Big Four could claim the sole direction. Talleyrand was quick to exploit this anomaly for his own advantage. The Allies had, by their inadvertence, placed themselves in a false position; it was a position from which Talleyrand only allowed them to extricate themselves at the price of admitting France into their inner council. And once he had succeeded in this, the whole controversy, as often happens with such initial controversies, quite suddenly petered out.

[2]

The discussion on procedure divides itself into two main periods, namely the period before Talleyrand's intervention and the period after his intervention. It must be realised also that Castlereagh, suspecting that Austria might at any moment desert to the Russo-Prussian block, was in his heart of hearts anxious to redress this uncertain balance by introducing into the councils of the Big Four, not France only, but if necessary Spain, Portugal and Sweden. It was with this in mind that on September 15 he suggested that the supreme direction of the Conference should be entrusted to the "six Powers of the first order." The Prussians countered by proposing, that whereas the "formal Cabinet" might consist of the Six, the right of "initiation" should be reserved for the Four. Castlereagh opposed this solution as being "rather repulsive against France."

The question then arose as to the method by which the Big Four or the Big Six could obtain from the Congress as a whole the necessary authority to assume the supreme direction. On the one hand it was suggested that the whole Congress should be summoned on October 1 and should be invited to accord the required mandate. On the other hand it was suggested that the Four or the Six should merely announce that all preliminary decisions would be made by them and that the other Powers would be "consulted when necessary."

These two proposals, representing as they did the extremes of democratic and authoritarian procedure, induced Castlereagh to advance a third and middle scheme and to justify it by an interesting statement of principles. His argument can be summarised as follows:

1—"It appears clear," he wrote, "upon the first assembling of a body as numerous as the plenipotentiaries deputed to the Congress of Vienna, that no effectual progress can be made in business until some plan of European settlement can be prepared ready to be submitted for their consideration."

11—"It is equally clear," he continued, "that such a plan or report cannot advantageously originate with any individual plenipotentiary unaided by the counsels and suggestions of others; and that it can still less be expected to originate in the body at large."

III—Thus "a limited body of plenipotentiaries must be charged to prepare and bring forward the same." How was this body to be composed?

IV—It was evident that such a limited body could only be constituted from "among those who have borne the principal share in the councils and conduct of the war" and by those who framed the several treaties which, under the secret article of the Treaty of Paris, were recognised to form the basis of the future peace.

V—Castlereagh proposed, therefore, that the plenipotentiaries of Austria, Russia, Prussia, Great Britain, France and Spain should "charge themselves with this preparatory duty." And that until their plan was ready the meeting of the Congress, fixed for October 1, should be adjourned.

VI—That in the meanwhile a special committee consisting of the representatives of Austria, Prussia, Bavaria, Würtemberg and Hanover should be appointed to consider German affairs.

VII—And that so soon as the general plan was ready the credentials of the other delegates should be examined and approved, and that they should then be individually summoned by Metternich who would present them the plan which had been drafted by the Big Six.

In presenting this middle scheme to his colleagues Castlereagh justified it as follows: "The advantage of this mode of proceeding is that you treat the plenipotentiaries as a body with early and becoming respect, you keep the power by concert and management in your own hand, but without openly assuming authority to their exclusion. You obtain a sort of sanction from them for what you are determined at all events to do, which they cannot well withhold and which cannot, in the mode it is taken, embarrass your march." "The good-sense of the proceeding," he concluded, "will establish its own purposes as we advance, the understanding being honestly to tranquillise Europe and by every reasonable and becoming sacrifice to preserve the concert between the Four Powers who have hitherto saved Europe."

Hardenberg and Humboldt saw at once that this scheme

would introduce two alien bodies into the balance of the Big Four. They therefore evolved a fourth scheme under which the business of the Congress should be divided into three main categories, namely territorial questions, questions of regional interest, and questions of general interest. As regards the first category of territorial adjustments, the Big Four should constitute a "directing committee" and in fact keep the whole business entirely within their own hands. Regional arrangements, such as the Federation of Germany, should be dealt with by the Powers immediately interested. General European questions (such as the slave trade, international rivers and diplomatic precedence) could well be left to the Six Great Powers.

Castlereagh, as was to be expected, was not in favour of this scheme. He considered that it "too broadly and ostensibly assumed the right to do what may be generally acquiesced in if not too offensively announced, but which the secondary Powers may protest against if recorded to their humiliation in the face of Europe."

As a result of these proposals and counter-proposals a compromise scheme was agreed to on September 20. It can be summarised as follows:

i—The Big Four should sign a protocol reserving to themselves the final decision in all territorial questions.

ii—This protocol to be first communicated to France and Spain and thereafter to the Congress as a whole.

iii—A special committee of the five German Powers to draft a scheme for a Germanic Federation.

iv—The future arrangements for the formal Congress to be discussed by the Big Six.

It was at this stage, on September 23, that Talleyrand arrived.

[3]

A week later, by which time he had taken his soundings, he was invited by Metternich to a "private conference" with the Big Four. At 2 P.M. on the afternoon of September 30 he

arrived at Metternich's house on the Ballplatz accompanied by
the Spanish representative, Don Pedro Labrador. He found the
Four already assembled under the chairmanship of Castlereagh
and took his seat next to Hardenberg. He then, as Gentz records, proceeded to "rate them soundly" for a space of two
hours.

Why had he been invited alone and without his fellow plenipotentiaries? Because it had been thought more convenient to
confine these preliminary and informal discussions to the heads
of the delegations. Then if so, why had Hardenberg been
accompanied by Humboldt? Because, unfortunately, Hardenberg was very deaf. "We all," replied Talleyrand, "have our
infirmities and can exploit them when necessary." Very well, he
could bring the Duc de Dalberg with him next time. Talleyrand
had won his first point.

Why were the Portuguese and Swedish representatives not
present? After all, they also were signatories of the Peace of
Paris and as such two of the convening Powers. There was no
answer to this question and an embarrassed silence followed.
Talleyrand had won his second point.

He was then handed the protocol which embodied the results
of the previous discussions of the Four. Several of the para-
graphs contained the words "The Allies." Talleyrand pounced
on this expression immediately. What Allies? Were they back
at Chaumont? And Allies against whom? Not against Napoleon
—he was in Elba. Surely not against Louis XVIII—he was
their main guarantee of peace. "Let us speak frankly, gentlemen, if there are to be Allies in this business then this is no
place for me." They explained that the expression "Allies" had
been introduced for purposes of brevity. "Brevity," snapped
Talleyrand, "should not be purchased at the price of accuracy."

After this preliminary sparring, Talleyrand started to read
the protocol which had been handed to him. "I do not understand," he murmured, and then started to read it through a
second time. "I do not understand," he repeated. "For me," he
said, "there are two dates only; between those two dates there
is nothing. The first date is that of May 30 on which it was

agreed to hold this Congress; the second date is October 1 on which it was proclaimed that the Congress would open. Nothing that may have taken place in the interval exists so far as I am concerned." The Quadruple Alliance, he argued, had ceased to have any meaning on the day the Peace of Paris was signed; the assumption of control by the Big Four possessed no historical, legal, logical or moral justification; if they had pledged themselves to anything, they had pledged themselves to summon the whole Congress on October 1; there was no escape from that position. The Big Four could find no reply to this argument. They agreed to tear up the protocol which they had signed and to start, with Talleyrand's assistance, all over again.

"The intervention of Talleyrand," Gentz records, "hopelessly upset our plans. It was a scene I shall never forget." "Thus France," wrote Talleyrand with some complacency, "by the sheer force of reason and the power of principles, broke an alliance which was only directed against herself."

Having thus pierced the Allied front on a weak and unprepared sector of its defences, Talleyrand proceeded rapidly to fan out. On his return that evening he addressed an official note to the four Ministers in which he argued, first that the only directing body with any semblance of legality must be the eight convening Powers signatory to the Peace of Paris, and secondly that their authority must be confirmed by the whole Congress in plenary session. The Four were enraged with Talleyrand for having embodied in an official note the results of a private discussion. They agreed, however, that the Six should now become the Eight, but refused obstinately to summon the whole Congress. Talleyrand in the meantime had held a meeting of the small Powers and had obtained their ardent support. Thus encouraged he informed the Four on October 5 that he would only agree to the postponement of the Congress provided they accepted a formula which in effect would have included Saxony among the negotiators but excluded Murat. "I ask for nothing," he informed them, "but I bring you something important—the sacred principle of legitimacy." He insisted moreover that all their discussions, actions and procedure should be based upon

the foundations of "public law." The only hope, in dealing with
so logical and determined an antagonist, was to retreat and to
regroup. The four Ministers therefore played for time. Gentz
was instructed to draft a communiqué which was published on
October 12 and was issued in the names, not of the Four, not
even of the Six, but of the Eight signatories to the Peace of
Paris. It announced the postponement of all plenary sessions of
the Congress until November 1 and expressed the hope that by
then the questions at issue would have matured "in harmony
with public law, the provisions of the recent Peace and the
expectations of the age."

Talleyrand was not satisfied with this communiqué. He called
it "a bad bit of paper." At a subsequent meeting of October 30
the Eight decided to postpone the plenary sessions of the Congress indefinitely. In fact, as Gentz subsequently remarked, there
never was a Congress of Vienna. It was only constituted eventually to sign the Final Act of June 9 and that Act had been
almost wholly drafted by the Great Powers. But Talleyrand
none the less had gained his point. As spokesman, as champion,
of the smaller Powers, he had prevented the Quadruple Alliance from directing the Congress to the exclusion of France.
Having secured that main objective, he rapidly abandoned all
his small allies. The nature of his achievement is vividly con-
densed by Duff Cooper in his classic biography of Talleyrand.
"He had," he writes, "succeeded in getting his foot into the
door of the European Council Chamber. . . . Very soon those
who were already ensconced there were glad enough that he
should come in and shut the door behind him, leaving his
former partners in the passage."

This manoeuvring for position may seem to the reader a most
unworthy affair. It was more serious than that. There was a real
danger that the four victorious Allies, under pressure from
Russia and Prussia, would seek to impose their will upon the
whole Congress. There was a real danger that, if this occurred,
Metternich would surrender to the combined power of Russia
and Prussia and that Castlereagh, without support at home,
would find himself in a permanent minority of one. By exposing

the legal and moral fallacies of such a contention, by asserting
the principles of legitimacy and public law, Talleyrand did more
than win a point of procedure for his own advantage; he
established and changed the principles upon which the deliberations of the Congress were thereafter conducted. The skill with
which he exploited the position he had thereby gained will be
apparent in what follows.

[4]

Although Talleyrand had by these ingenious manoeuvres
prevented the Big Four from assuming the unquestioned direction of the Congress, he did not, at least until January 9, 1815,
secure the admission of France as an equal partner into the inner
councils of the Quadruple Alliance. There intervened an uncertain and wholly empirical period in which various directing
bodies acted without authority or logical justification. The Four,
basing their right upon a secret article of which only France
had been informed, reserved for themselves the discussion of
the central problem of the Congress—namely the Polish-Saxon
dispute. The Eight, as signatories to the Peace of Paris, assumed
the formal direction of the Congress without authorisation from
any of the other Powers. The German Committee, although
illegally constituted, discussed not only the problems of German federalism, but also territorial adjustments between the
Germanic Powers.

This *de facto* distribution of functions, moreover, was not
observed with any logical consistency. Thus the Eight, at their
meetings of December 9, 10 and 14, approved the allocation of
Genoa to the Kingdom of Sardinia but were forbidden to discuss
any other Italian problems. It was the Eight also who appointed,
without formal sanction from the Congress as a whole, the committees which dealt with international rivers and diplomatic
precedence. They would also, but for the opposition of Spain
and Portugal, have appointed a committee to discuss the abolition of the slave trade. On the other hand the committee which
dealt with the Swiss problem, and on which our own expert was

Stratford de Redcliffe, was appointed, not by the Eight, but directly by the Four.

In the end ten separate committees were chosen as follows:

(1) The German Committee.
(2) The Slave Trade Committee which called itself a Conference.
(3) Swiss Committee.
(4) Committee on Tuscany.
(5) Committee on Sardinia and Genoa.
(6) Committee on the Duchy of Bouillon.
(7) Committee on International Rivers.
(8) Committee on Diplomatic Precedence.
(9) Statistical Committee.
(10) Drafting Committee.

These ten committees varied considerably in their status and composition. On some of them the plenipotentiaries of the Great Powers sat by themselves; to others the representatives of smaller Powers, and even officials and experts, were admitted. Thus the Committee on International Rivers, which was originally confined to the Great Powers, eventually admitted to its sittings the representatives of the riverain States. But sufficient has been said to indicate that the process of "methodizing" to which Castlereagh had so optimistically looked forward proved neither easy nor unimportant. The Congress, as is the way with all international conferences, never had a settled or agreed plan of procedure. It functioned in spurts of improvisation interspersed with pauses during which the Big Four sought to discover which of the many lines open to them was the line of least resistance.

[5]

It remains only to refer to the Statistical Committee which, although it was created on the spur of the moment and almost by chance, proved eventually one of the most efficient and useful of all the bodies which the Big Four appointed. It was, moreover, through the Statistical Committee that Talleyrand eventually managed to insinuate himself into the inner council of the Quadruple Alliance.

It had at an early stage become apparent that there was considerable uncertainty as to the numbers of population in the territories under dispute. Castlereagh suggested therefore that a Statistical Committee should be created for the purpose of ascertaining the facts. Talleyrand, with the support of Castlereagh and Metternich, was permitted to have a representative on this committee. The Spanish Representative, Don Pedro Gomez Labrador, had already made such a general nuisance of himself that he was not admitted; the Swedish and Portuguese representatives were ignored. Thus almost inadvertently it came about that a new figure—the figure Five—was substituted for the previous figures of Four and Eight; and by the time that the supreme crisis had arrived the Four, and the Congress as a whole, had accustomed their minds to this new grouping.

The Statistical Committee worked rapidly and well. They were appointed on December 24 and entrusted with a task of making a complete enumeration of all the territories conquered from Napoleon or his satellites. The guiding spirit in the committee was the Prussian J. G. Hoffman who possessed a wide knowledge of the subject; Professor Martens acted as its secretary. By January 19 the committee were able to provide the Big Four with complete population statistics for the territories under dispute. Talleyrand, it is true, contended that this purely quantitative "enumeration of souls" bore no relation to the actual human value of the territories transferred. He contended that it was a mistake to assume that the inhabitants of the Rhineland were qualitatively equal to a similar number of Galician Poles. Hardenberg refused to accept any such sophistication; souls were souls to him, whether educated or the reverse. And it was in this way that purely quantitative standards for the "transference of souls" became the yard-stick which the Congress adopted.

The Four, having thus become accustomed to the exclusion of the intolerable Labrador and the ineffective Swede from important business, were not unprepared, when the final crisis arose early in January, to admit Talleyrand as one of their number. From January 9 onwards therefore the Council of

Four became the Council of Five. It was the latter body which in effect became the directing organ of the Congress. It held forty-one meetings whereas the Eight held only nine meetings. By February 8 the Council had so far progressed with their work that they were able to appoint a Drafting Committee to draw up the Final Act.

But long before this final stage was reached acute dissension had broken out between the Powers on the questions of Poland and Saxony. And since these two interlocked problems constituted the essence of the whole Congress they must be examined with such clarity as the immense complexity of the facts, and the continuing veering and shifting of the several protagonists, will permit. For when once these two central problems had been disposed of, the remaining work of the Congress fell comparatively easily and comparatively rapidly into place.

10. The Approach to the Polish Problem

[October 1814]

Result of the partitions—Attitude of the Tsar, of Metternich, of Hardenberg and of Castlereagh—A compromise is almost reached in October 1814—Talleyrand intervenes to frustrate this arrangement—Estimate of Talleyrand's diplomatic ingenuity—His essential consistency—His fear of Prussia—His conception of the Russian difficulty—His realistic view of the balance of power—The instructions which he drafted for himself—His championship of the King of Saxony—His insistence on the principles of public law and legitimacy—Complication introduced by the Tsar's insistence on being both a negotiator and an autocrat—Comparison with President Wilson's position at the Paris Conference—The resultant confusion—The general atmosphere of the Vienna Congress—The social background—Festivities and gossip—The figure of Castlereagh in this uncongenial setting.

THE POLISH PROBLEM became the central test, even as it constituted the essential crisis, of the Vienna Congress. If we are to see it in its true proportions it is first necessary to repeat once again the several stages by which, during the latter half of the eighteenth century, Poland had been expunged from the map of Europe.

In 1750 Poland possessed a vast area of territory and a population of some ten and a half millions. Her frontiers were indefensible, her constitution fantastic, and her leaders divided by internal dissension and family feuds. She proved incapable of maintaining her independence against the expansive tendencies of her three powerful neighbours, Russia, Austria and Prussia. Under the first partition of 1772 her population was reduced to 8,746,000. Under the second partition of 1793 it was further reduced to 3,500,000. Under the final partitions of

1795-1796 Poland was completely absorbed by Russia, Austria and Prussia; she ceased to exist.[1] After the defeat of Prussia in 1807 Napoleon reconstituted a tiny area of Polish territory, composed only of 1,850 square miles, which he called The Duchy of Warsaw, and placed under the nominal suzerainty of the King of Saxony. After the defeat of Austria in 1809 he took the areas of Western Galicia and Cracow from the Hapsburg monarchy thus adding to his Grand Duchy a further area of 900 square miles. It may be noted in anticipation that the Kingdom of Poland which eventually emerged from Vienna and which became known as "Congress Poland," comprised an area only three-quarters as large as Napoleon's tiny Grand Duchy. This gives some idea of the extent to which the Tsar's humane but imperialistic plan was defeated by the combined opposition of Austria, France and Great Britain.

So much for the actual dates and figures. But what were the motives and ambitions which, in the late autumn of 1814, inspired and inflamed the several protagonists?

The Emperor Alexander, as has been abundantly suggested, was a schizophrenic, and as such sought to conceal the contradictions of his split personality in a cloud of mystification which before long became a fog of mysticism. On the one hand he saw himself as the conqueror of the greatest military genius of all ages; as the soldier-Tsar who, by the might of his armies and the tenacity of his own leadership, had rendered Russia the dominant physical force upon the continent of Europe. From this aspect he desired to create an enlarged Kingdom of Poland which, being wholly subservient to himself, would extend the boundaries of Russia to the very banks of the Oder. On the other hand he saw himself as the evangelist of progress, as the great Christian Liberator who, in the very plenitude of his power and renown, would as a "moral duty" recreate the Polish nation and restore to suffering Poland her ancient liberties and independence. The gestures which he made during this period, and which so perplexed contemporary observers, were made, now under the impulse of one set of theories, and now under the impulse of another set of theories. At one moment he would send his brother the Grand Duke Constantine to Warsaw to raise and equip a Polish army to fight on his side against the Western Powers; at another moment he would write to Jeremy Bentham asking that philosopher to draft for him a model constitution for Poland on the most advanced lines. The strain of caution which was within him, the memory of his father's fate, made him hesitate none the less to push either of his two contradictory theories to its logical conclusion. He was aware that his army was exhausted, that his generals were dissatisfied, and that if Russian opinion desired any further imperial adventures they would prefer him to seize this immense opportunity by driving towards Constantinople and the East rather than to provoke European combines by indulging in continental dreams. He was aware also that Russian opinion, the opinion that is of the army and the great landowners, was bitterly opposed to any democratic experiments in Poland or to the establishment in a neighbouring province of liberal institutions which would be bound to produce an unsettling effect in Russia itself. Thus while constantly asserting his strength in such a manner as to cause suspicion and alarm to his former European allies, he was dimly aware that he was seeking to use that strength for two contradictory purposes and that owing to the exhaustion of his armies and the need for rapid reconstruction at home his power was in itself a diminishing and not an increasing asset. His attitude during the crucial months at Vienna was thus one of moody and secretive uncertainty, punctuated by sudden gestures of irritable violence or by the impulsive pronouncement of vapid sentimental words.

In considering the attitude adopted at the outset of the Congress by the other members of the Quadruple Alliance, it is necessary to realise that for them the Polish problem was indissolubly linked with the problem of Saxony. If an enlarged Kingdom of Poland were to be created, then Austria and Prussia would be bound to surrender to it the large provinces they had acquired from the partitions and would have to seek compensation elsewhere. Austria could without undue disturbance find such compensation in Italy and Illyria; but if Prussia were to be compensated she would demand the whole of Saxony. And this annexation would in its time entail a fundamental disturbance in the balance of continental power.

Austrian opinion was not at first united on the subject. Metternich, owing perhaps to his extreme personal antipathy to the Tsar, did not care so much if Prussia obtained Saxony but was determined at any cost to prevent Russia from getting Poland. Stadion and Schwarzenberg on the other hand, while comparatively indifferent to the fate of Poland, were filled with alarm at the prospect of Prussia increasing her weight in the Germanic body by the acquisition of Saxony.

The attitude of Prussia was almost avowedly opportunist. King Frederick William, it is true, was prepared to make severe sacrifices for the benefit of his idol Alexander; but Hardenberg and the Prussian generals were determined that whatever happened Prussia should emerge from the Congress with such additions of territory as would render her a Germanic Power of the first magnitude.

Castlereagh, and with him British public opinion, would have preferred a solution which would have seen an enlarged Poland restored to complete independence. Realising that this was in practice impossible he hoped to achieve his "just equilibrium" by the creation of a strong Prussia, allied to Austria, and thus forming a powerful counterpoise, on the one side against an imperialistic Russia and on the other side against any revival of French militarism. In shaping the pattern of his policy, however, he was hampered by the fact that progressive opinion in Great Britain, in spite of the disillusion caused during the Tsar's visit to London, still believed in the beneficence of Russian intentions towards a reconstituted Poland; whereas to rob the King of Saxony of his dominions in order to pay compensation to Prussia would, he well knew, be regarded by the British press and Parliament as a denial of the high purpose and professions of the Quadruple Alliance and as a cynical abandonment of the principles of justice and legitimacy which had been proclaimed.

In October 1814 it might have seemed to an unbiassed observer that these half-intentions and half-objections would cancel each other out and that a compromise solution would in some manner be reached. Metternich by then had relinquished his extreme contention that he "would perish" rather than admit even a modified Russian solution of the Polish problem. Castlereagh had come to realise that his original conception of an enlarged and independent Poland was in fact impracticable. And Alexander, in the face both of external and internal opposition, was prepared to relinquish his former idea of a Russian Poland comprising all the Prussian and Austrian provinces and to accept instead some enlargement of Napoleon's Duchy of Warsaw. All of them, however, seem to have taken it for granted that the King of Saxony, with or without compensation elsewhere, would lose his dominions and that in return for the surrender of Warsaw, Prussia would obtain the whole of Saxon territory. Each party to this adumbrated arrangement was, however, dissatisfied with such a compromise. It was Talleyrand who, with his clear-cut principles and irrefutable logic, prevented any scheme from being accepted which would put Prussia in possession of the whole of Saxony. It was not so much that he provided any new ideas or raised any original objections; it was rather that he was able to give to existing dislike a precision and a consistency from which a firm negative emerged. The others did not know exactly what they wanted or how far they dared to go; Talleyrand with his lucid persistence showed them the way.

[2]

Some historians, it is true, have tended to exaggerate the insight and prescience which Talleyrand displayed. It is evident from his despatches and letters at the time that he often misjudged the situation and that there were moments when he also became bewildered and confused. But the difference between Talleyrand and the others was that whereas they were apt to gallop round and round in meaningless circles he, when once he realised that he had lost the scent, darted back to the spot where he had first missed it; and that, having once recovered the correct principle, he resumed the chase with such unswerving certitude that they were tempted, and indeed, obliged, to follow in his wake.

France had little to lose at the Congress of Vienna; she had already abandoned her conquests under the Peace of Paris. But she had much to gain, namely her position and influence as a Great Power. The ingenuity with which Talleyrand, as has been described in the last chapter, forced himself into the inner council of the Four Allies enabled him to play a leading, and in the end a decisive, part in the settlement of the Polish controversy. The fact that France desired nothing more than the creation of conditions of European stability and repose brought him inevitably into union with Castlereagh, who also had the same objectives in view. But whereas Castlereagh became disconcerted and hesitant once he discovered that the facts of the situation refused to adjust themselves to his ideal of a just equilibrium, Talleyrand,—who had learnt from long experience that in the world of affairs ideal solutions can never be fully attained,—concentrated upon arranging and re-arranging the facts until they formed a pattern corresponding, if only approximately, to that which he desired.

The reader may be tempted, in perusing this story of forgotten but most educative controversies, to curl the lip of righteousness and to dismiss the statesmen of the Vienna Congress as mere hucksters in the diplomatic market bartering the happiness of millions with a scented smile. Yet at every international conference it is the duty of a Minister, first to defend and further the interests of his own country and secondly to adjust those interests to the requirements of the community of nations. It would be an error, as I have said, to imagine that the statesmen of 1814 were more cynical or selfish, more ignorant or unintelligent, than their successors of 1919 or 1946. Their common aim was to secure the stability, and therefore the peace, of Europe; and, before indulging in irritation or contempt, it is salutary to reflect that they did in fact prevent a general European conflagration for a whole century of time. Similarly, it would be incorrect to dismiss Talleyrand as a cunning opportunist; undoubtedly he was both versatile and corrupt; but in his desire to give peace to France and Europe he was abundantly consistent and sincere. He saw with a lucidity not given to his contemporaries that it would be a mistake to assess the elements of future danger in terms of those factors which had caused disturbance in the past. He knew that after twenty years of military glory France longed only for repose, and that for three generations at least Europe had no cause to fear a revival of French militarism. To his clear mind the dangers which were liable to threaten continental stability were to be looked for, not in the West, but in the East and North. The spectre of the Russian colossus did not inspire him either with defeatism or panic fear; he knew that a united attitude of combined conciliation and firmness would suffice to halt the wave of Russian aggrandisement; and that if Europe could only gain sufficient time, the vast tide of Muscovy would be sucked back again by the Asian moon. A more constant, a more immediate and a more durable danger was to his mind the military might of Prussia. If once this highly disciplined and gifted Power could obtain the mastery over Germany, then indeed would the liberties of Europe be exposed to danger. It was with this in mind that he laboured, with skill and logic, to create a united front between the three sedative or civilian Powers of France, Great Britain and Austria, against the disturbance threatened by Prussia in the first place and by Russia in the second. His success in creating this combination constitutes one of the most useful achievements in all diplomatic history. For in Talleyrand the sense of proportion and the sense of occasion transcended opportunism; they amounted to genius.

His views, for instance, upon the true nature of the balance of power were more realistic and more practicable than any which Castlereagh had hitherto entertained. "The general equilibrium of Europe," he wrote, "cannot be composed of simple elements: it can only be a system of partial equilibrium. An absolute equality of power between all the States, not only can never exist, but is not necessary to the political equilibrium and would perhaps in some respects be hurtful to it. That equilibrium consists in a relation between the power of resistance and the power of aggression. If Europe were composed of States being so related to one another than the minimum of resisting power of the smallest were equal to the maximum of aggressive power of the greatest, then there would be a real equilibrium. But the situation of Europe is not, and will never be, such. The actual situation admits solely of an equilibrium which is artificial and precarious and which can only last so long as certain large States are animated by a spirit of moderation and justice which will preserve that equilibrium."

Thus whereas Castlereagh dreamt of an ideal equilibrium, calculated almost mathematically in terms of population and power, Talleyrand realised that any balance of power must be relative. It was this more realistic conception which enabled him to confront the facts with peculiar lucidity, elasticity and speed.

His original foresight and subsequent consistency are demonstrated by the instructions which he prepared for himself at the time when the Allied monarchs were squabbling and feasting in London. He then laid it down that the establishment of a large Poland would only be beneficial to Europe provided three essential conditions were fulfilled. In the first place Poland must be absolutely independent. In the second place she must be strong enough to maintain that independence. And in the third place the enlargement of Poland must not entail undue compensations to Austria or Prussia. Obviously these three conditions could not possibly be secured and for several reasons. "In the first place," he wrote, "Russia does not wish for the re-establishment of Poland in order to lose what she has acquired of it: she wishes it so as to acquire what she does not possess of it. . . . Thus to re-establish Poland in order to give it entirely to Russia . . . and to extend her frontiers to the Oder, would mean creating so great and imminent a danger for Europe that . . . if the execution of such a plan could only be stopped by force of arms, not a single moment should be lost in taking them up." Since therefore Poland could not be expected to maintain her independence against Russia, and since any form of "constitution" which Alexander might accord her would be bound to lead to internal dissension and anarchy, the only advantageous solution was to return to the situation as it had existed after the last of the three partitions.

On his arrival in Vienna Talleyrand sought, apparently without success, to convince Metternich of the logic of this argument. "How have you the courage," he said to him on September 23, "to put Russia like a belt around your principal and most important possessions in Hungary and Bohemia? How can you allow the patrimony of an old and worthy neighbour such as Saxony to be given to your natural enemy, Prussia?" Metternich, as was his custom, returned polite but equivocal answers to these leading questions. Talleyrand felt it wise to provide himself with more precise instructions from his sovereign. On October 25 Louis XVIII signed these supplementary instructions with his own hand. In view of the fact that "the aggrandisement of Russia by Poland's being subjected to her rule, and the union of Saxony to the Prussian monarchy would be equally contrary to the principles of justice and public law and to the establishment of a system of solid and durable equilibrium in Europe," he authorized Talleyrand to inform Great Britain, Austria and Bavaria that they could count upon "the most active military co-operation" on the part of France in opposing any such plans.

It is evident moreover that Talleyrand's opposition to the compromise arrangements which had almost been accepted by the Four Allies in October 1814 was based more on suspicion of Prussia's future intentions than upon any fear of the effect which the Tsar's Polish plan would have upon the interests of Western Europe. His hatred of that plan was due to the fact that it implied as its corollary that Prussia should receive compensations in Saxony. He did not in any sense agree with Castlereagh that a strong Prussia would constitute a valuable make-weight in the European balance. Such was the subservience of King Frederick William to the Emperor Alexander, that so far from restraining Russian imperialism he would be likely to encourage it. If the Prussian generals obtained their desires, then Prussia "would in a few years form a militarist monarchy which would be very dangerous to her neighbours." "The exiguity of her monarchy," he wrote, "makes ambition a sort of necessity to her. Any pretext seems good to her. No scruples stop her. Her convenience constitutes her right. . . . It is said that the Allies have agreed to re-establish her in the same degree of power as she possessed before her fall, that is to say with ten million subjects. If that were permitted, she would very soon have twenty and the whole of Germany would be subjected to her. It is thus necessary to put a rein on her ambition, first by restricting as much as possible the amount of her possessions in Germany, and thereafter by curtailing her influence by means of a Germanic Federation."

And in any case, what right had the Powers to defy the principle of legitimacy and deprive the lawful King of Saxony of his throne? "He has governed his subjects for forty years like a father, serving as an example of the virtues both of a man and of a prince." He may, by his blind loyalty to Napoleon, have committed errors; but "those who reproach him with those errors have committed graver errors themselves and with less excuse." Talleyrand, being well aware that the principle of legitimacy was one of his strongest weapons,—knowing well that public opinion in Germany and even in Great Britain had much sympathy for the aged monarch whom it was intended to despoil—became therefore one of the most ardent champions of Frederick Augustus. Even at the crisis of the Congress, when the Tsar angrily brushed aside Talleyrand's defence of the King of Saxony by accusing him of being "a traitor to the common cause,"—"That, Your Imperial Majesty," answered Talleyrand, "is a question of dates."

It was with such an attitude of mind, an attitude at one and the same time flexible and rigid, that Talleyrand intervened in the fierce controversy which arose in Vienna on the subject of Saxony and Poland. He did not, at first, obtain much encouragement from either Castlereagh or Metternich. He regarded the Big Four with contemptuous impatience. "Too frightened to fight each other," he commented acidly, "too stupid to agree."

[3]

One of the misfortunes of the Vienna Congress was that it was directed in fact by two separate bodies. There was in the first place the Council of Ministers, known as the Council of Four, or, subsequent to the admission of Talleyrand, as the Council of Five. It was their general custom to meet in the morning in Metternich's office in the house on the Ballplatz. But in addition to this there were the daily meetings of the Allied sovereigns who gathered together in the Hofburg every afternoon. To a certain extent the Emperor Francis and King Frederick William could be counted on to support in the afternoon the arrangements to which their ministers had agreed in the morning. No such consistency was to be expected from Alexander who, in fact as well as in name, regarded himself as his own sole plenipotentiary. In assuming this dual function of autocrat and negotiator he created a situation of extreme diplomatic complexity. The Ministers, at their morning meeting, and in order to obtain Nesselrode's agreement, might have made certain concessions to the Russian point of view; that afternoon the Tsar, while taking note of the concessions offered, would withhold his consent to the corresponding undertakings given by Nesselrode. A somewhat analogous situation arose at the Paris Peace Conference in 1919, when President Wilson was invested with the functions of a negotiator while retaining his position as Head of a State. Thus concessions were continually being made to the President's point of view which would not have been made had he been a mere negotiator and not also Chief Executive; whereas his simultaneous position as Head of the State rendered it difficult for his fellow-negotiators to question whether his promises would be endorsed by the people of the United States in Congress assembled. All negotiation must be based upon the interchange of dependable concessions; if the concessions made by one side are held to be valid and the corresponding concessions made by the other side are thereafter repudiated, then all negotiation becomes impossible. And if the practice becomes established whereby the undertakings entered into by plenipotentiaries can subsequently, at the time of "ratification," be repudiated by their legislatures, then assuredly the future for the new diplomacy is dark indeed.

From the account given in the next chapter of the actual progress of the Polish negotiations at Vienna, of the constant proposals and counter-proposals which were almost daily exchanged, it will be seen that one of the major difficulties under which the statesmen laboured was the element of uncertainty introduced into their agreements by the Tsar's duality. It is probable that, had the five Ministers been able to work uninterruptedly and dependably together, a solution would have been found without extreme measures having to be adopted; it was the protean conduct of the Emperor Alexander which obliged them to substitute for the reasonable arguments of diplomacy the dangerous expedients of force.

It must be remembered also that the atmosphere of the Vienna Congress was still further vitiated by the fact that, whereas the Big Five and their staffs suffered from appalling overwork, the innumerable monarchs and delegations of the smaller Powers had practically nothing at all to do. As has already been noted, it was found necessary to occupy their attention by a round of festivities the extravagance of which has brought the whole Congress into disrepute. Although the social amenities of the Vienna Congress have been much exaggerated, yet there is little doubt that by their excessive accumulation they increased lethargy and diminished concentration. Before therefore we examine the hard work which was put in between October 1814 and February 1815 it is necessary to give some indication of the tinsel background against which these sombre labours were conducted.

[4]

The burden of all this entertainment fell primarily upon the Emperor Francis, who was by nature averse from all social amenities. In the Hofburg itself he was obliged, day in and day out, to entertain an Emperor, an Empress, four Kings, one

Queen, two Hereditary Princes, three Grand Duchesses and
three Princes of the blood. Every night dinner at the Hofburg
was laid at forty tables; special liveries and carriages were
provided for all the royal guests; the horses in the stable numbered no less than 1,400. Each monarch or head of a family
had brought with him a crowd of chamberlains and equerries,
and the royal consorts were attended by mistresses of the robe
and ladies-in-waiting. The members of the Tsar's suite caused
special preoccupation and were in fact described in a contemporary report as not being house-trained or *"stubenrein."* As the
Congress dawdled on to its devitalised close the visiting potentates contracted the habit of taking their meals in their own
apartments, thus throwing an additional strain upon the Emperor Francis' household. It was estimated at the time that the
cost to the Austrian civil list of this lavish hospitality was no
less than thirty million florins, approximately three and a half
million sterling in our modern currency.

Apart from the reigning dynasties who were accommodated
in the palace itself there were present in Vienna some 215
heads of princely families. The diplomatic delegations, as has
been seen, were also very numerous. In order to amuse this
horde of miscellaneous visitors the Emperor Francis had appointed from his court officials a Festivals Committee who were
driven to distraction by the task of inventing new forms of
amusement and by the excruciating problems of precedence. In
the Hofburg itself it had wisely been laid down that the guests
should take precedence according to their age, with the result
that the King of Würtemberg, who had been born in 1754,
was obliged night after night to give his arm to the Empress
of Austria. No such rule had however been adopted for the
minor royalties whose resentment at being seated below other
minor royalties created a whole series of small typhoons and
whirlwinds which weighted the atmosphere with the thunder of
a sultry July.

There was present at Vienna during this time an unattached
Frenchman of the age of thirty-one bearing the name of Count
Auguste Louis Charles de La Garde-Chambonas. This plump,

snobbish and extremely self-satisfied young man subsequently published a detailed memoir of the social amenities of the Vienna Congress. He recounts with horrible gusto the unending series of drawing-rooms, balls, banquets and gala performances which took place. There were large and small redoubts; there were tombolas and faked tournaments; there were amateur theatricals; there were *tableaux vivants* at which the young ladies of Viennese society and the attachés to the several delegations and embassies would give representations of "Louis XIV at the feet of Madame de La Vallière" or "Hippolytus defending his virtue before Theseus." There were sleighing expeditions to the Wienerwald from which the assembled guests would return in darkness flanked by the mounted footmen in special liveries carrying flaming torches in their hands. There were public balls in the Apollo Hall and private representations at the *Kärnthnerthor* theatre. The ballet of *Flore and Zéphire* was performed again and again at the Opera House with Signora Bitottini in the principal part; and the Tyrolean singers were much in vogue. On October 28 a performance was given of Beethoven's *Fidelio;* and on Tuesday, November 29, took place, in the presence of the Tsar and Frederick William III, a gala concert of Beethoven's music. The Seventh Symphony was given, followed by the piece which Beethoven had just written in celebration of Lord Wellington's victory at Vitoria. Beethoven, although by then completely deaf, himself conducted the latter composition; he stood there, among that distinguished but unappreciative audience, a "short and stout" figure waving his baton triumphantly.

From time to time hunting parties would be instituted and at the Luxemberg an elaborate drive of game was arranged under which, according to Chambonas, "a countless number of wild boar, stags, hares and other species of game fell, amidst the plaudits of the spectators, to the fowling pieces of the privileged few." A popular festival was also instituted in the Augarten, when the visiting monarchs had the occasion to mingle democratically with the Vienna crowds, and when the aviator Kraskowitz made a balloon ascent, rising over the roofs and gardens of Vienna waving from his basket the flags of the united nations. Sir Sidney Smith, much to everybody's amusement, organised a subscription picnic which proved a disastrous failure. He insisted on that occasion in recounting every detail of the siege of Acre to the Prince de Ligne [2] who in revenge referred to him thereafter as "Long Acre." And meanwhile Lord Stewart, magnificently arrayed, drove his English four-in-hand through the Prater.

More intimate and more important were the smaller parties given by the leaders of Viennese society. Princess Metternich received on Mondays; Princess Trautmansdorf on Thursdays; whereas Saturdays were reserved for the receptions of Countess Zichy. The monarchs and the ministers would meet each other in the boudoirs of Princess Esterházy, Princess Thurm and Taxis, Princess Fürstenberg and Madame Fuchs. Talleyrand, in the Kaunitz Palace, would hold a morning reception while his two barbers attended to his elaborate coiffure and his valet would pour vinegar over his lame foot. And in the evenings the Comtesse Edmond de Périgord, his niece, would ravish the attendant potentates with the brilliance of her beauty, with the quick dartings of her "pretty serpent's head," and the supreme excellence of the food provided. Inevitably, in an atmosphere of such frivolity, scandal was rife. The incessant and sometimes disreputable flirtations of the Emperor Alexander were the subject of constant gossip, which La Garde-Chambonas retails with succulent lips. And it was in fact true that the relations between the Tsar and Metternich were embittered by amatory rivalries and intrigues.

Amid this crowd of foreigners one catches a glimpse now and then of Castlereagh, austere, handsome, undecorated and shy. Chambonas, who had evidently not been invited to the Minoritenplatz, spoke with disparagement of the social attainments of the Castlereagh household. He laughs at Castlereagh attempting to dance with huge long legs; he refers to his "long, bored face"; he pokes fun at Lady Castlereagh and her sister Lady Matilda. Yet it is evident that even during the worst days of the crisis both Castlereagh and his wife endeavoured to pander to the prevailing fashion. "The Emperor," wrote Edward Cooke to Lord Liverpool in December, "danced polonaises with Lady Castlereagh, country dances with Lady Matilda. The Archduchess Catherine polonaised with Planta." Yet Castlereagh, during those unending nights, when the smell of guttering candles mingled with the scent of hot-houses, had more important things to brood upon than polonaises.

11. The Polish Negotiations

[September 1814-February 1815]

The dividing line between diplomacy and foreign policy, between conciliation and threats—How far were Castlereagh and Talleyrand justified in crossing that line?—The five main stages of the negotiation—Previous commitments—Castlereagh's attempts to reach agreement with the Tsar—He fails, and Metternich then takes up the negotiation—As a result all personal relations between him and the Emperor Alexander are broken off for three months—Hardenberg then tries and also fails—Castlereagh seeks to still the growing anxiety in the British Cabinet and Parliament—His justification of his own policy—He receives precise instructions not to push matters to a point where war may threaten—He ignores these instructions—Talleyrand then intervenes and secures the Secret Treaty of January 3, 1815, under which France, Austria and Great Britain pledge themselves to resist Russia and Prussia by force of arms—This threat becomes known in Vienna and Alexander and the Prussians at once modify their demands—A compromise is reached on February 11 under which "Congress Poland" is created and Prussia acquires only a portion of Saxony—Castlereagh leaves Vienna on February 14.

I is useful, even when dealing with a remote historical episode, to consider where diplomacy ends and foreign policy begins. Each of them is concerned with the adjustment of national to international interests. Foreign policy is based upon a general conception of national requirements; and this conception derives from the need of self-preservation, the constantly changing shapes of economic and strategic advantage, and the condition of public opinion as affected at the time by such diverse factors as energy or exhaustion, prejudices or sympathies (whether ideological or humane), future ambition or past pride. Diplomacy, on the other hand, is not an end but a means; not a purpose but a method. It seeks, by the use of reason, conciliation and the exchange of interests, to prevent major conflicts arising between sovereign States. It is the agency through which foreign policy seeks to attain its purposes by agreement rather than by war. Thus when agreement becomes impossible diplomacy, which is the instrument of peace, becomes inoperative; and foreign policy, the final sanction of which is war, alone becomes operative.

When a negotiation between sovereign States reaches a point where pressure on the one hand and resistance on the other have created an abnormal condition—a condition, that is, which is liable to lead to war—then diplomacy must cease to function and foreign policy comes into play. The phase of appeasement, for instance, which culminated in Munich was essentially a diplomatic phase; Hitler's seizure of Prague in March 1939 marked the transition from the phase of persuasion to the phase of action, and the conflict became one, not of diplomacy, but of foreign policy.

In few self-contained negotiations is this transition between diplomacy and foreign policy so difficult to disentangle, or so interesting to observe, as that which, towards the end of 1814, marked the crisis between Russia and Western Europe on the subject of Poland. Even today, when we possess almost all the documents in the case, it is difficult satisfactorily to determine whether the pressure of Russia on the one hand, and the resistance of France and Great Britain on the other, had in fact created the "abnormal condition" which alone justifies the abandonment of the curative methods of diplomacy for the surgical necessities of foreign policy. The fact that the threat of war did lead to a solution of the problem does not provide a complete answer. For we are left at the end with two questions —"Was Castlereagh justified in threatening war with Russia against the instructions of his Government and against the wishes of the British people?" "Was Talleyrand's sole objective the creation of stable conditions in Europe, or was he profiting by a confused situation to re-establish France's influence by dangerous means?" However much one may esteem Castlereagh's courage and honesty of purpose, however much one may admire the brilliance of Talleyrand's intellect, it is impossible to answer these two questions in a sense flattering to either. Success is never, either in diplomacy or in foreign policy, an ultimate justification.

In tracing the intricate negotiations which took place at Vienna between September 1814 and February 1815 on the connected problems of Poland and Saxony, it will be necessary to divide them into successive periods or phases each dominated in its turn by a single protagonist. Without some such process of simplification, the present chapter would become wholly unreadable. Yet it must be realised that the texture of any international negotiation is formed of diverse strands, some stretching back into the remoter recesses of national tradition, some being derived from previous commitments, and some owing their presence within the fabric to personal antipathies, chance misunderstandings, incidental ignorance or lethargy, and sudden improvisations. The structure of any international crisis is organic rather than artificial; it is the result of gradual growth; and however much one may seek to detach and mount the specimens for purposes of exposition, it must never be forgotten that at the time they were part of the thought, feeling and action of sentient beings, exposed to all the impulses and fallibility of human nature.

[2]

Subject to this important reservation, the development of the Polish crisis at Vienna can be divided into five main compartments. In the first place come the previous commitments which governed the contractual relations between the several disputants. The first period of actual negotiation begins in September 1814 and lasts until the middle of November; during this period it was Castlereagh who sought to play a leading part. There followed a second and most embittered phase during which Metternich endeavoured, rather vaguely and very shiftily, to come to a direct arrangement with the Emperor Alexander. From November until December 19 it was Hardenberg who, after the rupture of all intercourse between the Tsar and Metternich, tried to reach an agreed solution. And finally Talleyrand, by creating a united front between France, Austria and Great Britain, and by concluding between them the secret alliance against Russia of January 3, 1815, imposed on all the disputants a compromise solution which in effect endured for the next hundred years.

The previous commitments, although they had an important bearing upon the subsequent alignment of the Powers, need not long detain us. There was in the first place the Convention of Kalisch which had been signed between Russia and Prussia on February 28, 1813, neither Austria nor Great Britain being parties to this arrangement. Under the Kalisch Convention the King of Prussia agreed in effect to surrender a large part of his Polish provinces in return for a promise on the part of Russia that the Prussian Kingdom would be restored to the position of power which she had possessed prior to her overthrow by Napoleon in 1806. It was generally understood that this meant that Prussia would receive equivalent compensation in the Rhineland and in Saxony for the areas which she surrendered to a reconstituted Poland. It was this Convention of Kalisch, apart from the sentimental and often subservient bonds which attached Frederick William to Alexander, which formed the basis of the united front displayed by Prussia and Russia throughout the conflict.

In the second place there was the Treaty of Reichenbach of June 1813 which had been concluded at the time when Austria was contemplating armed mediation between Napoleon and the two northern courts and which established the conditions which Metternich was to offer to France as the basis for peace. Under this treaty it had been provided that the Grand Duchy of Warsaw and the Confederation of the Rhine should be abolished; that Prussia should be replaced in her previous position of power; and that the Illyrian provinces should be restored to Austria. As generally happens when a coalition wishes to entice a powerful neutral, those provisions of the Treaty of Reichenbach which might have discouraged Austria were left purposely vague. It could not be said that, in so far as Poland was concerned, they either confirmed or denied the tacit arrangement come to at Kalisch. Great Britain, it must be noted, was not a party to the Treaty of Reichenbach.

The Treaty of Teplitz of September 9, 1813, displayed an equal avoidance of precision. It merely provided that the future of Poland would be decided by "amicable" arrangement between the three Powers concerned. The difficulty of achieving such amity was made clear shortly after Napoleon's abdication when on May 5, 1814, Hardenberg produced his memorandum in which he interpreted the Convention of Kalisch as implying that Russia should obtain the whole of the Duchy of Warsaw minus the districts of Cracow and Tarnopol which should be given to Austria. Prussia for her part would surrender most of her Polish provinces in return for the whole of Saxony. The Tsar, while accepting the majority of Hardenberg's suggestions, refused under any conditions to accord Cracow and Tarnopol to Austria.

The conflict had thereby been stated in its most extreme form; it had not been solved. The Peace of Paris of May 30, 1814, merely provided that the settlement of questions affecting the balance of European power would "be regulated at the Congress upon principles determined by the Allied Powers themselves." And as has been seen, such conversations as took place during the London visit achieved no result other than an agreement that no irremediable action should be taken by any of the Allies in the areas at that time in their military occupation.

In so far therefore as any previous commitments were concerned, Russia and Prussia were distinctly bound together by the Convention of Kalisch; Austria was indistinctly bound to the Russo-Prussian solution under the Treaty of Reichenbach; and Great Britain was bound only to settle these grave problems in consultation with her three major Allies. France was bound only in so far as her adhesion to the Peace of Paris implied that she would accept any arrangement agreed to by Russia, Prussia, Austria and Great Britain. The situation, in other words, presented as bad a diplomatic pattern as can be conceived, namely, a pattern in which the two demanding Powers were tied together by a precise previous commitment, whereas the three resisting Powers were not united by any specific undertakings towards each other.

[3]

The first round in the negotiations was opened by Castlereagh who, owing to the fact that Great Britain had no previous obligations in the matter and no direct interest either in Poland or in Saxony, might be presumed to occupy a neutral, if not a mediatory, position. He began by making an appeal to the Tsar's better nature. This particular gambit failed completely.

In an interview which he had with Alexander at the end of September, Castlereagh sought to persuade him that in granting a constitution to a recreated Poland he would be placing his allies Prussia and Austria in an invidious position in regard to their own Polish populations. The Tsar was unmoved by this argument. Castlereagh then suggested that in seeking to create an independent Poland endowed with liberal institutions the Emperor was acting in disregard of the wishes and apprehensions of his own people. The Tsar countered this by saying that in opposing the liberation of Poland and the grant to her of a constitution drafted by Jeremy Bentham Castlereagh was totally misrepresenting the hopes and ideals of the British Parliament and of the British people. At this Castlereagh shifted his ground. He indicated to Nesselrode that the Tsar's acquisition of Poland would place him in a position of dominion in Europe such as Napoleon himself had not enjoyed. On October 12 he had a further long audience with the Emperor Alexander. He contended that His Imperial Majesty's attitude of intransigence was contrary to the whole spirit of the Treaties of 1813 and 1814. He indicated moreover that if the Tsar felt so sensitive regarding his "moral duty" towards Poland, then he could better fulfil that duty by surrendering some portion of the Russian shares of the three partitions rather than by insisting that the only sacrifices to Poland should be made by Austria and Prussia. The Tsar answered coldly that in any case he was in occupation of Poland, that he possessed a large army, and that, if England did not care for the settlement, it was for England to come and turn him out. Castlereagh replied to this that he was confident that His Imperial Majesty "could not wish to rest his pretensions on a title of conquest in opposition to the general sentiments of Europe." He followed up these somewhat ineffective remarks by a letter which he addressed to the Tsar that very evening of October 12. In this he pointed out that Russia had already acquired Finland, Bessarabia and a large slice of Poland and asserted that he must protest "against this fourth instance of Russian aggrandisement." It rested with His Imperial Majesty whether the Congress of Vienna would prove a blessing to mankind or "exhibit a scene of discordant intrigue and a lawless scramble for power."

Castlereagh soon realised that these personal appeals to the Emperor had but little effect. "He thought," commented Talleyrand, "that he was in a position to bend the Emperor of Russia, but only succeeded in irritating him." Castlereagh was not unaware of the fact that there were moments when the Tsar was impervious either to emotional suggestions or to appeals to high moral principle. He therefore fell back upon the idea of composing the difference between Austria and Prussia and presenting Russia with a united negative. Throughout the month of October he worked with commendable patience and resource at cementing a union between Hardenberg and Metternich. He managed with some difficulty to induce the Prussian Minister to promise that if Austria would consent to giving him the whole of Saxony he would be prepared to oppose to Russian ambitions "such resistance as prudence might justify." This was not much, but it was something. On October 9 therefore Hardenberg formally demanded the whole of Saxony plus the fortress of Mainz. Metternich agreed to Prussia obtaining Saxony "subject to satisfactory settlement of the Polish question," but contended that Mainz must go to Bavaria. Hardenberg was dissatisfied with this reservation but at a subsequent meeting in Castlereagh's house it was agreed to shelve the question of Mainz for the moment and to present the Tsar with a joint refusal on the part of all the Powers to agree to Russia's plan for Poland. It was suggested that this joint resolution should be presented to the Tsar by Metternich.

The choice of the Austrian Minister as a negotiator was unfortunate. On the one hand his personal relations with Alexander, which were never of the most confiding, had of late been embittered by feminine influence. On the other hand Metternich was so entranced by his own ingenuity that he ruined even the simplest cause by preferring the diplomacy of stratagem to the diplomacy of sound principle. He thus assured Alexander that Austria would further his Polish scheme if only he would prevent Prussia from obtaining Saxony; and at the same time he told Hardenberg that the Tsar was prepared to abandon his previous support of Prussia's claims to Saxony in return for the agreement of the other members of the Quadruple Alliance to an enlarged Poland. This stratagem, as generally happens with stratagems, was exposed. At his first audience with the Emperor Alexander Metternich informed him that Austria would have no objection to a free Poland being created by Europe; what she objected to was a puppet Poland created by the Tsar; and if it came to that, Austria had as much right to create a puppet Poland as Russia herself. Alexander at this burst into one of his hysterical fits of rage. He treated Metternich, as Talleyrand reported home on October 31, "with a pride and violence of language which would have been thought extraordinary even towards one of his own servants"; he accused the Austrian Minister of being "rebellious." Metternich withdrew confounded.

The three monarchs thereafter proceeded on a visit to Buda Pesth. The Tsar endeavoured to induce Francis I to dismiss Metternich from his post as Foreign Minister. He informed the Prussians that Metternich had told him that Prussia was seeking to make a deal with Austria and Great Britain behind his back. The Prussians retorted by saying that Metternich had assured them that on the contrary it was the Tsar himself who had opened treacherous negotiations. When confronted with this accusation Metternich could only reply that Hardenberg, owing to his total deafness, must have misunderstood what he had said. The Tsar did not accept this explanation. He threatened Metternich with a duel and in fact refused to speak to him again for a period of three unhappy months. And King Frederick William formally forbade Hardenberg to have any further consultations either with Austria or Great Britain. As a result, Castlereagh's plan for a common front between Austria, Great Britain and Prussia completely broke down.

In the meanwhile, during those October weeks, Talleyrand had been employing all his powers of persuasion to convince Castlereagh that any deal with Prussia over Saxony would be a grave political error. He recalled to the memory of the British Minister the iniquities and treacheries of which the Prussians had been guilty during the last sixty years; he asked him how Great Britain, with her immense commercial interests, could place a European mart of the importance of Leipzig in the hands of a possibly hostile Power; by means of maps and plans he showed him that if Prussia once obtained Saxony the very heart of the Austrian monarchy would be exposed to sudden aggression; and he assured him solemnly that whatever happened Louis XVIII would never sign a treaty which sanctioned the "revolting immorality" of despoiling the legitimate owner of the Saxon Kingdom.

Castlereagh was not unimpressed by these arguments. Realising that a common front between Austria and Prussia was in fact impossible to achieve he made one further despairing effort to redress the shattered balance. In a memorandum of October 24 he proposed to his Prussian and Austrian colleagues that the correspondence which had passed with Alexander upon the whole Polish problem should be laid before the Congress as a whole and that "the several Powers of Europe should be invited to declare to the Emperor of Russia to what extent, and upon what conditions, Europe in Congress can or cannot admit His Imperial Majesty's pretensions to an aggrandisement of Poland." "It is desirable," he added, "that the Emperor should be made distinctly to understand . . . that it would rest with the Powers in Congress assembled to decide upon the measures which should be called for by so alarming an infraction of treaties." The Tsar received this intimation in sullen silence which lasted for more than three weeks. In the end, on November 21, he replied to Castlereagh claiming three-quarters of the Duchy of Warsaw plus the towns of Thorn and Cracow. They were back exactly where they had started in September: a complete deadlock had been reached.

[4]

Castlereagh was aware that his endeavour to bring Austria and Prussia together by sacrificing Saxony would not be favourably viewed, either by his Government, or by public opinion in Great Britain. The British public did not appreciate the danger of Russian aggrandisement, and if they thought of Poland at all they thought that it would be an agreeable thing if that unhappy country were restored to independence and granted liberal institutions upon the British model. Conversely they felt sorry for the King of Saxony and regarded the transference of his dominions to Prussia as a most cynical bargain wholly inconsistent with high motives which the Allies had proclaimed and with the accepted principles of public law and legitimacy. Even if his scheme had succeeded, it would not have been easy for Castlereagh to explain his action to the House of Commons; the fact that he had sacrificed a principle without securing any advantage, and with the result that the unity of the Alliance had been still further disrupted, rendered his explanation even more difficult. In a despatch to Lord Liverpool of November 11, 1814, he sought, in his frank if intricate manner, to justify his attitude:

Since I have been on the Continent [he wrote], in my intercourse with the several Cabinets, I have conceived my duty to keep in view the following principles, considering them to be those on which it was the intention of His Royal Highness' Government that I should act. In the first place, so to conduct the arrangements to be framed for Congress, as to make the establishment of a just equilibrium in Europe the first object of my attention, and to consider the assertion of minor points of interest as subordinate to this great end. Secondly, to use my best endeavour to support the Powers who have contributed to save Europe by their exertions in their just pretensions to be liberally established upon the scale to which their treaties entitled them to lay claim, and not to be deterred from so doing by the necessity of adopting, for this end, measures which, although not unjust, are nevertheless painful and unpopular in themselves. And thirdly, to endeavour to combine this latter duty to our friends and Allies with as much mildness and indulgence even to the offending States as circumstances will permit. . . .

I deemed it of great importance, [he added] to contribute, as far as depended upon me, to this Austro-Prussian concert, considering the establishment of Russia in the heart of Germany, not only as constituting a great danger in itself, but as calculated to establish a most pernicious influence both in the Austrian and Prussian Cabinets. I also foresaw that if these two Powers, from distrust of each other, gave up the Polish point as desperate, the contest in negotiation would then turn on Saxony, Mainz and other German points, and that through the contention of Austria and Prussia the supremacy of Russia would be established in all directions and upon every question; where as an understanding previously established on German affairs gave some chance of ameliorating the Polish arrangement, and, in case of its failure, affording the best, if not the only, means of counteracting Russian influence in other European arrangements.

Now that Castlereagh and Metternich had both failed, it became the turn of Hardenberg to seek a solution. On November 27 he induced the Tsar to agree that the cities of Thorn and Cracow should not be incorporated in his new Poland but should be declared independent and neutral. In return Prussia was to receive the whole of Saxony whereas Mainz was to be held jointly by Austrian and Prussian garrisons. On December 2 he put this proposal to Metternich, who was not accommodating. He insisted that Austria must retain Cracow and that Prussia must only acquire a small slice of Saxony or in any case none of those Saxon areas which would give her a common frontier with Austria. On December 15 Hardenberg replied to this contending again that Prussia must receive the whole of Saxony and suggesting that King Frederick Augustus should receive compensations either in Westphalia or the Rhineland. "I witness every day," moaned Castlereagh to Liverpool, "the astonishing tenacity with which all the Powers cling to the smallest point of separate interest."

Meanwhile, and when the deadlock seemed insoluble, three events occurred, the first two of which increased the danger, and the third of which seriously diminished Castlereagh's ability to cope with it. It became known in Vienna that on November 8 Prince Repnin, the general commanding the Russian army of occupation in Saxony, had handed over the administration of that Kingdom to the Prussian authorities. A few days later news was received that the Grand Duke Constantine in Warsaw had issued a proclamation calling upon all Poles to unite and fight for their independence. As a result, Austrian troops were moved to the Galician frontier and a partial mobilisation was decreed in France. And at the same moment the Cabinet in London began to display marked symptoms of timidity.

For some time it had been evident that parliamentary and public opinion in Great Britain were interpreting Castlereagh's policy as a perverse desire to maintain the pernicious partitions of Poland and as an equally perverse desire to despoil the good old King of Saxony. In the Cabinet itself the chief advocate of appeasement was the Chancellor, Vansittart. He addressed a memorandum to his colleagues, criticising the policy being pursued at Vienna, and insisting that "we ought to avoid irritating Russia by a pertinacious opposition which is unlikely to be successful." Castlereagh sought in reply to persuade Liverpool that the Russian menace was not imaginary and that the Tsar's ambitions must be resisted rather than humoured. "You must make up your mind," he wrote to him on November 11, "to watch him and to resist him as another Bonaparte. You may rely upon it—my friend Van's philosophy is untrue as applied to him. Acquiescence will not keep him back, nor will opposition accelerate his march." To Vansittart himself he addressed a reasoned letter replying to the criticisms of his memorandum. He assured him that never would he himself be a party to assisting "a Calmuck prince to overturn Europe."

The uneasiness in the Cabinet was increased so soon as it was learnt that Castlereagh's endeavours, instead of bringing conciliation, had increased disunity. On November 27 Bathurst addressed on behalf of the Cabinet an official despatch to their plenipotentiary at Vienna. It contained the following decisive sentence. "It is unnecessary for me," wrote Bathurst, "to point out to you the impossibility of His Royal Highness consenting to involve this country in hostilities at this time for any objects which have been hitherto under discussion at Vienna."

Castlereagh himself was prepared, as will be seen, to ignore these formal instructions. But it became known in Vienna that the attitude which he was adopting did not command the support of his Government at home. And his authority, at a crucial moment, was thereby diminished.

[5]

It was then that Talleyrand intervened. He had for long been viewing with increasing impatience both Castlereagh's caution and Metternich's unbearable habit of twisting the issues into small cat's-cradles of string. "Prince Metternich," he had written after the meeting of November 1, "has shown at this sitting the full extent of his mediocrity, of his taste for petty intrigues and an uncertain and tortuous course, as also of his marvellous command of words that are vague and void of meaning." The time had come to sweep away all these hesitations and arabesques: the time had come to return to fundamental principles. In two notes of December 19 and 26 he insisted that the dethronement and spoliation of the King of Saxony was a flagrant violation of the principle of legitimacy. Frederick Augustus might, if he saw fit, make certain territorial concessions to Prussia; but the cession of Saxon territory could only legitimately be accomplished by Saxony's lawful monarch after he had been reinstated on his throne. At the same time he let it be known that he had arranged with all the minor German States that they should address to the Congress a collective note protesting against the annexation of Saxony by Prussia. In conversation with the Emperor Alexander he warned him that by persisting in his attitude he "might sacrifice his fame as the pacificator of Europe."

The Prussians, as might be expected, were so enraged with Talleyrand for intervening that they lost their heads. Hardenberg on December 29 announced that if Prussia's claim to Saxony were any longer denied he would regard it as a declaration of war. In replying "to this most alarming and unheard-of menace," Castlereagh warned the Prussian Minister, "that if such a temper really prevailed, we were not deliberating in a state of independence and it were better to break up the Congress."

There were few who doubted during those anxious December days that war might at any moment break out between the former Allies. It was during the panic which ensued that Talleyrand struck his final blow. He proposed to Metternich and Castlereagh that they should sign a secret treaty of alliance against Russia and Prussia. In what Sir A. Ward in the *Cambridge Modern History* describes as "a moment of what might almost be called infatuation" the Austrian and British ministers consented. The treaty between France, Austria and Great Britain was signed on Tuesday, January 3, 1815. Under Article I the three Powers agreed to furnish mutual support in the event of any one of them being attacked "on account of the proposals to which they had mutually agreed for the completion of the Treaty of Paris." Under Article II Austria and France pledged themselves to provide 150,000 men and Great Britain agreed to furnish the equivalent either in subsidies or in mercenary troops. Article III provided that any attack upon Hanover or the Low Countries would be regarded as an attack upon Great Britain. Article IV provided that Hanover, Sardinia, Bavaria and Hesse Darmstadt would be invited to accede to the treaty. And Article V made provision for a military commission to be appointed to prepare joint plans in the event of an advance of the Russian armies upon Vienna.

Talleyrand did not conceal his jubilation at this signal triumph. "The Coalition is dissolved," he wrote to Louis XVIII.

"France is no longer isolated in Europe." "So great and so fortunate a change," he added humorously, "can only be attributed to that protection of Providence which has been so plainly visible in the restoration of Your Majesty." Castlereagh, having flagrantly and in a vital issue ignored his instructions, was more composed. "The alarm of war," he wrote to Liverpool on January 5, "is over."

It may be argued of course that the Secret Treaty of January 3 was a gigantic bluff. It was doubtful whether Austria, preoccupied as she then was with Italian affairs, would have been prepared to embark upon a war with Prussia and Russia; it was quite certain that France, in her present condition of exhaustion, would be unable to furnish the contingent which Talleyrand had promised; it was more than doubtful whether the British Parliament would for such purposes vote the subsidies stipulated by Article 11. Had Prussia and Russia really been determined to impose their will upon Europe, there is little doubt that in spite of the Secret Treaty they would have accomplished their desires. In fact, however, neither the Tsar nor Frederick William were prepared to face a renewal of hostilities. Alexander was aware that his troops were disaffected and that his generals were anxious only to return to their homes; he could not venture to alienate his army for purposes which were regarded by Russian opinion as fantastic and unwise. The Prussians for their part were most disinclined, when the moment came, to place themselves in opposition to the united sentiments of the Germanic body. It was not so much that the Secret Treaty was in itself a bluff; it was rather that its conclusion called the bluff which had so long been practised in concert by Alexander and his Prussian friends.

Although the actual terms of the treaty remained secret,[1] it was generally known in Vienna that it had been signed; Freiherr vom Stein moreover acquired definite, although somewhat highly-coloured information regarding its contents which he immediately communicated to the Emperor Alexander. From that moment, with rapid dissolution, the crisis melted away.

On January 28 Metternich proposed that Austria and Prussia

should jointly agree to an unsatisfactory Polish frontier and that Prussia in return should obtain a portion, but not all, of Saxony. The remainder of the former kingdom would be restored to its lawful sovereign. On February 3 these principles were accepted and the Drafting Committee were instructed to put them into treaty form.

The final agreement was reached on February 11. As regards Poland, it provided that Prussia should retain the province of Posen and that Austria should retain the province of Galicia. Cracow, with a surrounding area of 1,000 square kilometres and a population of 95,000, was constituted a free city. The remaining areas of Napoleon's Duchy of Warsaw, representing 127,000 square kilometres with a population of 3,200,000 souls, was formed into the Kingdom of Poland under the Tsar of Russia. Under the "Principles of the Constitution of the Polish Kingdom" which was drawn up by Adam Czartoryski and published in Vienna on May 25, 1815, promises were given that the new kingdom would be wholly independent, that the judicature would be released from dependence on the executive, and that full rights should be accorded to the peasants and the Jews. On June 20, 1815, the creation of this new kingdom was formally proclaimed in Warsaw. Its constitution was thereafter carefully elaborated; it contained seven chapters and 165 articles. Under this constitution full independence and a separate political structure was guaranteed "to the Polish people." A Polish diet was also provided for. But it was made clear from the preamble that this constitution was not a right inherent in the Polish people but a favour granted to them by the All-Russian Tsar. It was stipulated moreover that the new kingdom would be the hereditary appenage of the House of Romanoff and that the foreign policy of the kingdom should remain in Russian hands. Scarcely had the new kingdom been established when Adam Czartoryski was relieved of all further authority and Novosiltsov put in his place with the title of Commissar for the Tsar. The fiction of independence was maintained for several years, but in the end the fiscal difficulties which developed and the increasingly reactionary disposition of the Tsar and his successors rendered this independence wholly illusory. It was in this manner that "Congress Poland" or, as it was known locally, "*Kongresowka*," was born and died.

Prussia, in return for the surrender of Warsaw, received most valuable compensations. In the first place she acquired two-fifths of Saxony with a population of 850,000 souls; the remainder of Saxony was restored to its ancient dynasty. Prussia also obtained the fortresses of the Elbe, much of the left bank of the Rhine, the Duchy of Westphalia and Swedish Pomerania. She thus became the leading Power in northern Germany and Metternich was sharply criticised by Stadion and the Archdukes for having irresponsibly abandoned Austria's former dominance within the Germanic body. In return for such concessions, Austria herself obtained the Tyrol and Salzburg, further promises in Italy, and the Illyrian provinces upon the Adriatic. It may not have been an ideal settlement; but it prevented a major war and remained in all its essentials intact for three generations.

Meanwhile the Cabinet in London had been clamouring for Castlereagh's return; as leader of the House of Commons it was essential that he should be in his place to defend the Government against the attacks which were being made. Now that the common danger was over, now that they were no longer united by fear, the British public had returned with delighted gusto to their accustomed pastime of party recrimination. It was galling, nay it was intolerable, for the Opposition to admit that it was a Tory Government which—through years of effort, enterprise and inventiveness—had achieved overwhelming victory; they sought by every means in their power to belittle past achievement, to discredit present policy, and to sow distrust of future intentions. They had started to assail the Government with violent, if ill-combined, ferocity.

"I can assure you," wrote Lord Liverpool to the Duke of Wellington on January 15, 1815, "that I have not known for some years such party spirit and rancour as exist at present. The restoration of general peace, though it may relieve the country of great difficulties, does not make the government more easy to be conducted in the House of Commons. During a war so eventful as the last, all minor questions, however subordinate, will create a conflict, and if the Government in the House of Commons should lose credit, and be considered as beat in debate before Castlereagh returns, it will be no easy matter for him or for any man to recover the ground which has been lost."

On February 3, 1815, therefore, the Duke of Wellington arrived at Vienna to succeed Castlereagh as first British plenipotentiary. On February 6 in a final despatch Castlereagh was able to assure Lord Liverpool that "the territorial arrangements on this side of the Alps are settled in all their essential features." Having introduced his successor to the Congress, Castlereagh left Vienna on February 14. After spending two busy days in Paris, he returned to London.

12. The Italian and German Settlements

LORD CASTLEREAGH's arrival had been awaited with impatience both by his opponents and by his supporters in the House of Commons. When we read the *Hansard* of 1813-1815 it may seem at first sight that parliamentary opinion was more concerned with the conduct of the American War, the Irish Glass Duties Bill, and the Court Martial of Colonel Quentin, than it was with the great European problems under discussion by the Congress of Vienna. This is a misleading impression. The Opposition were all too anxious to discredit Lord Castlereagh, and through him the Tory Government, by accusing them of having at Vienna betrayed the principles for which the people of Britain had fought so gloriously and so long; they were, however, inhibited by two circumstances. In the first place the admirable custom had not at that date become established under which the leaders of His Majesty's Opposition are kept confidentially informed of the main lines of foreign policy being pursued by His Majesty's Government. They were bound to rely upon information supplied them, either by the agents of unsatisfied foreign potentates, or by those of their political friends who happened, often in very subordinate positions, to be attached to military or diplomatic staffs abroad. They knew that such information was generally biassed and often unreliable and this rendered them hesitant in pressing their attack.[1] In the second place the theory still persisted that the conduct of Foreign Policy was part of the royal prerogative, that the Government of the day were fully entitled to withhold information, and that no international treaties could properly be discussed in Parliament until ratification had been exchanged; until, in other words, it was too late to hold any useful discussion at all. These two circumstances give to the debates which took place an atmosphere of petulance and unreality.

In spite of this the Opposition, although often divided among themselves, had for the past months been exposing the Government of Lord Liverpool to repeated and not always ill-founded criticism. Their protests centred upon the spoliation of Saxony, the unwillingness of Castlereagh to support the Tsar in his plan for a large and independent Poland, the alleged betrayal of the Republic of Genoa, and the arrangements come to with Joachim Murat, King of Naples.

In the debate on the address of November 8, 1814, Samuel Whitbread had expressed the view that the annexation of Saxony by Prussia would be "as unprincipled a partition as the world ever saw." Mr. Lambton a few days later referred to "the acts of rapine and aggression of the club of confederated monarchs at Vienna, who appear to have met, not to watch over the interests of Europe, but as contemners of public faith and justice, as the spoliators of Saxony and the oppressors of Norway." Mr. Whitbread on November 28 renewed his attack. "It was impossible," he said, "to contend for an instant that this act of robbery had not been perpetrated in the very spirit of Buonaparte." He read aloud the preamble to Prince Repnin's proclamation in which it was stated that Great Britain had agreed to an Austro-Russian Convention under which Saxony would be handed over to Prussia. Had Lord Castlereagh really assented to such an act of brigandage? If so, it was "a humiliation and a degradation of this country, so low as to be beneath expression." Whereas the transfer of Saxon territory as compensation to Prussia appeared to the Whigs an act of cowardly cynicism, the unwillingness of the British Government to assist the Tsar in his Polish schemes seemed to them a proof of blind reaction. "If," Mr. Whitbread exclaimed, "the Emperor Alexander, beside the splendid triumphs he has gained, has added this fresh glory to his character, in what disadvantageous contrast must the noble Lord appear who is resisting this plan of liberty and happiness." "The rumours are," Mr. Whitbread continued on November 28, "that the Emperor Alexander has strenuously contended for the independence of Poland and that he has been opposed in his benevolent views by the British Ministers. We now live in an age when free nations are not to be sold and transferred like beasts of burthen, and if any attempt of the kind is made the result will be a bloody and revengeful war."

Mr. Horner, on November 22, had launched an even more direct and personal attack. He had criticised Lord Castlereagh for acting without authority and for not keeping his own Government properly informed of the Vienna transactions. Had the Foreign Secretary agreed to Metternich's secret treaty with Murat or had he not? Had he, or had he not, agreed to Prince Repnin transferring the administration of Saxony into Prussia's hands? He had demanded an answer. The Government, who were in fact not fully aware of what Lord Castlereagh was up to in Vienna, were in some difficulty how to reply. Charles Bathurst, the Chancellor of the Duchy of Lancaster, pleaded with the House on the ground that "it was plain that no negotiations could with honour or advantage be carried on if they were subject to partial examination in detail by questions put across the table." Vansittart was more explicit, and from Castlereagh's point of view, more indiscreet. When Ponsonby accused the Government of violating, in their consent to the transfer of Saxony, the very principles which formed the pre-

amble to the Treaty of Chaumont, and when he arraigned
Castlereagh personally for having "disgraced his title and betrayed the honour of his country," Vansittart blandly assured
him that no Saxon settlement had as yet been come to since the
Congress itself had not been formally inaugurated; and that in
any case "no British Minister would be a party" to any decision
involving the suppression of Saxony. It was high time that
Castlereagh should return to London and answer for himself.

[2]

In regard to Poland and Saxony he was now in a strong
position. By the arrangements come to at Vienna a large portion
of Poland had been rendered nominally independent under the
Tsar, whereas only a proportion of Saxon territory had been
ceded to Prussia. In regard to Genoa and Murat his position was
weak; on these two questions he did not inform the House with
that frankness which we or they would have expected.

Lord William Bentinck [2]—the progressive but unmanageable
Minister in Sicily—had at the beginning of 1814 been instructed
to "take possession of Genoa in the name of His Sardinian
Majesty." Castlereagh had had previous experience of Bentinck's
imaginativeness and warned him from Dijon on March 30,
1814, "studiously to abstain" from committing His Majesty's
Government to any general support of Italian nationalism. On
March 14, however, Lord William had already issued from
Leghorn a proclamation calling upon all Italians to rise in the
defence of their liberties. Castlereagh on learning this wrote to
Lord William reminding him of his previous instructions and
warning him that proclamations of this nature might be interpreted as applying to the future political destiny of the Italians
rather than to their immediate task of turning out the French
garrisons. Lord William replied that the Genoese would strongly
resent annexation to Piedmont and their incorporation within
the dominions of His Sardinian Majesty. He enclosed in this
letter a further proclamation which he had addressed specifically
to the Genoese on April 26, 1814, promising them "in conform-

ity with the principles recognised by the high Allied Powers"
their liberty and independence and the restoration of their constitution of 1797. This was not in accord with Castlereagh's own
intentions. At a meeting of the Eight on November 13, either
ignoring or forgetting Bentinck's proclamation of the previous
April, he agreed that Genoa should be incorporated in Piedmont
on the ground that any other solution would entail "the weakness and therefore the insecurity of Italy." And for this, as was
to be expected, he was bitterly attacked in the House.

In an able speech delivered on February 13, 1815, Samuel
Whitbread contended that the Allies had done their best to
"unholy" the Congress of Vienna. He instanced Genoa as a
specific case. After reading the text of Lord William Bentinck's
proclamation of April 26, 1814, he protested that for Great
Britain, who during the war had been regarded as the champion of true liberty, to consent to the annexation of Genoa by a
monarchy "equally imbecile as it is corrupt" was a further
condonation of public brigandage. Lord Castlereagh, for consenting to this further act of spoliation, should be "arraigned
before the tribunal of the world." The Government for the
moment were able to parry this thrust by falling back on the
by then threadbare contention, that since the articles of the
Vienna Congress had not yet been ratified, it would be improper
for them to reply in matters of detail to questions which could
not properly be judged unless and until the whole series of
agreements come to could be envisaged as a whole. Whitbread
remained unsatisfied and on March 20 he renewed his offensive
along the whole line. In Paris, he contended, the Allies had
pledged themselves to the liberation and independence of small
countries. Had Castlereagh defended the independence of Saxony? Had he defended the independence of Poland? Had he,
or had he not, repudiated Lord William Bentinck's promise of
independence for Genoa? "In this one transaction," he said, "is
brought together all the perfidy, baseness and rapacious violence
that could disgrace a country."

Castlereagh, who had by then returned to face his critics, rose
to reply with that handsome demeanour, that cool calm voice,

that exquisite courtesy and that attractive oratorical ineptitude which even his most rabid political opponents, such as Creevey, were forced to admire and forgive. He reproved the House for having, on information supplied them by foreign agents, embarrassed His Majesty's Government in the midst of vitally important negotiations. So far from disclaiming responsibility, he accepted it. He had been obliged to take action even without reference to his own Cabinet since had he delayed his decision "the whole machine of Europe would have been arrested." Lord William Bentinck's promise to Genoa had been totally unauthorised; Mr. Whitbread's habit of broadcasting accusations based upon insufficient information was "both dangerous and indecent"; the absorption of Genoa within the Kingdom of Sardinia had been essential to the security of Europe and it was on those grounds that he had consented to it. The Republic of Genoa could not expect to be immune from the law of conquest. "The Congress of Vienna," he added in reply to Sir James Mackintosh, "was not assembled for the discussion of moral principles, but for great practical purposes, to establish effectual provisions for the general security."

The rumbles of this controversy then passed onwards from the House of Commons to the House of Lords. On April 20, 1815, Lord Grey opened the debate by saying that "although it was the practice of Parliament during the pendency of all foreign negotiations to leave the management and direction in the hands of the executive Government," yet there were occasions when "cases of great importance occurred, in which the justice, the good faith and the honour of the country were involved. It then became the duty of Parliament to intervene." Such cases were Genoa, Saxony and Murat. If rumours which had reached him were true we had behaved in each of these cases in a manner "which exceeded everything of treachery and fraud which I have yet witnessed in that new diplomatic school of which the noble Lord, Lord Castlereagh, might be considered as the founder." Five days later Lord Buckingham renewed the attack. He described the Genoa settlement as "foul and disgraceful." Lord Liverpool's reply was lame. He again evaded the main issue by saying that he would only be in a position to give the full facts when the whole body of agreements come to by the Vienna Congress had been ratified and laid upon the table. As regards Genoa, it had been necessary to incorporate that republic within the dominions of His Sardinian Majesty since the latter was the natural guardian of the Alpine passes. When asked by Lord Buckingham why, if that were the case, some of the more vital passes had been handed over to Bourbon France, Lord Liverpool could find no adequate reply.

The Government had thus been able to evade criticism, rather than to answer it. It is questionable whether, if the full story of their shifting policy towards Murat had been fully known, they would have been able, even in the face of a divided and uncertain Opposition, to have secured even a comparative parliamentary success.

[3]

Castlereagh's personal attitude towards the Italian problem was perfectly lucid and consistent. He had little belief either in Italian unity or in the capacity of the Italians in general, and the Sicilians in particular, to establish parliamentary or constitutional government. While desiring to exclude French influence, whether Bonapartist or Bourbon, from the Italian peninsula, he was inclined to regard Italy as a purely geographical area in which Austria could find compensation for such sacrifices as might be entailed upon her elsewhere. He thus sought to adapt his Italian policy to that of Metternich. So long as the latter showed a predilection not unconnected with the fact that Queen Caroline had once been Metternich's mistress, Castlereagh was quite willing to maintain King Joachim upon the throne of Naples. So soon, however, as Metternich came to regard Murat as a danger to Austrian influence in Italy, Castlereagh assisted him in his efforts to replace Ferdinand upon the throne of the Two Sicilies.[3] His inconsistency, although unavowable, was due, partly to the fluctuation of Metternich's own policy, and partly to the disorder and contradictions introduced into British action by the temperamental conduct of Lord William Bentinck in his capacity of British Minister at Palermo.

In order to understand the intricate situation which had developed it is necessary to return for a moment to January 1815. Castlereagh had not realised in time that Lord William was, as even so dispassionate a historian as Professor Webster admits, "a brilliant and unbalanced egoist." He should have been warned by the example of Lord Aberdeen that when a British representative abroad is a novice in diplomacy, is possessed of powerful family or political connections at home, is afflicted with extreme personal ambition and immeasurable righteousness, it is advisable at once to recall that representative to London. Lord William had forced King Ferdinand to grant a constitution which his Sicilian subjects were totally unable to operate; he had forced him to abdicate temporarily in favour of his eldest son and to send away his domineering wife, Queen Maria Carolina. He had gone further. In what he subsequently excused as a "philosopher's dream" he had suggested to the Sicilian Regent that Sicily might with advantage become an appenage of the British Crown. Castlereagh did not recall Lord William Bentinck. He allowed him to remain on in the Mediterranean. He allowed him to exercise general authority over the British forces and auxiliaries in the whole area; and to follow a personal line which introduced distrust and confusion into Castlereagh's own policy of co-operation with Austria in all Italian affairs.

Joachim Murat, who had fought with superb dash and courage during the Russian campaign, realised so soon as Napoleon had left the *Grande Armée* at Smogorni that it was high time that he himself returned to Italy. "The King of Naples," wrote Berthier to Napoleon, "is very unsettled in his ideas." The Emperor was enraged. "You are a good soldier in the field," he wrote to Murat on January 26, 1813, "but elsewhere you have neither energy nor character." "Your husband, the King of Naples," he wrote to Caroline, "deserted the army on the 16th. He is a brave man on the battlefield, but he is weaker than a

woman or a monk when he is not in sight of the enemy. He has
no moral courage."

On his return to Naples in January 1813 Murat had done
everything possible, by showing himself in public and by touring
the provinces, to conciliate the affections of his subjects. He
decided at the same time to reinsure himself with the Allies and
to open negotiations with Austria and Great Britain. In April
1813 he sent Prince Cariati as Neapolitan Ambassador to
Vienna; he also sent an agent of the name of Cerculi to get into
touch with Colonel Coffin, commanding the Anglo-Sicilian
forces on the island of Ponza. Colonel Coffin referred to Lord
William Bentinck for instructions and the latter authorised him,
on May 16, 1813, to assure Murat that Great Britain would
agree to his remaining King of Naples until some other principality was found for him elsewhere.

Rumours of these intrigues reached the ears of Napoleon who
sent a fulminating order to Murat summoning him to send a
Neapolitan army to his assistance and insisting that this army
must reach Bologna not later than July 15, 1813. Murat promised that if Austria joined the Coalition he would send 25,000
men to assist Napoleon on condition that this army remained
under his own command. The reply was a curt summons to
meet Napoleon at Dresden. Murat obeyed. On his way to
Dresden he crossed a courier from Vienna bearing a letter from
Metternich assuring him that if he joined the Coalition he
would be guaranteed the throne of Naples and also offering him
an extension of territory in the direction of Ancona. It was then
too late.

Having, as usual, fought with great personal gallantry at
Leipzig, Murat accompanied Napoleon in his retreat as far as
Erfurt, where he again deserted him. Hurrying across the
Simplon and through Milan he reached Naples on November 4.
From there he resumed his negotiations with the Austrians and
the British, promising once again to assist them in driving the
French armies out of northern Italy. Metternich, with the
consent of Castlereagh, sent General Neipperg to Naples to
negotiate a definite treaty. This treaty was signed on January 11,

1814. Murat undertook to place an army of 30,000 men at the disposal of the Allies; in return Austria agreed to guarantee him the throne of Naples with an extension of territory. Metternich promised at the same time to obtain British adherence.

It was at this stage that Lord William Bentinck's independent attitude introduced an element of confusion. In spite of his instructions, he refused to adhere to the Treaty which Neipperg had signed on January 11. It was only grudgingly that he agreed to conclude an armistice between Murat and the Anglo-Sicilian forces under his command. The King of Naples by then had advanced with his army as far as Bologna and was preparing, unwillingly it is true but in accordance with his treaty with Austria, to attack the French armies in northern Italy under the Viceroy Eugène. Bentinck did everything within his power to obstruct these operations. It is not surprising that Murat should by then have felt some doubts regarding the sincerity of British intentions and that he should have sought, with characteristic vacillation, to play with both sides. On March 1, 1814, he wrote to Napoleon protesting his loyal affection and ending "Love me always. Never was I more worthy of your affection. Your friend till death." At the same time he entered into secret communication in the hope of arranging some sort of truce with Eugène. The Austrians warned him that this attitude of "neutrality" was a violation of the Treaty of January 11 and might cost him his throne. On March 6 therefore he ordered his Neapolitan forces to attack the French armies under Eugène. Three days later Lord William Bentinck landed at Leghorn, issued the proclamation in which he called upon all Italians to rise in defence of their liberties and at the same time insisted that Great Britain would maintain the rights of the Sicilian Bourbons. On hearing of this Murat immediately resumed his negotiations with Eugène and the unavowed truce between the two armies was again concluded. The situation thus remained in a condition of confused suspension when news was received of the occupation of Paris and the abdication of Napoleon. A convention was then arranged between Prince Eugène and the Austrians under which the French armies retired from northern Italy; and Murat returned to Naples where he did everything possible to convince his subjects that in some manner he had won a glorious campaign and to conciliate the large number of English tourists who thereafter flocked to his capital. Such was the uncertain condition of affairs when Castlereagh arrived in Vienna.

Throughout the early months of the Congress Metternich was able to postpone any overt discussion of Italian questions on the ground that the Polish and Saxon problems must first be disposed of. During those months however his attitude towards Joachim Murat underwent a change. On the one hand he had come to realise that Murat, so far from being a pliant tool in the hands of Austria, might seek by stirring up Italian nationalism to create disorder and dissension in northern Italy itself. On the other hand he wished to purchase French assistance in the Polish and Saxon questions by sacrificing Murat to Louis XVIII's hatred of all the Napoleonids and to his desire to see the Bourbon dynasty restored to the Kingdom of the Two Sicilies. With his characteristic passion for the indirect method he worked behind Talleyrand's back, approaching Louis XVIII, not through his accredited representative in Vienna, but by direct negotiations with the Comte de Blacas, the King's favourite, in Paris. A secret agreement was reached by January 1815 under which an Austrian army, with or without French assistance, would expel Murat from his Neapolitan kingdom. In return for this Louis XVIII was to agree to those minor adjustments in northern Italy which Metternich desired. The details of this arrangement were confirmed by Castlereagh himself, who in this matter acted as Metternich's representative, during his short visit to Paris at the end of February 1815. The deposition of Murat had thus been agreed to between Louis XVIII, Metternich and Castlereagh, long before it became justified by his fantastic conduct during the Hundred Days. And when eventually the Bourbons were restored to their Kingdom of the Two Sicilies by an Austrian army it was provided in a secret treaty that King Ferdinand would not apply to his Neapolitan subjects the constitution which, under British pressure, he had granted in Sicily. It is not surprising therefore that Castlereagh should have felt it necessary to warn the Duke of Wellington that "there will be some nicety in giving to our line on this question a form most likely to prove satisfactory to Parliament."

[4]

With the settlement of the Polish crisis, with the removal from the area of acute controversy of the problem of Murat, and with the departure of Castlereagh for London, the Congress of Vienna settled down to that secondary stage familiar in all international conferences, when the committees and the experts concern themselves, not with major issues of high policy, but with the orderly arrangement of minor affairs. It is during this stage, when the high excitement of the earlier meetings has given place to general lassitude, when the several negotiators are anxious only to come to a conclusion and to return with a general treaty to their homes, that a mood of inattention descends upon the protagonists and when many subjects, which are in fact of extreme significance, are treated as if they were merely complementary or incidental. It is in these concluding, weary, hurried stages that negotiators are apt to evade further difficulties, to indulge in amiable imprecisions and to commit actual mistakes.

The process of "tidying up" the Vienna Congress was, with one important exception, neither unduly protracted nor unduly rushed. The several committees functioned with amity, accuracy and speed. When once the main pieces of the puzzle had dropped into place the smaller and more intricate portions were neatly fitted into the pattern. In the last weeks of February and the early weeks of March much useful and enduring work was accomplished. It suffices to summarise, as shortly as possible, the territorial conclusions that were reached.

In so far as the remainder of Italy was concerned, the fact that Austria, France and Great Britain were in general agreement and that Prussia and Russia could not assert any predominant interest, simplified what might otherwise have been a highly intricate transaction. In November, 1814, Don Pedro

Labrador had suggested that an Italian Committee should be constituted charged with the task of settling the Italian problem as a whole. This suggestion was firmly resisted by Metternich and on Talleyrand's advice it was agreed that each Italian problem should be dealt with on its merits.

It was tacitly assumed that Austria should obtain Lombardy and Venetia. The fate of Genoa was decided by its incorporation, under the King of Sardinia, within Piedmont. Cardinal Consalvi, on behalf of the Pope, claimed the restoration of all the territories, including Avignon and the Comtat Venaissin, which had belonged to the Holy See in 1790. Talleyrand was able to convince the Congress that it would be illogical to accord the Pope any enclaves in French territory and in the end Cardinal Consalvi was well content to obtain the old States of the Church with the three Legations of Ferrara, Bologna and Ravenna. Tuscany, in spite of Labrador's advocacy of the claims of the Infante Don Louis, was accorded to the Grand Duke Ferdinand III, who was also an Austrian Archduke. The Duchies of Modena, Reggio and Mirandola were accorded to Duke Francis IV, the grandson of Ercole III, the last Duke of the House of Este, and a faithful Austrian satellite. Some difficulty arose in regard to the disposal of Malta: under the Peace of Paris that island had been accorded to Great Britain, but Louis XVIII and the Congress generally felt that its previous owners, the Knights of the Order of St. John of Jerusalem, should at least be accorded compensation. At one moment it was suggested that the Order should be given the Ionian Islands in exchange; this suggestion was opposed by Capo d'Istria, who, as a Corfiote, was anxious that they should go to Great Britain in the justified hope that she would one day restore them to a liberated Greece. There remained the vexed question of Parma.

Under the Treaty of Fontainebleau it had been agreed that the Duchy of Parma should be accorded to Marie Louise with remainder to her son. Labrador contested this settlement by again advancing the claims of the Infante Don Louis; on this occasion he was supported by Talleyrand who did not desire to see any of the Bonapartes established in Italy. He advanced an elaborate scheme under which Parma, Guastalla and Piacenza should go to Don Louis or to his mother the Queen of Etruria, under which Lucca with part of Elba, should go to the Grand Duke of Tuscany, and under which Marie Louise should be compensated with certain Bohemian fiefs. In the end it was agreed that the Queen of Etruria should be given the Duchy of Lucca, and that Parma should go to Marie Louise, but that her son, the King of Rome, should be excluded from the succession. Everybody, and above all Metternich, was delighted by these arrangements which in fact ensured the predominance of Austrian influence throughout the Italian peninsula.

The Swiss problem⁴ was complicated by 'the fact that every one of the nineteen cantons had sent separate delegates to Vienna. La Harpe was able to influence Alexander in favour of the democratic cantons: Sir Stratford Canning supported Zurleder, the representative of the "aggrieved City and Republic of Berne." The Swiss Committee spent much time in discussing the conditions on which Geneva, ably represented by Monsieur Pictet, should be allowed to enter the Federation; and whether the Valtelline should or should not be incorporated within Swiss territory. Finally, on March 29, 1815, an agreement was come to under which a Confederation of twenty-two cantons was formed, the directorate of which was to be held successively, in biennial periods, between Berne, Zürich and Lucerne. This decision was resisted by Schwyz, Unterwalden and Appenzell and was only recognised by Zürich as late as May. More importantly the perpetual neutrality of Switzerland was recognised by the Five Great Powers by a joint declaration of November 20, 1815.

These, in comparison with the tremendous issues of peace or war which had been raised by the Polish problem, were secondary matters. The Federation of Germany was not, however, a secondary matter. It seems strange indeed that Metternich, so acute and prescient in many ways, failed to realise how important to Austria was the future balance of power within the Germanic body itself.

[5]

Metternich possessed a distaste for what Guizot called "the natural impurity" of nationalistic movements; he was thus inclined to underestimate both their durability and their force. His own early experiences had imbued him with so deep a realisation of the feuds and jealousies of the several German courts that he regarded any conception of a unitary German fatherland as a pathetic fallacy. To him the deep emotions released in Germany by the ardours and triumphs of the War of Liberation seemed little more than the hysterical excitement of a few students and intellectuals; he was so convinced that Germany desired "repose" above everything that he was satisfied that sooner or later this momentary effervescence would subside. Although he viewed with natural apprehension the increase of power which Prussia had obtained at Vienna, yet he did not share Talleyrand's certainty that Prussia would end by dominating the whole of Germany. He might, had he listened more readily to Stadion and Schwarzenberg, have sought to recast the Holy Roman Empire under the leadership of Austria and with the federal capital in Vienna itself. Europe would have been spared many misfortunes had Metternich grasped and realised this wider vision. As it was, he regarded the German problem as one of the comparatively minor issues of the peace settlement; he sought, in his intricate way, to create a German system in which, as he imagined, Prussia and Austria would hold the balance between the various states and in which the German Federation itself would not acquire sufficient identity or power to constitute a rival to either of the two. His failure to foresee the possible consequences was also due to his almost total ignorance of, and indifference to, economic factors. He seems to have imagined that Prussia, whose dominion would be dispersed in little packets throughout Germany, would be politically and militarily weakened by such dispersal: he did not foresee the immense economic domination which Prussia would acquire through her control of roads, waterways and markets;

a domination which in the coming decades was, with the additional control of railway communications, to establish her supremacy over the whole Germanic body.

Freiherr vom Stein was perhaps the only man at Vienna who either wanted or foresaw a unitary German Reich. The German liberals desired some form of federal union and the grant of constitutions in the several States; but they had little common idea as to how that union was to be formulated or what constitutions exactly should be established. The several German princes, relying upon the guarantee of sovereignty which had been given them by the Great Powers when they joined the Coalition in 1813, were unwilling either to pool that sovereignty or to share it with their peoples. In this general atmosphere of vague aspirations and regional selfishness a scheme was devised which, while it gave to Austria a purely formal or institutional hegemony, rendered the German Federation too weak and disunited to be able to resist the tremendous economic pressure exercised by Prussia throughout the nineteenth century.

The German Committee of the Vienna Congress was constituted on October 14, 1814, and consisted of Austria, Prussia, Bavaria, Würtemberg and Hanover. They already had before them two alternative proposals and on October 16 Metternich submitted a third. This scheme, which became known as the Twelve Articles, proposed a federal constitution on the following lines. Austria and Prussia were to enter the Confederation in respect of part only of their dominions; a federal Diet was to be created consisting of a Directory (shared jointly by Austria and Prussia), a Council of the Heads of the Circles (with eleven votes distributed between Prussia, Austria and the smaller States) and a Council of the Princes and Estates on which the remaining German principalities and cities would be represented. No provision of any sort was made for popular representation.

The smaller German States objected strongly to this constitution which would in their opinion curtail their independent sovereignties and give too much power to Austria and Prussia. Baron von Gagern—one of the two Plenipotentiaries for the Netherlands who was anxious to display his independence of

Great Britain—organised and headed this revolt. At a meeting held at his house the representative of thirty-one small German States drafted a counter proposal, known as the Proposal of November 16, in which they demanded representative constitutions for each of the German States, a judicial authority for the whole of thé Confederation and a federal leader with full executive authority. The Duke of Baden at this refused to surrender any of his sovereign rights and the Würtembergers proved even more obstructive. As a result the sittings of the German Committee were on November 24 suspended for a period of more than five months.

In the interval many ill-considered and varying solutions were canvassed. It was suggested that the Emperor of Austria should become German Emperor for renewable periods of five years, while the King of Prussia was to hold the vicariate for northern Germany. It was suggested that Francis I should be crowned German Emperor and that Frederick William should be concurrently crowned King of Germany. It was suggested that the King of Prussia should hold the post of imperial commander in chief under an Austrian Emperor. It was suggested that there should be two vicariates, one of which should be directed by Bavaria. It was even suggested that a Confederation should be created from which both Austria and Prussia should be explicitly excluded. Of all these conflicting and often fantastic theories the most concrete was that advanced by Prussia on February 10, 1815. Under this scheme every German should be guaranteed his fundamental rights and constitutions should be accorded in every State. There was to be a supreme judicial tribunal for the whole Confederation and two councils were to be created, the one consisting of the five major States being an executive council, and the other, on which all German states and principalities would be represented, having only legislative powers. This Prussian scheme remained on the table until the return of Napoleon imposed joint action upon all dissentients. The German Committee was for this purpose enlarged to include Saxony, Bavaria, Hesse-Darmstadt, the Netherlands (for Luxemburg) and Denmark (for Holstein). The representatives of the Princes and the Free Cities were also admitted. On June 9, 1815, this enlarged body adopted a final scheme drafted by Baron Wessenberg. Under this it was provided that a federal Diet should be constituted at Frankfurt under the presidency of Austria which should become the central organ for all the thirty-eight German States. This Diet was to draft the fundamental laws of the Confederation. Under Article XIII of this Federal Act each sovereign was obliged to grant a constitution to his subjects.

The Confederation of Germany, of which Stein and Arndt had dreamt such golden dreams, resulted therefore in a separation of powers which was so meticulously contrived that no central organ possessed any authority at all. Metternich was so delighted by this negative device that the subsequent futility, or abuse, of the functions of the Frankfurt Diet are justifiably attributed to his disastrous ingenuity. The high hopes of the German nationalists and liberals were doomed to disappointment; the opportunity was missed to create a German Confederation which might well have been liberal, civilised and humane; the unity of Germany could thereafter only be forged by blood and iron.

13. General Questions

MEANWHILE the social activities at Vienna, which had been
damped by the death of the Prince de Ligne and the extreme
tension of the Polish crisis, were resumed in an atmosphere of
increasing boredom and satiety. Even the lavish appetite of
La Garde-Chambonas appears for a moment to have been
assuaged; and the inventiveness of the Festivals Committee
became as strained as the Imperial Exchequer. The advent of
the Duke of Wellington, that to them mysterious hero, caused
a momentary revival of interest among all those unoccupied
people who had by then exhausted their powers of conversation
and their capacity for enduring late nights. The Duke himself,
although not in principle averse from social amenities, was hor-
rified by the carnival into which he was plunged. He contracted
a severe cold and for the first few days was able, on the plea of
illness, to remain in Castlereagh's apartments. On his recovery

he was lionised in the salons of Vienna. He accepted the process with obedient modesty; but he disliked it. "The hot rooms here," he wrote, "have almost killed me."

The painter Isabey[1] had established a thriving practice at Vienna and completed during those short months as many as fifty portraits; he chose the occasion of the Duke's introduction to the Congress as the main theme of his official picture. His first sketch for this picture, which displays his undoubted powers of composition, is reproduced as a frontispiece to this book. In his letters home Isabey complained of the difficulty of imparting to anything so sedentary as a group of men seated around a conference table the impression of animation and movement which his romantic principles demanded. He was hampered moreover by the inability of these preoccupied statesmen to afford him sufficient sittings; and he confessed that he found it hard accurately to portray their features without losing the tone of nobility and elevation which the occasion required. The Duke of Wellington, who was sensitive regarding his profile, tried to persuade Isabey to paint him full face; the artist was able to silence these objections by proving to the Duke that, when observed sideways, he bore an astonishing resemblance to Henri IV. From time to time Isabey would drive out to Schönbrunn and continue his portrait of the little King of Rome. And night after night he would hold receptions in his studio near the Café Jüngling and display to the visiting potentates the finished and unfinished portraits which were stacked around the walls.

It must be realised that this social energy, which appears to us so wasteful and so frivolous, filled a place which in our time would be occupied by press conferences and propaganda. These elaborate festivals and galas were not entirely purposeless; they were devised, not only as lubricants for the machine, but as a definite method of affecting what in those days was influential opinion. A European press, as we understand it, did not exist. Gentz would from time to time employ Pilat to write tendentious articles in the *Beobachter*, and Talleyrand made some use of the *Moniteur*. But such attempts as were made to influence opinion were directed, not at the masses, but at individual statesmen and politicians. The Emperor Alexander, for instance, instructed Prince Lieven to establish contact with the supposed appeasers in the British Cabinet, such as Vansittart and Bathurst. The Russian Ambassador in London was also advised to convince leading members of the Opposition, and the editors of the London journals, that in opposing the Tsar's scheme for an independent Poland Lord Castlereagh was allying himself with the reactionary forces in Europe. Castlereagh himself, through the agency of the Duke of Wellington, had endeavoured to exert pressure on Blacas and Louis XVIII behind Talleyrand's back. Yet these efforts of persuasion, intermittent and wholly individual as they were, bear but little relation to the pressure of mass propaganda which we enjoy today.

Nor were the social amenities at Vienna always so frivolous or so expensive as La Garde-Chambonas would have us believe. There exists another and less snobbish diary of the Congress written by Carl Bertuch of Weimar. Bertuch had been sent to Vienna as assistant to Cotta, the Augsburg publisher, and with the object of obtaining from the German Committee some reasonable copyright regulations applying to the German States. He arrived armed with a letter from Goethe addressed to Humboldt and he thereby obtained an unassuming entry into the edges of the great world of the time. Baron Hager, the Vienna police President, describes him in his reports as "provincial" or "*kleinstädtisch.*" This may well have been a correct description. Carl Bertuch was assuredly entranced by the great *redoute parée* which Prince Metternich gave on November 8 and at which Lady Castlereagh wore her husband's Garter entwined in her disordered hair. But Bertuch was interested in more serious things. It is from him that we obtain a picture of the concert which Beethoven conducted: it is evident that he, as other more serious people, spent most of their time walking quietly in the Prater or the Augarten, visiting museums and private collections, dining soberly with sober people in quiet restaurants, and spending patient hours with numismatists and geologists poring over cameos and coins, crystals and hardstones. The pages of Bertuch's diary and his sensible modest letters to his father provide an admirable antidote to the chubby greed of La Garde-Chambonas.

A curious aspect of the Vienna Congress was the elaborate system of espionage conducted by Baron Hager, President of the Austrian *Oberste Polizei und Censur Hofstelle*. Every morning the Emperor Francis, who possessed an infantile, and therefore prying, mind, would read with delight the secret reports with which Baron Hager's agents supplied him. These reports have since been discovered in the imperial archives and have been published by Commandant Weil. Their ineptitude is inconceivable. "The King of Prussia," we read, "this morning visited the Archduke Charles. In the evening he went out in civilian clothes with a round hat pulled down over his eyes: he had not returned at 10 P.M. The Emperor of Russia went out at 7 P.M. with one of his aides-de-camp. It is believed he went to visit the Princess Thurm and Taxis. Every morning a large block of ice is brought to the Emperor with which he washes his face and hands."

The agents employed by Baron Hager in these investigations were drawn from every class of society. There were a few penurious men and women who hung upon the fringes of the great world and relayed such gossip as they could extract during the course of the innumerable balls and banquets. There were the hall porters and coachmen attached to the several delegations. And more importantly there were the housemaids employed in the palaces and apartments of the leading delegates whose task it was to rummage in the waste-paper baskets and to extract any scraps of paper which they might find. "The British Mission," reports Hager, "owing to excessive caution, has engaged two housemaids on its own. Before I can get at the waste-paper which they throw into the baskets I must see whether I can count on these two women. . . . The box in Lord Castlereagh's room appears only to contain private papers. It would thus be best not to risk examining its contents in view of the length and danger of such operations."

The identity of the several agents was, even in the reports

sent to the Emperor Francis by Baron Hager, studiously concealed. There was no means, therefore, of judging the relative
value of the information they conveyed. Little useful knowledge was ever derived from these researches and much damaging suspicion was created. The Duc de Dalberg, for instance,
carelessly threw into his waste-paper basket a suggestion made
to the French Consul at Leghorn to the effect that it might be
possible to kidnap Napoleon from Elba by bribing the captain
of the brig in which he occasionally spent the night. It should
have been evident that Dalberg regarded the proposal as so
ridiculous that he merely cast it into the basket by his side;
but the circumstance that this document had been obtained by a
secret agent gave to it, in the eyes both of Hager and of his
Emperor, a significance which intrinsically it had never possessed. There is nothing in the whole of Hager's voluminous
reports which conveys any information of primary importance;
there is no mention, for instance, of the secret treaty of January
3; and the whole business demonstrates the futility of employing anonymous agents and the unnecessary suspicion and confusion which such a system of espionage creates. Far more
important was the fact that most of the diplomatic couriers, with
the exception of those employed by Castlereagh, were in Austrian pay and that all letters were opened and transcribed. It
was not so much that any valuable information was obtained by
this postal censorship; it was rather that the knowledge that all
couriers were corrupt and all letters opened hampered frank
communication between the several delegations and their Governments. It was not till 1817 moreover that England discovered that the Prussians had in their possession a copy of one
of her own most secret cyphers; and it has also been since
revealed that the Swedish cypher was available to the Austrian
Foreign Office.

Exaggerated emphasis has often been given to the part played
in diplomacy by secret service methods. There can be no doubt
that the information furnished by agents in regard to military
or naval matters, in that it relates to ascertainable facts, is often
of vital importance. But the reports of secret agents on political

and diplomatic matters are generally little more than personal inferences regarding the supposed tendencies or opinions of foreign statesmen; they depend for their value entirely upon the intelligence, knowledge and judgment of the agents themselves; and if these agents remain anonymous there exist no means of estimating the reliability of the information they provide. The positive advantages of secret service methods in diplomacy are therefore questionable; the negative disadvantages of such methods are great; they diminish confidence, they cause confusion, they create what is often wholly unnecessary and ill-founded distrust. No one can study the reports provided to his master by Baron Hager during the Vienna Congress without realising the dangerous futility of the whole system.

[2]

Foreign observers at the time were puzzled by the fact that the British plenipotentiaries at the Vienna Congress did not use the dominant position which they had acquired to further British interests. Gentz's bewildered commentary on Castlereagh's "aloofness" has already been quoted, and Gentz was not alone in his opinion. Napoleon himself, at St. Helena, remarked that Great Britain at the Congress of Vienna had missed a supreme opportunity to establish her predominance over the continent of Europe. Such criticisms display a misapprehension, on the one hand of the true nature of British ambitions, and on the other hand of the very valuable assets which were, in fact, obtained.

The main objective of British policy was, as it has always been, the achievement of "security." Castlereagh, as has repeatedly been shown, interpreted British security both in general and particular terms. In general, he believed that Britain's security could best be achieved by a system of a "just equilibrium" or balance of power upon the Continent; and it is this belief which explains the immense efforts which he devoted to the settlement of the Polish and Italian problems, neither of which could be described as a direct British interest. At the same time he was vividly and constantly aware that there were three particular interests which were vital to British security and which must at all costs be safeguarded. The first was British Maritime Rights or a solution in our favour of the freedom of the seas. The second was the creation in the Low Countries of a unitary State, closely allied to Great Britain, and capable of forming a barrier against any further French aggression. And the third was the exclusion, so far as was possible, of French influence from the Iberian Peninsula, or more specifically from Madrid and Lisbon. The fact that these three subjects were excluded in advance from what might be called the terms of reference of the Vienna Congress has obscured the extent to which we in the end secured the special objectives which we ourselves desired.

As described in Chapter 5, Castlereagh, on his very first visit to the Continent, was able to undo the harm which Aberdeen had perpetrated at Frankfurt and to secure the consent of the three Allied Sovereigns to the exclusion from any international conference of the question of British Maritime Rights. He was almost equally successful in arranging that the future of the Low Countries, with the attendant problem of the former Dutch colonies, should be left for direct settlement between His Majesty's Government and the parties concerned.

At Chaumont, and again during the London conversations, it had been agreed that a strong and enlarged Kingdom of the Netherlands should be created under British auspices. Castlereagh was above all anxious to create conditions which would remove all danger of the port of Antwerp and the estuary of the Scheldt again falling under French control. "The destruction," he wrote, "of the arsenal (of Antwerp) is essential to our safety. To leave it in the hands of France is little short of imposing upon Great Britain the charge of a perpetual war establishment." It was foreseen of course that the Belgian provinces would not spontaneously relish any union with their Dutch neighbours. "Depend upon it," wrote Lord Liverpool to Clancarty on May 30, 1814, "it will require the utmost management and indulgence to reconcile the people of Brabant to this connection." It was thus decided that the Act of Union should contain clauses guaranteeing to the Belgian populations complete religious toleration and commercial equality; and these stipulations, incidentally, represent the first Minority Treaties to figure in diplomatic practice. Further complications were created by the desire of Baron von Gagern, the self-assertive plenipotentiary of the Netherlands, to extend the Dutch frontier towards Cologne, and the attempts of Freiherr vom Stein and others to include the new Kingdom, at least partially, within the German Confederation under the guise of "a Burgundian circle."

Less successful was Castlereagh's endeavour to unite his new Kingdom of the Netherlands to Great Britain by a dynastic tie. It had been arranged, as has been said, that Princess Charlotte, the heiress to the British Crown, should marry the hereditary Prince of Orange; this arrangement was frustrated by the obstinacy of the young Princess, the intrigues of the Princess of Wales not unassisted by the Grand Duchess Catherine, and the general incompatibility of temper manifested by the British Court. The Princess, at first, showed a preference for her own cousin, the Duke of Gloucester: "I was very much afraid," commented the Duke of Cumberland, "that she would prefer the cheese to the orange." By February 1814, however, the betrothal had been arranged between the Prince Regent and the Prince of Orange, and was formally announced to foreign Courts. It was then that the Princess of Wales and the Grand Duchess Catherine intervened. They were assisted in their tactics, not only by some members of the Opposition, who missed no chance of embarrassing the Government, but by M. Tatisheff, Russian Ambassador in Rome and a close personal friend of the Princess of Wales. They pointed out to Princess Charlotte that if she married the Hereditary Prince she would have to leave England and spend the rest of her life in the Low Countries. Castlereagh, hearing of these intrigues, hurriedly summoned the Hereditary Prince to London; this was an inauspicious move: the Prince got so drunk at a dinner party at Carlton House that Princess Charlotte's distaste was much increased. The engagement was finally broken off in June 1814

and the Hereditary Prince of Orange, much to the Grand
Duchess's delight, thereafter married the Tsar's younger sister
Anne.

There remained the problem of the former Dutch colonies.
During the Napoleonic wars, when Holland had become a
dependency of France, Great Britain had captured all the Dutch
colonies including the East Indies. The Cape of Good Hope,
for instance, had been in British hands since 1806. Castlereagh,
who had little conception of Empire, did not wish to appear
grasping. A compromise settlement was thus negotiated which,
considering the proportions of power at the time, was by no
means ungenerous. Great Britain retained Guiana and the Cape,
and agreed in return to assume responsibility for one half of
Holland's debt to Russia and to pay in further recompense the
sum of two million pounds, this sum to be expended upon the
building of fortresses on the new frontier between the Netherlands and France. At the same time Sweden was paid an indemnity of one million pounds in return for the abandonment by
Bernadotte of his strange claim to Guadeloupe. The remaining
Dutch colonies, including the incredibly rich Dutch East Indies,
which Great Britain had acquired with such enterprise and
daring, were returned to the King of the Netherlands. With
all these important transactions the Congress of Vienna had
little or no concern.

Great Britain's relations with Spain and Portugal, the liberation of which she had secured by such gigantic efforts, constituted
a more difficult problem. King Ferdinand on his restoration was
so encouraged by the reception he received from his people, that
he repudiated the constitution, re-established the Inquisition,
and instituted a system of autocracy supported by a Church
camarilla. Don Pedro Labrador, his representative at Vienna,
behaved, as has been seen, with such excessive vanity and so
little judgment, that even Talleyrand, who had at one time
hoped to use him as a tool or satellite, was obliged to disentangle
himself from so embarrassing a connection. "It is somewhat
singular in itself," wrote Castlereagh, "that the only two Courts
with which we find it difficult to do business are those of the

Peninsula. There is a temper in both which makes it more arduous to settle a trifling matter with them than to arrange a great measure of European policy with other Powers. It seems as if the recollection of our services made it impossible for them to do anything without endeavouring most unnecessarily and ungratefully to display their own independence."

It thus came that the Spanish delegation in Vienna not only sought by all manner of inconveniences to assert their position as the representatives of a Great Power, but obstructed business by raising foolish claims. They endeavoured, as has been seen, to establish the rights of forgotten and obscure Spanish Bourbons to a number of Italian principalities. They even went so far as to seek to make a secret treaty with France under which Louis XVIII would agree to support these dynastic ambitions. They refused, without exaggerated compensation, to restore to Portugal the district of Olivenza. And they sought to make concession on this matter and in regard to the abolition of the slave trade conditional upon Great Britain's accepting their fantastic claim to Louisiana. It was only with great difficulty that Sir Henry Wellesley in Madrid was able to conclude a treaty between Spain and Great Britain. Under a secret clause of this treaty the Spanish Court undertook not to enter into any form of family compact with France. But all efforts to extract from them a treaty regulating Great Britain's future commercial relations met with an obstinate and often sullen refusal. Britain's eventual difficulties with Spain and Portugal, which became increasingly complicated as the memory of the Peninsular War receded, constitute, however, a later chapter of Europeon and American history.

[3]

It is a mistake, for these reasons, to assert that Great Britain, having for so many years stood alone against Napoleon, obtained nothing for herself from the resettlement which was negotiated at the Congress of Vienna. She retained her command of the seas; she obtained general and local security; she acquired important possessions. There was one object, however, to which Great Britain both during the Congress and throughout the years that followed, devoted unstinted effort. She sought to secure the total abolition of the slave trade; and her energies in this great cause were generous and humane. It was only after many years, and at the cost of serious sacrifices and gross misrepresentations, that her efforts were successful.[2]

As a young man Castlereagh had shared with many of his generation the impression that those who pressed for the abolition of the slave trade were little more than left-wing agitators or sentimental idealists. The more he studied the matter, the more convinced did he become that the trade was in truth a terrible evil, and that it was the duty of Great Britain to use her moral influence, her wealth and her maritime power to secure its general abolition. To this task, in the years that remained to him, he devoted commendable energy and resource. His change of heart had no doubt been accelerated by the fact that, once the danger of Napoleon had been removed, the missionary spirit of the British people became inflamed upon this subject. Petitions poured in upon him from all parts of the country; addresses were moved unanimously in both houses of Parliament; and he was warned by so placid a man as the Duke of Wellington of the "indescribable degree of frenzy existing here about the slave trade." He had been severely blamed for not having secured total and general abolition at the time of the First Peace of Paris. When he had laid that treaty upon the table of the House Wilberforce, amid murmurs of approval, had uttered a solemn protest. "I cannot but conceive," he had said, "that I behold in the hand of the noble lord the death-warrant of a multitude of innocent victims, men, women and children, whom I had fondly indulged the hope of having myself rescued from destruction."

Wilberforce was himself convinced of the sincerity of Castlereagh's intentions, even as he was aware of the obstruction of the several foreign Governments and interests concerned. He was the patient type of fanatic. "Against precipitancy," he noted in his diary, "Moses 80, Aaron 83 years old, when God sent them to lead out the Israelites from Egypt. Abraham 100 years old when Isaac born." Nor was he in the end ungrateful for what Castlereagh was able to accomplish. "I believe all done," he noted after an interview with Castlereagh upon the latter's return from Vienna, "that could be done." The tremendous power which Wilberforce exercised was due to his gentle fairness of mind.

Castlereagh had not, in fact, been inactive. Denmark had already decreed abolition; the Dutch were constrained to do so in return for the cession of the East Indies; Sweden, having been handsomely paid for Guadeloupe, followed suit. Prussia, Austria and Russia, having acquired no interest in this branch of commerce, were prepared, in the hope of gaining British support in other matters, to adopt an attitude of benevolence, not unmixed with scepticism. It was the three Catholic Powers who caused the difficulty.

Castlereagh, in that he possessed a realistic mind, foresaw from the outset that it would not be difficult to obtain from the Congress some general moral condemnation of the traffic in slaves; the difficulties would arise when it came to putting this general principle into practice. He was correct in this estimate. On December 10, 1814, on the motion of Talleyrand, a committee of the Eight Powers was appointed to consider the question of total abolition. On February 8, 1815, before Castlereagh's departure from Vienna, this committee produced an agreed declaration under which the inhuman traffic was unanimously condemned. This declaration received the approval of all the Powers and was eventually embodied in the Final Act. It did not prescribe, however, when or how the several States then engaged in the slave trade should decree its abolition. It thus became necessary for Castlereagh to negotiate direct treaties with all the interested Powers. And although the negotiation of these treaties took some years, and extends this narrative beyond the actual period of the Congress, yet no true estimate can be made, either of the influence which Great Britain was able to exercise, or of the personal part which Castlereagh himself played in this fine cause, unless the story of the abolition of the slave trade is continued a stage or two further.

At the time of the first Peace of Paris Castlereagh had obtained from the Government of Louis XVIII an assurance that France would suppress the slave trade within her own dominions within a period of five years and that she would assist Great Britain at the coming Congress in securing its abolition by all other European Powers. Although Louis XVIII personally, and to some extent Talleyrand also, were prepared to honour this assurance, they found themselves confronted with unanimous and obstinate obstruction on the part of French public opinion. The whole scheme was regarded in royalist and commercial circles as some hypocritical device on the part of Great Britain for stifling France's colonial trade. These suspicions were fostered by an ingenious argument. Great Britain, it was contended, had during the period of Napoleon's ban on British exports to the Continent accumulated vast stocks of colonial produce of which she was anxious to dispose. By abolishing the slave trade she hoped to reduce the colonial production of her rivals, and thus to dump her own accumulated produce upon a receptive European market.

Direct negotiations were carried out by the Duke of Wellington during the period when he was acting as Ambassador in Paris. He wrote long and patient letters to Wilberforce. He suggested to the French a modified scheme under which there should be an agreed quota of slaves annually exported, under which the trade would be totally abolished north of the equator, and under which the British Navy should obtain the right of visit and search in African waters. It was this latter stipulation, more than anything else, which cast doubts upon the sincerity of British intentions. Even in the United States ex-President John Adams described it as a typical piece of English self-seeking. Talleyrand exploited this advantage in the hope of obtaining something in return; he hinted to Lord Holland and Mr. Clarkson that French public opinion might be less unwilling to accept the proposal if Great Britain would pay an indemnity or offer to return one of the captured colonies. The Cabinet in London signified their willingness to cede the island of Trinidad, but French opinion had by then become so inflamed upon the subject that Talleyrand was forced to deny that he had ever suggested such a bargain and to assert that Lord Holland must have completely misinterpreted the desultory conversation which they had held. The Duke of Wellington's task was not assisted by the violence and vituperation of the English press. "The task," he wrote to Lord Holland, "is a most difficult one; and the more so because the object is really felt by every Englishman, and is urged by our newspapers and other publications with all the earnestness, not to say violence, with which we are accustomed to urge such objects, without consideration for the prejudices and feelings of others."

The direct negotiations between Wellington and De Jaucourt were thus still in a state of suspended animation when Napoleon landed in the Golfe Juan. One of his first acts on reaching the Tuileries was to declare the abolition of the slave trade in all French dominions. When eventually Louis XVIII regained his throne he felt obliged to substantiate this promise.

The negotiation with Spain and Portugal proved even more difficult. Castlereagh was faced indeed by an attempt on the part of all the Powers to barter their consent to, or their support of, abolition in order to obtain sacrifices or assistance from Great Britain in other directions. Even Cardinal Consalvi assured him that "the Pope will not lose a moment, *after his establishment in Rome,* to exert such influence as he may possess among the Catholic nations of the Continent." The Spaniards and the Portuguese were less subtle in their suggestions.

When Sir Henry Wellesley, our Ambassador in Madrid, approached the Spanish Government he was informed that the Spanish colonies, unlike those of Great Britain, were as yet not well stocked with slaves. The most Sir Henry could obtain was an assurance that, if Great Britain undertook not to supply arms to the rebellious Spanish colonies of South America, the Spanish Government would consider the suppression of this odious traffic "with all the deliberation which the condition of the Spanish colonies in America demands." When Castlereagh sought to press the subject further he could obtain no more than an assurance that if Great Britain would pay the Spanish Government a sum of £800,000 they would agree to suppress the traffic ten degrees north of the equator in ten years' time. It was upon this monetary basis that an agreement with Spain and Portugual was, after many years' delay, finally concluded. In September 1817 a treaty was signed with Spain under which she agreed immediately to abolish the slave trade north of the equator and to suppress it totally by May 30, 1820: in return for this promise the British Government paid Spain the sum of £400,000. The sum which Portugal demanded, and eventually obtained, for a similar agreement was £300,000. It was the British taxpayer who furnished these amounts.

It remains to note that in the course of these negotiations two new diplomatic devices were invented. It was suggested at one stage that the produce of those countries or colonies which refused to abolish the slave trade should be excluded from European markets. This suggestion was not adopted at the time but was revived by the Tsar in 1817 when he wished to exert pressure upon the rebellious Spanish colonies. This is the first appearance in diplomatic practice of the peace-time imposition of economic sanctions. A second device which was applied in connection with the abolition of the slave trade was the institution in London, sitting at the Foreign Office under Castlereagh's chairmanship, of a Conference of Ambassadors charged with the duty of watching the execution of the several agreements come to. It is true that this permanent Conference effected little nor did the several representatives do more than exchange courtesies and amicable little pieces of information. But the constitution of such a "watching committee" on the part of the Great Powers was at the time a startling innovation and provided a useful precedent for the future.

[4]

The slave trade was not the only general subject dealt with at Vienna. The Jewish community in Germany succeeded, by paying large sums to Gentz, in having the question of their rights inserted on the agenda of the German Committee. Such rights as they had already obtained in the several German States were formally confirmed together with a somewhat vague recommendation that these rights should be extended. It does not appear that the British delegation took any leading part in pressing for Jewish emancipation. Lord Liverpool, it is true, had forwarded to Castlereagh a memorandum from Mr. Nathan Rothschild calling his particular attention to the disabilities under which the Jewish community in Germany still suffered. "Mr. Rothschild," he wrote, "has been a very useful friend. I do not know what we should have done without him last year." There is no evidence to show that Castlereagh took any energetic action on this recommendation.

More definite and effective work was accomplished by the Congress in regard to the navigation of international rivers. A committee on this novel question was appointed by the Council of Eight on December 14, 1814, and held twelve sittings between February 2 and March 27. Not only were the Four Powers represented on this committee but representatives of all riverain States, and important commercial cities, were also admitted. Elaborate regulations were agreed to regarding the navigation of the Rhine, the Moselle, the Neckar and the Meuse. The principle was established that navigation should be free upon such rivers as served the traffic of several contiguous countries. Lord Clancarty, who was British representative on this committee, endeavoured to persuade his colleagues to recommend the destruction of all port installations at Antwerp; the Duke of Wellington, on learning this, expressed the opinion that any such action would be both foolish and unnecessary. An even more recalcitrant member of this committee was Count Münster, who as Hanoverian representative, complained to the Prince Regent that the interests of his German kingdom were being sacrificed "in favour of some vague ideas about the liberty of commerce." The committee none the less did much constructive work and its recommendations formed the precedent and the basis for many similar international agreements in the future.

There was another subject of general interest to which the Congress devoted much time and their recommendations in regard to which proved of lasting benefit. The problem of diplomatic precedence had for centuries created much unnecessary friction, hampered the rapid or even orderly conduct of international business, and exposed diplomatists to great inconvenience, odium and ridicule. Castlereagh himself regarded this subject with impatience, and even suspicion. He contended that any discussion of the precedence between States would raise many more problems than it would solve; and he seems to have feared that other Powers would profit by such a discussion to challenge the British claim to receive salutes from shore batteries as a recognition of our supremacy in the narrow seas. This claim was not founded upon, and was certainly not justified by, any international usage or enactment; it was little more than an arrogant pretension; and in the end the British were sensible enough, after 1818, to allow this foolish claim to lapse.

The question of diplomatic precedence was not, however, as trivial or as secondary as Castlereagh supposed. In the Middle Ages it had been assumed that the order of precedence among the several States should be fixed by the Pope, and in fact there exists a table or class-list, dating from 1504, by which the several Sovereigns are listed in their appropriate order. Under this table of precedence the German Emperor came first and the Duke of Ferrara last; the King of England figured seventh on the list, immediately after the King of Portugal and immediately before the King of Sicily. It was not to be expected that this arbitrary fixation of values would survive the changing proportions of national power. From the very first the Spaniards refused to accept the Pope's classification according to which Spain received a lower place than France. Unseemly pushings and poutings between the French and Spanish Ambassadors became an embarrassing element in the functions of every Court, and on September 30, 1661, when the Spanish Ambassador's coach tried to push in front of the coach of the French Ambassador at a procession in London, a regular street battle occurred which led to a rupture of diplomatic relations between Paris and Madrid and the actual threat of war. A further complication arose when Russia ceased to be an Asiatic, and sought to impose herself as a European, Power. At a court ball in London in 1768 the Russian Ambassador sat himself down beside the Ambassador of the Emperor; the French Ambassador, who was late in arriving, climbed round by the back benches and squeezed himself forcibly in between his two colleagues; a duel resulted in which the Russian Ambassador was wounded. The whole business was becoming a farce.

A more serious aspect of this constant and ill-regulated struggle for precedence and prestige was the complication it introduced into the conclusion of international treaties. Bitter animosities were aroused by the problem of the order in which the several plenipotentiaries were to sign. An elaborate device, called the *alternat,* was invented under which a separate copy of each treaty or document was provided for each plenipotentiary who signed his own copy first; this method, while it created much unnecessary labour and delay, gave to each plenipotentiary the satisfaction of feeling that at least on one copy his own name occupied the place of honour. The Congress of Vienna decided wisely that the time had come to put an end to so ridiculous a system. A committee was appointed which after two months' labour presented its report.

This report divided the several Powers into three classes, but this classification met with opposition from several of the smaller Powers and notably from the representatives of the republics. The common-sense method was therefore adopted by which the precedence of diplomatic representatives should be governed by their actual seniority, that is, by the date of the official notification of their arrival at the seat of their mission. The *Règlement* of the Vienna Congress at the same time divided diplomatic representatives into four distinct classes,—Ambassadors and papal legates, Ministers plenipotentiary, Ministers resident, and Chargés d'Affaires. It was further provided that the order in which plenipotentiaries should sign treaties should be determined by lot; this was subsequently amended at the Conference of Aix-la-Chapelle in 1818 when the more reasonable method was adopted by which signatures should be affixed in alphabetical order. The alphabet then chosen was, however, the French alphabet, a circumstance which rendered it for many years uncertain whether the United States should sign under the letter E or A or U. Yet apart from this slight imprecision the Vienna *Règlement*, in spite of Castlereagh's scepticism, did in fact settle the precedence problem for more than a hundred years. It may well be that some future congress will find itself obliged, in view of the multiplicity of Embassies which have since been created, to adopt a further *Règlement* under which Ambassadors are classified as of the first, second or third category. This, it is to be expected, will provoke a most invidious discussion.

14. The Second Peace of Paris

NAPOLEON, since his arrival in Elba on May 4, 1814, had
thought fit to surround himself with the apparatus of royalty.
He at first lived in the town hall at Porto Ferrajo, but thereafter he transferred his quarters to a house above the harbour
known as I Mulini. Here he constructed a large reception room
together with a small garden and terrace opening upon the bay.
At the same time he acquired a summer villa up at San Martino.
He summoned artists from Italy to decorate the ceilings and
the walls. The main reception room was painted in the Egyptian
style and was known as the *Salle des Pyramides;* it bore the
motto, engraved upon the base of one of the pictured columns,
"Ubicunque felix Napoleon." The ceiling of the adjoining
salon was adorned with an allegorical painting of two turtle-
doves, separated by wide spaces of sky and cloud, but joined
together by a ribbon indicating conjugal constancy during mis-

fortune. The bathroom which opened out of the bedroom was decorated with Pompeian frescos: above the stone bath ran another motto: "*Qui odit Veritatem, odit Lucem.*" Sometimes he would spend a night up at the rough hermitage at Marciana Alta: occasionally he would for a day or two occupy the rooms reserved for him in the citadel of Porto Longone. He flung himself into the administration of his little kingdom with restless, if intermittent, zest.

His mother was permitted to join him and established herself in a small house fronting the road and not far distant from I Mulini. His sister, Pauline Borghese, also spent some weeks upon the island. He received a secret visit from his former mistress, Countess Waleska, and on occasions English visitors of note would be admitted to an audience. The time, none the less, hung heavy on his hands. "My island," he sighed to Neil Campbell, when one evening they had climbed together to the ridge which dominates Porto Ferrajo, "is very small." His outward demeanour was resigned and calm. It was noted only that his increasing corpulence had much diminished his former physical alertness and that he would spend hours of lethargy soaking in his Pompeian bath.

In his desire to preserve his royal state he maintained a household which was in fact beyond the scope of his limited budget. There was Bertrand, the grand marshal of the palace; there was Druot, the military governor of Elba; there was Peÿrusse, the treasurer. He appointed four chamberlains from among the citizens of Elba: Doctor Lapi, Signor Traditi, the mayor of Porto Ferrajo, Signor Cantini, and the mayor of Rio Montagna who had lost one eye in a scuffle with the gendarmes during a period of brigandage. He employed two secretaries, a doctor, a chemist, a butler, the chef Ferdinand with seven assistants, two valets, three chasseurs, the Mameluke Ali, two ushers, eight footmen, one porter, a woman in charge of the linen, a washerwoman, a director of the gardens, and a director of music assisted by two female singers. His stables were lavishly equipped. He possessed twenty-seven carriages and employed thirty-five stable hands. Many of his famous horses had been sent over from France to join him. There was the dappled grey, Wagram, whom he had ridden at the battle of that name. There was Emir, on whose back he had entered Madrid; Gonzalve who had borne him at Brienne; Roitelet, who had shared the retreat from Moscow; and the two white horses, Intendant and Tauris, the gift of Alexander after Tilsit.

Under the Treaty of Fontainebleau he had been permitted to bring with him 400 men of the Old Guard who were placed under Cambronne. In addition to this he had fifty-four Polish cavalry and a local Elban militia of some 800 men. The budget for his army and navy (since he had been allowed to retain the brig *Inconstant*) amounted to 689,317 francs a year.

In the first months of his reign upon the island he attempted to create at least the semblance of a court society. The leading citizens of Elba—the notaries and the apothecaries, the managers of the tunny fisheries and the mines—were provided by the tailors of Leghorn with state uniforms of blue embroidered with silver; the sempstresses of Porto Ferrajo were kept busy stitching trains of yellow or violet cloth to evening gowns designed in the more recent Empire fashions. In the *Salle des Pyramides* the chamberlains whom he had recruited locally would endeavour to marshal these gaping women into a royal circle; the door would be flung open and the grand marshal would announce the Emperor; he would make the round of the circle addressing a few questions in Italian to each in turn. Ungainly and unkempt, these women would either gape in panic silence or giggle with panic volubility. Even Napoleon, who had small sense of incongruity, realised in the end that these court ceremonies were misplaced: he decided no longer to expose either his subjects or himself to such distorted imitations of the Tuileries. He remained thereafter within the circle of his own family and household.

In the evening his mother or his sister would keep him company. They would play dominoes together, or *vingt-et-un*, for nominal stakes. Napoleon, as usual, would cheat. His mother on one occasion reproved him sharply for this habit. "What does it matter?" he said to her. "You are far richer than I."

Night after night they would sit there in the *Salle des Pyramides* playing these heart-rending games. When the clock struck nine the Emperor would rise from the card table and walk slowly towards the piano; with one finger he would tap out the notes of a then famous lullaby. It was the signal for them to retire for the night.

He was not immune from personal anxieties. He was constantly afraid of assassination and a careful watch was kept upon all unknown characters who might reach the island from Corsica or the Italian mainland. In the early months he was terrified of being raided by Barbary corsairs and relied almost pathetically upon Neil Campbell's protection. In the end, however, the corsairs agreed to respect the Elban flag (a white flag with a bend of orange decorated with three enormous bees) and amicable relations were established. He was well aware, moreover, that he owed his kingdom of Elba solely to the magnanimity of Alexander, and that whereas the Bourbons resented his proximity to France, Metternich was rendered uneasy by his proximity to Murat and the Italian mainland. He knew that at the time of his abdication Talleyrand had pressed for his removal to the Azores, to Santa Lucia or some other West Indian Island, even to distant St. Helena. He learnt from his informers in Paris that secret negotiations were proceeding between Metternich and Blacas and he feared, not without reason, that one condition of such negotiations might be his removal to some more distant place of internment. A year later, on a damp evening at The Briars at St. Helena, he confessed to Las Cases that the fear of removal from Elba had been one of the determinant reasons for his escape.

His main preoccupation, however, was finance. He had brought with him from Fontainebleau a sum of frcs. 3,979,915. A large portion of this was pilfered on the journey and but little remained. The budget of his island kingdom was not ill-balanced. He received some 120,000 francs from customs and indirect taxation; the iron mines brought in a revenue of 300,000 francs, the salt mines produced an additional 20,000, and the tunny fisheries showed a profit of 30,000. These sums sufficed for the actual administrative expenses of the island. But there remained nothing over for the maintenance of his small army or for the personal expenses of his household. Under Article III of the Treaty of Fontainebleau it had been provided that, in return for his surrendering his private fortune, which was estimated at some eight million pounds sterling, he and his family would receive from the French exchequer an annual allowance of £100,000. This pension was never paid. The Allied Plenipotentiaries at Vienna, foreseeing that this violation of the Treaty of Fontainebleau might drive Napoleon to desperation, protested mildly but frequently to Talleyrand. "People," wrote the latter to Louis XVIII on October 13, 1814, "often wonder, and Lord Castlereagh plainly asked me, whether the treaty of April 11 is being put into execution. The silence of the budget in this respect is being remarked by the Tsar of Russia. Prince Metternich says that Austria cannot be expected to pay off the interest on the monies invested in the Mont de Milan bank if France does not execute the clauses of the treaty which are incumbent on her. On every occasion this matter always reappears under different forms and almost always in an unpleasant manner. However painful it may be to dwell on such money matters, I can but say to Your Majesty that it is desirable that something be done in this respect. A letter from M. de Jaucourt, who by command of Your Majesty should inform me of it, would certainly have a good effect." A reply was returned to this letter by Louis XVIII on October 21. He informed Talleyrand that he would be prepared to pay even a larger pension than that provided under the Treaty of Fontaine-bleau "if the excellent idea of the Azores were put into execu-tion." There is no evidence that Napoleon ever knew of this reply; he possessed his sources of information; but the fact remains that the money promised and guaranteed was never paid. It was the failure on the part of Louis XVIII and in-directly of the Allies to carry out the Treaty of Fontainebleau, or what Madame d'Arblay mildly calls "this general failure of foresight," which convinced Napoleon that he was morally absolved from his own signature to that treaty. Yet the deter-

minant factor was the information which reached him as the
months wore on regarding the internal condition of France. The
Bourbons, under the influence of Monsieur and the ultra-
royalists, under the lazy optimism of Louis XVIII, were displaying consummate ineptitude. The army and the dismissed
officers were seething with unrest. "France," commented Napoleon a year later at St. Helena, "was discontended. I was her
only resource. The illness and its cure were in accord."

In the last days of February 1815, Napoleon, accompanied
only by a handful of men, escaped by night from Elba. On
March 1 he landed in the Golfe Juan; on March 10 he entered
Lyons in triumph. The royalists in Paris, who had at first been
inclined to laugh at this "escapade," were seized with sudden
panic when they learnt of the reception accorded to the usurper
at Lyons. A flood of liberal decrees were issued in the *Moniteur;*
all manner of promises were lavished upon the half-pay officers
and the old Imperial Guard. On March 16 Louis XVIII drove
to the Palais Bourbon wearing for the first time the rosette of
the Legion of Honour. He received a rapturous welcome from
the assembled deputies. "How can I," he said to them, "at the
age of sixty better terminate my career than by dying in defence
of my country?" On the next morning news was received of
the defection of Marshal Ney; Napoleon, it was reported, had
already reached Auxerre unopposed. On the night of Sunday,
March 19, Louis XVIII shambled in his velvet slippers across
the parquet of the Tuileries towards the Pavillon de Flore.
His carriage was waiting for him at the side-door. The cande-
labra which they held to guide his slow steps guttered in the
wind and rain that slashed around them. He drove off into the
darkness on his way to Ghent.

On the night of Monday, March 20, which was again a night
of rain and wind, a carriage escorted by Polish cavalry carrying
torches galloped into the capital. The crowd surged round the
Tuileries. They carried Napoleon upon their shoulders up the
grand staircase and into the throne room. His face was deathly
pale: he wore a slight, an almost contemptuous, smile upon
his lips.

[2]

The news of Napoleon's escape from Elba reached Vienna in the early morning of March 7. The circumstances are best recorded in the words of Metternich himself:

On the night [he writes] of March 6-7 there had been a meeting in my rooms of the plenipotentiaries of the Five Powers. This meeting had lasted until three in the morning. I had forbidden my valet to disturb my rest if couriers arrived at a late hour of the night. In spite of this prohibition, the man brought me, about six in the morning, an express despatch marked "Urgent." Upon the envelope I read the words, "From the Imperial and Royal Consulate General at Genoa." As I had only been in bed for about two hours I laid the despatch, without opening it, upon the table beside my bed. I tried to go to sleep. But having once been disturbed I was unable to rest again. At about 7.30 I decided to open the envelope. It contained only the following six lines: "The English Commissioner Campbell has just entered the harbour enquiring whether anyone had seen Napoleon at Genoa, in view of the fact that he had disappeared from the island of Elba. The answer being in the negative, the English frigate, without further delay, put to sea."

I dressed myself in a flash and before 8 A.M. I was with my Emperor. He read the above mentioned despatch; he then, with that perfect calm which never deserted him on great occasions, said to me: "Napoleon appears anxious to run great risks; that is his business. Our business is to give to the world that repose which he has troubled all these years. Go at once and find the Emperor of Russia and the King of Prussia; tell them that I am prepared to order my armies once again to take the road to France. I have no doubt that the two Sovereigns will join me in my march."

At 8.15 I was with the Emperor Alexander who used the same language as the Emperor Francis. At 8.30 King Frederick William III gave me a similar assurance. By 9 o'clock I had returned home. I had already summoned Field Marshal Prince Schwarzenberg to come to my house. At 10 the Ministers of the Four Powers had gathered at my invitation in my study. At the same hour aides-de-camp were flying in all directions carrying to the several army corps, who were retiring, the order to halt.

In this way war was decided on in less than an hour.

Talleyrand was also summoned to the meeting of the four Ministers in Metternich's study. He was the first to arrive. It was an elderly Talleyrand who entered the room; formidable, almost frightening in his impassivity. It was the Talleyrand of the Ary Scheffer portrait: the Talleyrand in whose features Mary Berry, a few months later, was to recognise "a mass of physical and moral corruption"; the Talleyrand, whose appearance in July of that same year Croker described in startling terms: "He is fattish for a Frenchman; his ankles are weak and his feet deformed and he totters about in a strange way. His face is not at all expressive, except it be of a kind of drunken stupour; in fact he looks like an old, fuddled, lame, village schoolmaster, and his voice is deep and hoarse."

It was this Talleyrand who, on that for him early morning of March 7, 1815, limped into Metternich's study, casting a cold glance at the astronomical and chronological instruments with which it was encumbered. Their interview was short and to the point. Metternich read him the message received from the Austrian Consul General at Genoa. Not a flicker of surprise appeared upon the Frenchman's impassive features. The following dialogue took place:

Talleyrand: Do you know where Napoleon is making for?
Metternich: The report makes no mention of that.
Talleyrand: He will land on some part of the Italian coast and will then fling himself into Switzerland.
Metternich: No. He will make straight for Paris.

And at this the other Ministers, Hardenberg, Nesselrode and Wellington, arrived.

One of Napoleon's first remarks upon landing in France was, "The Congress is dissolved." This was an inaccurate estimate. In the first place the Congress continued to function throughout the following months while the Drafting Committee cast into shape the several agreements which had already been come to and which nine days before the battle of Waterloo, were completed as the Final Act. And in the second place the Eight acted during the weeks which followed with unexpected agility.

On the afternoon of March 8, Wellington, accompanied by Metternich and Talleyrand, dashed off to Pressburg in the hope of extracting from the King of Saxony his acceptance of the arbitral award imposed upon him. The King refused. "He treated with contempt," Wellington reported, "and a good deal of vivacity, the recommendation which I gave him not to allow himself to delay his decision from any hopes he might entertain of the success of Buonaparte's plans. Upon the whole I conceived that he was inclined to endeavour to excite a popular compassion in his favour, notwithstanding that his case is so bad, and His Majesty knows that we think so." On their return to Vienna the Five decided that in spite of the King of Saxony's protests the areas agreed on should at once be ceded to Prussia.

On March 12 Castlereagh wrote to Wellington suggesting that the Allied Sovereigns should issue a joint declaration against Napoleon. "Your Grace can judge," he added, "where your personal presence is likely to be of most use to the public service. The Prince Regent, relying entirely upon Your Grace's zeal and judgment, leaves it to you, without further orders, either to remain at Vienna or to put yourself at the head of the army in Flanders."

Wellington had already anticipated these instructions. On March 13 a declaration, signed by Austria, France, Great Britain, Prussia, Russia, Spain, Portugal and Sweden, was publicly issued. Under this declaration the Eight undertook to furnish "to the King of France and the French nation" the assistance to re-establish public tranquillity. At the same time they proclaimed that "Napoleon Buonaparte had placed himself outside the pale of civil and social relations" and that "as the disturber of world repose he had exposed himself to public indictment (*vindicte*)."

On March 18 a treaty was drafted to reaffirm the Coalition formed at Chaumont. The signature of this new document which recreated the Grand Alliance was somewhat delayed by the anxiety of the Sovereigns to obtain further subsidies from England. It was eventually signed by Austria, Russia, Great Britain and Prussia on March 25. France, Spain, Portugal, the

Low Countries, Sardinia, Bavaria, Hanover, Würtemberg, Baden, Hesse and Brunswick were invited to adhere. Article IV of this treaty solemnly reaffirmed the compact entered into at Chaumont. Article III expressly provided that none of the parties to the treaty would lay down their arms until Napoleon had been rendered totally incapable of stirring up further trouble or of seizing supreme power in France. In a supplementary clause Great Britain undertook to place at the disposal of her allies the sum of five million pounds sterling.

The armies, which were in process of dispersal, were rapidly regrouped. "I am going," wrote the Duke of Wellington to Lord Burghersh on March 22, "into the Low Countries to take command of the army." He reached Brussels on the night of April 4.

Yet beneath this seeming unison and decisiveness ran tremours of doubt and apprehension. In vain did Pozzo di Borgo proclaim that within a few days Napoleon would be arrested and hanged. In vain did Metternich maintain his courtly smile of placid scepticism and Talleyrand confront the world with an impassive mask. "A thousand candles," records La Garde-Chambonas, "seemed in a single instant to have been extinguished." "It was not difficult," wrote Lord Clancarty, who succeeded Wellington as head of the British delegation, "to perceive that fear was predominant in all the Imperial and Royal personages."

[3]

Napoleon meanwhile was well aware that his own position was precarious. The declaration of March 13 by which he had been proclaimed a world outlaw had produced its effect. He was conscious that a chill of general apprehension had succeeded the early raptures of delight. "I had no longer within me," he confessed at St. Helena, "the sense of final success. . . . I had an instinctive feeling that the outcome would prove unfortunate." He sought desperately to appeal to the liberal sentiments of the French people. He hurriedly proclaimed an *Acte Additionel*, under which he promised to provide France with a legislature consisting of two chambers. He submitted this act to a plebiscite, and although he only obtained one half of the votes he had secured in 1802, he solemnly ratified his new charter on June 1 at an imposing and dramatic ceremony which he entitled the *Champ de Mai*. At the same time he sought by every means in his power to disrupt the Coalition which had so rapidly been reformed against him. He endeavoured at once to open secret communications with his father-in-law, the Emperor Francis: he was enraged when Murat's escapade put an end to all such overtures. In the hope of conciliating British opinion he abolished the slave trade with a stroke of the pen. He knew that the Prussians would prove obdurate and he therefore concentrated his attention on the Tsar. The Russian chargé d'affaires, Boutiakine, had not followed Louis XVIII to Ghent but had remained in Paris. He was despatched to Alexander bearing, not only a conciliatory letter from Napoleon, but also a copy of the secret treaty of January 3, 1815, by which Castlereagh, Metternich and Talleyrand had pledged themselves to resist the Tsar's Polish scheme, if necessary by war. Castlereagh, the moment he heard that the Marquis de Jaucourt had run so hurriedly from the Tuileries that he had left all his secret papers behind him, foresaw this embarrassing disclosure; he comforted himself with the reflection that the Tsar must have had a shrewd idea at the time that some such compact had been concluded. He may have been correct in this estimate; but the revelation when it came did much to disturb the Tsar's confidence in British democracy; Capo d'Istria, who saw him just after he had read the document, records that the Emperor paced the room in such fury that his ears turned red with rage.

Napoleon certainly had some prospect of retaining his throne. It would take some time before the Austrian armies, who were already involved in Italy, would be able to take the offensive; the Russian troops had for the most part returned home and had no desire whatsoever to be driven into another European war. Wellington's detachment in Flanders represented, as Napoleon well knew, only a scratch affair, since the majority of the Peninsular veterans were still tossing on the Atlantic. If only Napoleon could deal a sudden secret blow at Wellington and Blücher before they could unite, then he might gain time till his new levies were fully conscripted and he possessed an army of half a million men.

He knew that opinion in Great Britain, in spite of the firm attitude adopted at Vienna, was uncertain and divided. Castlereagh himself had hesitated to "march into France for the purpose of restoring a sovereign who had been abandoned and betrayed by his own troops and subjects." Even the Duke of Wellington, who cherished a strange personal affection for Louis XVIII, was uncertain. "Notwithstanding," he wrote to Castlereagh from Brussels on April 11, "the respect and regard I feel for the King, and the sense which I entertain of the benefits which the world would derive from the continuance of his reign, I cannot help feeling that the conduct of his family and his government during the late occurrences, whatever may have been his own conduct, must and will affect his own character, and has lowered them much in the public estimation." [1]

The British people were quite prepared to fight Napoleon; they were not, however, equally willing to engage in a further war in order to restore the Bourbons. In Parliament the Opposition were divided; the Grenvilles realised that war was in fact inevitable; Whitbread, however, believed that a lasting peace could now be made with Napoleon and bitterly attacked the treaty of March 25 by which the Coalition had been reformed. As a result the Government decided to declare war, not upon France, but upon Napoleon personally. It was not, they asserted, their wish to make war for the purpose of imposing any particular dynasty on the French people. This led to all manner of complications regarding the calling up of the militia and the treatment to be accorded to French commerce and to the French colonies. Gradually, however, public opinion rallied behind the Government and the Duke of Wellington was able to build up his army from the drafts that dribbled hurriedly across.

On June 12 Napoleon left Paris determined at any price to prevent the junction of the Prussian and the British armies. On June 18 was fought the battle of Waterloo. On June 21

Napoleon returned to Paris a defeated man. On June 22 he signed a declaration by which he abdicated in favour of his son. On June 25 he retired to Malmaison which he left secretly on the night of June 29. For a few days he disappeared completely. On July 8 Louis XVIII re-entered Paris. On July 15 Napoleon boarded H.M.S. *Bellerophon* (Captain Maitland) in the Basque Roads.

[4]

It is beyond the scope of this study to consider whether Napoleon did in fact surrender to Captain Maitland or whether he merely flung himself upon the generosity of the British people,—even as Themistocles, having been ostracised by the citizens of Athens, flung himself upon the mercy of the Persians. For Napoleon, in any case, there was to be no Anatolian refuge. Had he managed to escape to the United States, had he been able even to surrender to the Emperor Francis or the Tsar, he might have been spared the long bitterness of St. Helena. On the other hand, had he been captured by the Prussians (as he was almost captured while lingering at Malmaison) he would certainly have been shot. Our first intention was to intern him at Fort St. George in Scotland. The reception accorded to him by the British public while the *Bellerophon* was at anchor in Torbay and later at Plymouth, coupled with an attempt on the part of the Opposition to serve a writ of habeas corpus, determined the Government to remove him to a more distant prison. It was thus almost by chance that Great Britain for a hundred years had to bear the full odium of his captivity.

The problem of his successor might, but for the Duke of Wellington's masterly activity, have caused grave dissension between the Allies. There were those who were in favour of a French republic; there were those who believed that tranquillity could best be restored to France if Napoleon's son were installed under a regency; there were those again, and the Tsar was among them, who felt that the only hope was to establish the Duke of Orleans as the "King of the Revolution."

The news of Waterloo reached the Emperor Francis and the

Tsar at Heidelberg on June 21. Each of them wrote to Wellington complimenting him upon his decisive victory. Metternich was more cautious. "I hasten to congratulate you," he wrote from Mannheim on June 24, "on the brilliant opening of the campaign." Alexander soon realised, however, that the British victory had in fact been complete. Leaving the Emperor Francis and Frederick William at St. Dizier he pushed on to Paris with only a small escort of Cossacks, in the hope of re-affirming the arbitral position which had been his in April 1814. On this occasion Louis XVIII was careful to flatter the Tsar's vanity; he loaded him with civilities; he even conferred upon him the Order of the Holy Spirit. But Alexander arrived too late.

Wellington had realised at once that, if the Bourbons were to be restored, it would be essential to secure the services both of Talleyrand and Fouché. The former was summoned from Vienna, was provided with £10,000 from British Secret Service funds, and was forced upon Louis XVIII at an interview which took place at Mons. It was with even greater difficulty that the Duke persuaded Louis XVIII to dismiss Blacas and to accept Fouché. "If," he remarked subsequently to Sir John Malcolm, "I had not settled with Fouché when I did, the Duke of Orleans would have been proclaimed King next day, and that would have been a new trouble." It was by such direct and rapid action that Louis XVIII was for a second time restored to his throne.

There remained the problem of concluding a second peace with France. The controversy which arose on this subject was embittered and prolonged; whereas the first Peace of Paris had taken only two months to negotiate, it took five months to negotiate the second. It is important also to realise that the Battle of Waterloo had shifted the incidence of immediate power; the conflict which followed thus became one between the two victors, Great Britain and Prussia; the Austrians, the Russians and the French were relegated to a secondary role.

The Prussians, almost avowedly, were out for revenge and loot. Their General Staff, with the full support of Marshal Blücher, demanded fantastic reparations and indemnities. The civilian Ministers were powerless to resist them. "I find myself," Hardenberg confessed to Cathcart, "in the midst of praetorian bands." The Prussian Generals demanded Alsace-Lorraine, the Sarre Valley, Luxemburg, and Savoy; they demanded a war indemnity of twelve hundred million francs; they wanted to blow up the Pont d'Iena; and their troops in occupation of French territory behaved so outrageously that the Duke of Wellington at one time suggested that the occupation should be confined to the British, Austrian and Russian armies.

Castlereagh crossed to Paris to assist the Duke in these negotiations. He arrived there on July 6 and remained until November 23. During the whole of this period he lived in the palace of the Princess Pauline Borghese which is still the British Embassy. Wellington took up his own quarters on the ground floor of the Hôtel de La Reynière, which belonged to the banker Ouvrard.

At no time in his career was Castlereagh's consistency so effective as during the five months in which he shaped the second Peace of Paris. He found himself in a position of supremacy as dominant as that which the Emperor Alexander had enjoyed, and vitiated, during the spring of 1814. It was not merely that the final defeat of Napoleon had this time been due almost entirely to British arms; it was not merely that in the previous two years his unruffled fortitude, his cool reasonableness, had earned him the respect and confidence of Europe; it was also that his several antagonists and allies were almost totally exhausted and that the differences which existed between them cancelled each other out. Castlereagh, in that summer and autumn of 1815, could, had he so desired, have acquired for his country important accessions of colonial and continental territory and immense financial and commercial benefits. In placing the ultimate interests of Europe above the immediate advantage of England he displayed qualities of imagination and understanding such as have not been sufficiently applauded either by foreign or by British historians.

Reading of these events at St. Helena, Napoleon, who was temperamentally incapable of understanding any politics other than power politics, could only ascribe Castlereagh's splendid moderation to treachery or corruption, to ignorance or folly. Why had he not reduced France to a tiny central kingdom surrounded by independent principalities in Normandy, Brittany and Provence each possessed of rulers subservient to British influence? Why had he not rendered Belgium a British colony under a King chosen from the Hanoverian family? Why had he not obtained for England strategical and commercial bases in Italy and the Baltic? Why had he not imposed by force upon Spain and Portugal commercial treaties so advantageous to Great Britain that they would have indemnified her for the vast sums she had lavished during twenty years of war? "One cannot understand," he said, "how a sensible nation can allow herself to be governed by such a lunatic."

"After twenty years of war," he said, "after all the wealth which she has expended; after all the assistance which she gave to the common cause; after a triumph beyond all expectation; —what sort of peace is it that England has signed? Castlereagh had the continent at his disposal. What great advantage, what just compensations, has he acquired for his country? The peace he has made is the sort of peace he would have made if he had been beaten. I could scarcely have treated him worse, the poor wretch, if it had been I who had proved victorious! . . . Thousands of years will pass before England is given a second opportunity equal to this opportunity to establish her prosperity and greatness. Was it ignorance, was it corruption, that induced Castlereagh to take the line he did? Nobly, so he imagined, did he distribute the spoils of victory to the sovereigns of the continent, while reserving nothing for his own country. He handed round presents of immense territories; Russia, Austria, Prussia, —all of them acquired millions of new subjects. Where did England find her equivalent? England, who had been the very soul of victory, who had paid the whole cost, must now reap the harvest of European 'gratitude'; the harvest of the blunders, or the treason, of her plenipotentiary."

Castlereagh, had he heard or read these words, would have replied quite simply. "But I was only," he would have answered, "carrying out what Pitt advised us all to do in 1804." In a world enured to brilliant opportunism, to the sensational politics of power, such consistency was in truth remarkable. His main thesis, throughout those months in Paris, was "security but not revenge." Reparation could be rendered, partly in the form of a moderate indemnity plus the costs of occupation, and partly by the restoration of those works of art which France had generously been allowed to retain in 1814. Security could be achieved by two processes, the one particular and the other general. On the one hand immediate strategic safety could be guaranteed by the occupation of the northern fortresses of France and the cession of a few frontier districts. On the other hand the peace of Europe could be maintained by uniting in a lasting alliance the forces of power which victory had left predominant in Europe.

Such were the general conceptions which guided Castlereagh in framing the second Peace of Paris.

[5]

The main issue, as has been indicated, lay between the Prussian theory of a punitive peace, dictated to France and maintained by compulsion, and Castlereagh's theory of a moderate peace, which would in the end receive the consent of the French people. Before leaving London Castlereagh had obtained the agreement of his colleagues to the general principle that the "integrity" of France should be respected. With the surrender of Napoleon and the utter collapse of French resistance public opinion in Great Britain had however begun to stiffen. "The prevailing idea in this country," wrote Liverpool on July 15, "is that we are fairly entitled to avail ourselves of the present moment to take back from France the principal conquests of Louis XIV." Fortunately, however, British opinion was less concerned with territorial concessions than with the punishment of war criminals and collaborators such as Fouché. The desire for personal vengeance was, however, soon assuaged by the arrest of Marshal Ney [2] and British opinion ceased thereafter to wish for any further blood-letting. The British people are not by nature punitive and one or two judicial murders will suffice to glut their momentary clamour for personal retribution. This particular movement of public opinion was not, therefore, either sufficiently deep or sufficiently lasting seriously to complicate Lord Castlereagh's task. He set himself, with his customary disregard both of popular clamour and of Cabinet opinion, to secure a just and reasonable peace with France, and in so doing he displayed unusual and uncharacteristic tactical skill.

In opposition to the excessive demands of Prussia he first devised a scheme which, he well knew, was too moderate to obtain the support of his own colleagues in the Government. It provided only for the dismantling of the French frontier fortresses, the temporary occupation of French territory, and the renewal of the Quadruple Alliance. He induced the Emperor Alexander to put forward this scheme as his own. The Cabinet in London disapproved of such moderation. Castlereagh was warned not to commit himself too far with Alexander and was told that, whereas the Government agreed that the Prussian demands were excessive, they favoured some middle line such as had been suggested by Austria. Castlereagh thereupon brought forward a second scheme under which France would be reduced to the frontiers of 1790 and would surrender those additional territories which she had acquired by 1792, namely a small slice of territory on the Belgian frontier and a part of Savoy. Two complications then developed. Count Münster persuaded the Prince Regent, and through him certain members of the Cabinet, that Castlereagh was being sentimental about France, and too suspicious of Prussia. Lord Stewart was sent over to London bearing a memorandum in which Castlereagh exposed the danger of Prussian militarism and its ultimate effect upon Hanover and the Netherlands. The Cabinet were impressed by these arguments and the diversion staged by Count Münster thereafter collapsed.

A second diversion was then created by Baron Gagern of the

Netherlands who weighed in with a bright idea that Prussia should obtain Luxemburg and that the Low Countries should be compensated by additional French territory beyond the Belgian frontier. Castlereagh was infuriated by this intrusion; he could not tolerate the endeavours of the small esurient Powers to snip pieces from the stricken body of France. "The more I reflect upon it," he wrote on August 31, 1815, "the more I deprecate the system of scratching such a Power. We may hold her down and pare her nails so that many years shall pass away before they wound us. I hope we may do this effectually and subject to no more hazards of failure than must, more or less, attend all political or military arrangements. But this system of being pledged to a continental war for objects which France may any day reclaim from the particular States that hold them, without pushing her demands beyond what she would contend was due to her own honour, is I am sure a bad British policy."

Gradually such diversions were eliminated and Castlereagh was able to obtain the support of Russia and Austria to a scheme, which, although not so moderate as that which he and the Tsar had at first advocated, was none the less an immense improvement upon the extreme partitions for which the Prussians had worked. On one point, however, he was obliged, against his will, to make concessions to vindictiveness. France was obliged to restore to their owners those works of art which Napoleon had taken as the spoils of his campaign. The Prussians, without awaiting the signature of any treaty or the consent of their Allies, had already packed their own works of art into wagons and sent them off to Berlin. The King of the Netherlands recovered those Flemish masterpieces which Napoleon had housed in the Louvre. The Venus of the Medici went back to Florence; the horses of St. Mark's were, on September 30, taken down from the arch of the Carrousel and restored to Venice; and the Pope sent Canova on a special mission to Paris to catalogue and recover the treasures which had once been his. The rage of the

Parisians at what they regarded as the despoiling of their capital was turned, not against those who had secured the restoration of their possessions, but against the British who obtained nothing at all.

The Second Peace of Paris, as thus negotiated, was signed on the afternoon of November 20, 1815. Under its provisions France lost a few small strips upon the Belgian frontier, the fortresses of Landau and Saarlouis, a few areas on the Swiss frontier in the region of Geneva, and most of Savoy. She was obliged to pay an indemnity of seven hundred million francs and to support for five years an allied army of occupation consisting of 150,000 men. In 1817, however, the total of this army of occupation was reduced to 30,000, and after the Congress of Aix-la-Chapelle in 1818 the occupying forces were completely withdrawn. It cannot be said that the Second Peace of Paris was, considering the circumstances, a punitive dictation; in all essentials the integrity and honour of France had been preserved.

Castlereagh had always felt, in the true Pitt tradition, that no frontier rectifications and no disarmament clauses, would in themselves suffice to maintain security unless backed by overwhelming force. The problem of a Treaty of Guarantee under which all the Powers should pledge themselves to the maintenance of the general settlement was one which had much exercised his mind and which will be examined in the next chapter. Meanwhile he succeeded in obtaining from his four Allies a special Quadruple Alliance guaranteeing the Peace of Paris.

Capo d'Istria, who was by then the leading figure in Alexander's councils, had sought to turn the new Quadruple Alliance into a specific guarantee of the Bourbon dynasty. Castlereagh was wisely opposed to this, feeling that it savoured too much of interference in internal French affairs. What he wanted was a treaty which "would make a European invasion the inevitable and immediate consequence of Buonaparte's succession, or of that of any of his race, to power in France." It was with this end in view that the Quadruple Alliance was signed at the British Embassy on the same day as the Treaty of Paris. Under Article VI of this alliance it was provided that the Powers would renew their meetings at fixed periods for the purpose of discussing what measures would be "most salutary for the repose and prosperity of nations and for the maintenance of the peace of Europe."

It was in this manner that the conference system was created.

15. The Holy Alliance

[September 26, 1815]

The drafting of the Final Act of the Congress of Vienna—Its
signature on June 9, 1815—Castlereagh raises the question of a
Treaty of Guarantee—His motives in so doing—He attempts to
induce Russia to guarantee the integrity of the Ottoman Empire
—This endeavour fails owing to Russian designs against Turkey
—The Nesselrode memorandum—Opposition in London to any
Treaty of Guarantee—Castlereagh drops the idea and falls back
upon the Quadruple Alliance—The effectiveness and acceptability
of this diminished by Alexander's conception of the Holy Alliance—Origin of the Tsar's conception—Baroness von Krüdener
—The Heilbronn interview—The review upon the plateau of
Vertus—The Tsar's draft of the Holy Alliance—Its reception by
Castlereagh and Metternich—Immediate reaction against it of
progressive opinion in Europe—Its conclusion marks the beginning of a rift between Great Britain and Russia—Metternich
seeks to create suspicion between Castlereagh and Alexander—
Castlereagh's general attitude towards the Russian menace—The
suggestion of a disarmament treaty—Its failure—Castlereagh
sees in the conference system the only hope of maintaining the
Concert of Europe.

THE ESCAPE of Napoleon from Elba, the drama of the
Hundred Days, the battles in Brabant, and the concentration
of diplomatic activity upon the negotiation of the Second Peace
of Paris and the Quadruple Alliance of November 20, 1815, all
combined to divert attention from the Congress of Vienna. Yet
the Congress had continued. The two Emperors, King Frederick
William III, Metternich and Talleyrand, remained on after
Wellington's departure until the end of May. It had been
Alexander's wish that no general treaty should be concluded
but that the several Powers should make separate treaties as
between themselves embodying the regional settlements which

had been arrived at. Lord Clancarty, under instructions from the British Government, insisted however that the results of the Congress should be embodied in some comprehensive form. He was supported by Metternich and the Tsar gave way. The task of drafting the main treaty was entrusted to Gentz who was able to incorporate the conclusions reached by the several committees into a single document of one hundred and twenty-one articles. The physical labour of making the number of copies required proved exacting; it was calculated that it took the time of twenty-six secretaries to make a single copy even if they worked all day. By the beginning of June, however, copies of the treaty had been prepared for signature by the plenipotentiaries of the Eight Great Powers. Don Pedro Labrador, who remained true to form throughout the Congress, refused to sign the treaty unless he were allowed to attach to it reservations regarding the rights of the Spanish Bourbons to the several Italian principalities. It was wisely decided that the treaty could not carry any reservations and that if Spain objected, then Spain must be left out. The Final Act of the Congress of Vienna was therefore signed on June 9, 1815, by the representatives of the Seven Powers alone. The smaller Powers were invited to adhere separately; and eventually they all did so, with the exception of Turkey and the Holy See.

The conclusion of this tremendous treaty attracted but slight attention. Castlereagh himself predicted that it would maintain the peace of Europe for at least seven years. As a matter of fact all the main provisions of the Vienna Final Act remained unaltered for a space of forty years; and the settlement arrived at preserved Europe from any general conflagration for all but a century.

Castlereagh had always retained at the back of his mind the recommendation which Pitt had made in 1804 that the new European order should be stabilised and perpetuated by some general Treaty of Guarantee. Pitt's idea had been that the rights and possessions acquired by the several Powers should be "fixed and recognised" and that the signatories to the guarantee treaty should "bind themselves mutually to protect and support each

other against any attempt to infringe these rights and possessions." Metternich, who was becoming increasingly alarmed by
the intrusion of Russia into Europe, sought with Talleyrand's
assistance to persuade Castlereagh that it would be preferable
to renew the secret treaty of January 3, 1815, under which
France, Great Britain and Austria had pledged themselves to
resist Russian expansion. Castlereagh was opposed to this suggestion, fearing that it would divide Europe into two potentially
hostile camps. He suggested to the Emperor Alexander that
the seven Powers who had signed the Final Act should declare
their determination to uphold the general settlement arrived at
by the Congress and should publicly announce "their determination to unite their influence, and if necessary their arms,
against the Power that should attempt to disturb it." A draft
treaty to this effect was prepared by Gentz. Castlereagh remained
for some time under the impression that this draft had been
accepted by Alexander and the Ministers of the other Powers.
This expectation was optimistic. For it was at this stage that a
fissure appeared in the fabric of the united nations which as the
months passed widened rapidly into a gulf.

Castlereagh's undeviating objective was the preservation of
peace. He conceived the maintenance of peace in terms of European stability and he interpreted that stability as a system under
which each of the Five Great Powers, having obtained from the
war all reasonable satisfactions and rewards, being almost exactly
balanced against each other in military strength, should form a
Security Council to safeguard the stability which had been so
painfully achieved. The balance of power was thus only one
element in his theory; treaties such as those of Chaumont, the
Quadruple Alliance of November 20, 1815, and even the
Vienna Final Act, were valuable expedients devised to deal with
a contemporary situation; what he really desired was to create
some permanent institutional device which would enable the
united nations to co-operate indefinitely in preventing the threat
of war wherever it might arise.

He was unable to realise this far-seeing project owing to three
main factors of which at the time he was strangely unaware. He

failed to foresee that the Russian tide, having been stemmed in one area of the Continent, might seek for outlets in other directions. He failed to foresee that his Security Council would deteriorate into a Pact of Sovereigns intent, not so much upon the prevention of war, as upon the repression of all democratic and nationalist movements. And he failed to foresee that the British people, who only become conscious of foreign policy when in imminent danger from external aggression, would relapse into a mood of isolationism hostile to any foreign or long-term commitments.

He was aware of course that if his Treaty of Guarantee were to apply solely to the general settlement embodied in the Final Act of the Vienna Congress it would not cover the Near East. He was aware that Russia, now that she was the dominant military Power in Europe, would wish to modify to her own advantage the Treaty of Bucharest [1] which, with British assistance, she had hurriedly concluded with Turkey, under the threat of the Napoleonic invasion of 1812. What he did not foresee was the extent to which Russia, having been balked in Poland, would desire compensations and rewards in the Near and Middle East. It was with some naïveté therefore that he suggested to the Tsar that a clause should be inserted in the Treaty of Guarantee including the Ottoman dominions within its scope. Alexander replied that the difficulties between Russia and Turkey, which had been left unsettled by the hasty Treaty of Bucharest, must first be re-examined; he indicated that he would be willing to accept the good offices of Great Britain, Austria and France in reaching an accommodation with the Turkish Government. The three Ambassadors at Constantinople were instructed accordingly and an hour before he departed from Vienna Castlereagh had a conversation with Mavrojeni, the Sultan's representative, in which he urged him to persuade his master to accept such mediation.

Alexander, having disappointed the hopes both of his Russian and his Polish subjects, had begun meanwhile to dream of finding in the Balkans and the Levant the rewards which had been denied him in central Europe. It was observed that Capo d'Istria, who looked to the Tsar as the liberator of all orthodox Christians, was becoming increasingly influential and that the counsels of Czartoryski and Stein were on the wane. A memorandum was drafted by the obedient Nesselrode from which it became startlingly clear that what Russia wanted from Turkey was something far more than a rectification of the frontiers established by the Treaty of Bucharest. The territory now demanded would firmly have established Russian strategic dominance over the Black Sea and the Caspian. Even more disturbing was Nesselrode's claim that to Russia should be accorded the right of "protecting" all the Christian subjects of the Sultan of Turkey. If such claims were admitted, then Russia would not only obtain bases from which to threaten Constantinople and the Straits, but she would acquire on religious, and even racial, grounds, a vast and indefinable zone of influence in the Adriatic, the Aegean and the Levant which would provide her with inexhaustible excuses for future intervention. The Sultan, as was to be expected, refused to accept mediation on such terms. And the idea was therefore abandoned of including the Ottoman Empire within any treaty which might guarantee the general settlement arrived at in Vienna.

On his return to London Castlereagh found that his colleagues in the Cabinet were by no means enamoured of his suggested guarantee treaty. They pointed out that any such agreement would have the effect of committing Great Britain to go to war in defence of Russia's European acquisitions without in any way curtailing Russia's expansion in the Near and Middle East. The British people, moreover, now that the Napoleonic menace had been removed, were becoming increasingly suspicious of continental entanglements. Thus when the inevitable leakage occurred and Gentz's draft of the Treaty of Guarantee was published in the London newspapers, Castlereagh was obliged to state in the House of Commons that this draft was not to be regarded as an official document.

Having in this way abandoned, and thereafter repudiated, his original conception of a general guarantee, Castlereagh decided that the only way in which the Concert of Europe could be maintained would be to stipulate for periodic conferences between the great Powers. It was with this in mind that he secured the insertion into the Quadruple Alliance of November 20, 1815, of Article VI which provided for regular meetings between the Allies. He believed sincerely that this device would transform the methods of the old diplomacy and create a new and useful system of intercourse between sovereign States. He did not explain to his colleagues in the Cabinet the intention underlying this article; he kept his plan to himself. But whatever prospect (and it was small indeed) that Castlereagh may have had of inducing the British public to accept and thereafter to support the conference system was prejudiced, and eventually destroyed, by the mood of spiritual exaltation which at this stage took possession of Alexander's mind and produced the Holy Alliance.

[2]

Barbe Julie von Wietgenhof was born at Riga in the year 1764. While still a girl she married Baron von Krüdener, Russian minister in Venice, Copenhagen and Berlin. Being an assiduous woman she neglected her domestic and diplomatic duties and concentrated upon emulating the example of Madame de Staël. The amatory adventures in which she indulged, whether in her Latvian homeland or in the smaller watering places of the Continent, were recorded in her autobiographical novel *Valérie*, which caused a slight and momentary stir. The passage of years, coupled with her failure to establish her reputation as a European woman of letters, induced a mood of repentance; her final conversion was affected when, gazing one morning from the parlour window of her house in Riga, she observed one of her admirers raise his hat to her and thereafter fall dead in the street. Shocked by this episode, she experienced a change of heart. She embraced the pietist movement with uncritical fervour; she fell under the influence of the impostor Fontaine and his medium Maria Kummrin. She became an evangelist. "Everything," she confessed, "requires a certain amount of charlatanism."

Her mystic faith in Russia and in the Emperor Alexander was, however, perfectly sincere. For her the Russian people were "the sacred race"; they were "dear in the sight of the Almighty"; they were "a simple folk, who had not drunk the cup of iniquity." More specifically she was obsessed by the pre-ordained mission of the Emperor Alexander. He was "the elect of God"; he "had walked in the paths of renunciation"; he was the "Conqueror of the Dragon"; he was "a living preface to the sacred history which is to regenerate the world." For years Baroness von Krüdener had been addressing evangelical letters to Mdlle Stourdza, lady-in-waiting to the Empress of Russia. These letters predicted the day when Alexander, "regenerated in the stream of life," would "partake of the marriage supper of the Lamb"; they also predicted that Napoleon would before long escape from Elba. Mdlle Stourdza showed these letters to the Tsar: he was flattered, comforted, impressed. But he refused for the time being to see the Baroness.

During those spring months of 1815 Alexander had much need of spiritual comfort. He was no longer young: he was becoming stout, he was becoming bald, he was becoming increasingly deaf: even his eyesight was failing him and he would conceal in the sleeve of his uniform a monocle with a tortoise-shell handle which from time to time he would raise to his left eye. He was no longer the liberator of Europe, the idol of the multitude, the Agamemnon of Kings. His people were disappointed, his army disaffected, his generals sullen, his Ministers disloyal, his Allies suspicious. And now that Napoleon had escaped from Elba the final decision would pass into other hands; into the hands of Wellington, who had had the audacity to oppose the suggestion that he, the Tsar, should be appointed Allied commander in chief; into the hands of Blücher, that "drunken corporal," whom only a year ago he had patronised and disliked.

It was Alexander's habit, when confronted by obstacles or disappointments, to appeal to some higher, or at least to some other, authority. When Metternich flouted him, he would have recourse to Francis I; if Hardenberg proved obstinate, he would exercise pressure on Frederick William III; when opposed by Castlereagh, he would appeal to the Prince Regent and the Whigs. And now that the enjoyments and the glories of this natural world had turned to dust and ashes, he sought with pathetic evasiveness to invoke the assistance of the supernatural.

He had always been addicted to moods of mysticism; these moods had increased when Napoleon reached the Kremlin; they had been stilled during his two years of triumph; they had returned to him after the disappointments of the Vienna Congress. Leaving the Austrian capital on May 25, he had travelled via Munich to join the Emperor Francis and the vanguard of the eastern armies at Heidelberg. On the night of June 4 he reached Heilbronn in a mood of deep dejection. At any hour he expected to hear that Wellington and Blücher had engaged, and possibly defeated, Napoleon; and this at a moment when the Russian armies had not yet crossed the Rhine. He had contracted the habit of seeking guidance or divination in the New Testament; he had been reading the Book of Revelations. "And there appeared," he read, "a great wonder in heaven: a woman clothed with the sun." His mind veered round to the letters which Mdlle Stourdza had shown him from that unknown Baroness von Krüdener who believed with such prophetic ecstasy that he, the Tsar, who seemed so out of things, was in fact the predestined instrument of divine intention. And it was at that moment, at midnight on June 4 in the inn at Heilbronn, that his aide-de-camp informed him that a woman had arrived and demanded instant audience. This was no coincidence; it was a sign, a portent; he remained closeted with the Baroness for several hours. She abjured him to repent his sins and to prove himself worthy of his mission. They prayed in ecstasy together and he wept.

On his arrival in the French capital the Tsar installed himself in the Palace of the Elysée. Baroness von Krüdener and her attendants occupied the Hôtel Monchenu next door. A hole was knocked in the wall separating the two gardens and night after night the Tsar would attend prayer meetings in the Baroness's house. By the beginning of September, ten weeks after Waterloo, the Russian armies reached French territory. On September 10, 1815, the Emperor staged a tremendous review upon the plain of Vertus to which he invited the Emperor of Austria, the King of Prussia and all the allied generals. Eight altars had been erected upon the plateau with the whole Russian army dispersed around them. Baroness von Krüdener, arrayed quite simply in a blue serge dress and a straw hat, acted as high priestess on this occasion. "It was," writes Sainte-Beuve, "as the Ambassadress of Heaven that he received her and conducted her into the presence of his armies." Waving her arms in wide gestures of prophecy and dedication the Baroness passed from altar to altar accompanied by her acolytes and her Emperor. The foreign monarchs and generals watched this spectacle with disquiet. "This day," wrote the Tsar to the prophetess on his return, "has been the most beautiful in my life. My heart was filled with love for my enemies."

[3]

The ceremony upon the plateau of Vertus marked the climax of Baroness von Krüdener's ascendancy. It may be that she overplayed her part; it may be that Alexander became bored by her ecstatic vocabulary as by her constant prophecies that Napoleon, this time, was on the verge of escaping from St. Helena. It may be that he was annoyed by her demands for money. He escaped from the Elysée as soon as he was able and took refuge in Brussels. "Here I am," he wrote to his sister on October 1, "away from that accursed Paris." In vain did the Baroness seek to renew their spiritual relationship; the Tsar had come to regard her exhortations with distaste not unmixed with alarm; he refused her permission to come to St. Petersburg; and after a few more years of penurious wandering she returned to Latvia where she died.

Baroness von Krüdener always claimed, and Gentz believed, that she was the authoress of the Holy Alliance. It may well be that she invented the title even as she stimulated the mood in which it was conceived. It may well be that her surprising, but carefully planned, irruption into the Tsar's tavern at Heilbronn on the night of June 4 confirmed him in the idea that, having ceased to be the military or political arbiter of Europe, he could become the moral leader of evangelical opinion. The fact remains that the general conception of the Holy Alliance had for long been germinating in the Tsar's mind. As early as 1804 he had suggested to Pitt some pact under which all States should renounce war as an instrument of policy. As late as 1812 he had confided to Countess von Tisenhaus at Vilna his idea of a spiritual compact under which the sovereigns of Europe would agree "to live like brothers, aiding each other in their need, and comforting each other in their adversity." He had recently been reading a book by François Baader which advocated that the only cure for the evils of the French Revolution was a close identity between politics and religion; and he had been much impressed by Chateaubriand's *Génie du Christianisme*. Some such league, some such affirmation of Christian principles, had moreover been already suggested in other quarters. There had been the Abbé de Saint Pierre's *Projet de Paix perpetuelle;* there had been the pamphlet published by Augustin Thierry in 1814; even Napoleon assured Las Cases at St. Helena that he had himself conceived of some such universal compact. It had been contemplated also that a declaration of Christian principle should figure in the Final Act of the Congress of Vienna and Castlereagh himself had tried his hand at drafting some preparatory clauses before the escape of Napoleon had diverted his attention to more mundane affairs. The particular shape which was eventually given to these current theories was, however, due entirely to the Tsar's own mood at the time. To him must be attributed the tone of mystic pietism in which the document was drafted; to him above all must be attributed the fatal error of concluding the Holy Alliance in the name of the sovereigns personally, and not in the name of their governments or peoples.

The document that Alexander drafted, and which caused such havoc to the Quadruple Alliance and the whole conference system, does not strike us today as either more or less meaningless than the Kellogg Pact of 1928. It established that henceforward the relations between sovereigns should be based "upon the sublime truths which the Holy Religion of Our Saviour teaches." It affirmed that "the precepts of justice, Christian charity and peace . . . must have an immediate influence on the councils of princes and guide all their steps." It announced that the three monarchs would remain united "by the bonds of a true and indissoluble fraternity" and would regard themselves "as fathers of families towards their subjects and armies." Governments and peoples must from now on behave as "members of one and the same Christian nation." All those Powers who should "choose solemnly to avow the sacred principles which have dictated this Act" were invited to join the Holy Alliance. Most of them did so. The Pope and the Sultan felt unable, none the less, to accede to a pact subscribed to by so many sectarians and infidels. The Prince Regent refused to sign on the ground that under the British Constitution any signature of his would be invalid unless accompanied by that of a responsible Minister. He none the less addressed a letter to the Tsar assuring him of his "entire concurrence with the principles laid down by the august sovereigns," and promising that it would always be his endeavour to conform his policy "to their sacred maxims."

The Holy Alliance was not at first taken very seriously by any of those who adhered to it, nor did the Ministers concerned seem to have foreseen at the time the influence which it would exercise either upon policy or upon public opinion. Castlereagh deemed it "a piece of sublime mysticism and nonsense." He confessed that when the Tsar first produced the draft to the Duke of Wellington and himself "it was not without difficulty that we went through the interview with becoming gravity." If he was worried at all, he was worried by the constitutional problem which the adhesion of the Prince Regent to a monarchical trades union was bound to raise. "This," he wrote, "is what might be called a scrape." Even Metternich appears at first not to have realised how valuable an instrument the Holy Alliance would prove for the purposes of his own policies. He called it a "loud-sounding nothing."

Progressive opinion throughout Europe was from the outset alive to the potential dangers of the Holy Alliance. The fact that it had been concluded between Russia, Austria and Prussia, and only adhered to by the other Powers, suggested that in some manner it represented an attempt on the part of the Three to dominate the Continent. The fact, above all, that it had been concluded as a personal pact between the sovereigns and princes created extreme prejudice and alarm. For against what or whom could these potentates be allying themselves unless it were against the liberal movement and the spirit of the age? It may well be true that Alexander did not at first intend that his Alliance should become a formula of repression; it only became so when Metternich, playing adroitly upon the Tsar's increasing repudiation of his former liberal sentiments, used it as an organ of reaction. And as such it rapidly cast a blight upon the Quadruple Alliance and brought the whole conference system on which Castlereagh had staked so much, into universal suspicion and disrepute.

It is interesting to note how quickly the Holy Alliance led to a divergence of theory between Russia and Great Britain. In April 1816 the Tsar was already writing to Princess Lieven to defend his Alliance against the imputations cast upon it by liberal opinion or, as he phrased it, "by the genius of evil." It signified no more, he explained, than an attempt to "confirm the contracting sovereigns in the principles of political and social conservation." Not even the Whigs could have given it a more damning definition.

[4]

In spite of these misfortunes and disillusions Castlereagh maintained his conviction that at any cost the unity between Russia, Austria and Great Britain must be preserved. Metternich sought, by exploiting the distrust of Russia which was now affecting official and even popular feeling in England, to revert to his old idea of an anti-Russian front between Austria, Great Britain and France. Talleyrand himself had been alarmed by Russian ambitions. "When," he wrote to Jaucourt, "unfortunately for Europe, Russia meddles in this way in every concern and takes a tone of authority and seems inclined to dictate to everyone else, it is deplorable and scandalous that no single Power except France should dare to object, not even England who contents herself with vague grumbles." This disquiet increased as the years went by. The day was to come when even Creevey, who had once shared the confidence of his Whig friends in the Tsar's progressiveness and magnanimity, could write: "We long-sighted old politicians see a fixed intention on the part of Russia to make Constantinople the seat of her power and to re-establish the Greek Church upon the ruins of Mohammedanism. A new crusade, in short, by a new and enormous Power, and brought into the field by our own selves, and one that may put our existence at stake to drive out again."

Rumours of Russian intrigues and intentions poured into the Foreign Office from every quarter. The Tsar's agents at Naples were, it appeared, encouraging the *Carbonari* to look for Russian support. Through his family connections with Würtemberg and Baden Alexander was seeking to oust both Austrian and Prussian influence from the Germanic Confederation. The Russian Ambassador in Turkey issued a sort of Monroe doctrine on his own, intimating that Russia would not permit the interference of other Powers in her relations with the Porte. Even more disquieting news was received from Spain. A marriage contract was, it appeared, being negotiated between the Spanish and Russian Courts. Russia, in return for the cession of Minorca, had agreed to deliver some of her fleet to the King of Spain and to assist him in suppressing the revolt of the Spanish colonies in South America. Rumours reached England of a projected Russian landing at Buenos Aires. And in fact a few old and most unseaworthy vessels were actually transferred from the Russian to the Spanish flag.

The Duke of Wellington was not unduly disturbed by such rumours. "What the Russians are looking to everywhere," he wrote to Sir Henry Wellesley in March 1815, "is general power and influence. But as they have neither wealth nor commerce, nor anything that is desirable to anybody except 400,000 men (about which they make more noise than they deserve) they can acquire these objects in a distant Court like Spain only by bustle and intrigue."

Castlereagh himself was more than imperturbable; he sought to allay the perturbation of others. "The true interests of Russia," he wrote to our Ambassador in Vienna, "dictate a pacific policy." He described the anti-Russian agitation, which he admitted "must exist in all Governments against a State as powerful as Russia has latterly become," as a mere *cri de bureau* or as we might say a Foreign Office ramp. This attitude of distrust on the part of the professionals might, unless sternly suppressed by Ministers, create the very dangers which all wished to avoid. He urged our agents in foreign countries to avoid suspicion and not to credit rumours. "It will be the province of Ministers abroad," he wrote to our representative in Madrid, "to inculcate in all quarters the importance of union, to [*sic*] the preservation of peace for which the Powers have for so long and so gloriously contended, and to keep down as far as possible the spirit of local intrigue which has proved no less fatal to the repose of States than the personal ambitions of their sovereigns." "My wish," he wrote on January 1, 1816, to our Minister in Naples, "is that while you watch with all due attention whatever the Russian agents be about, that you do not suffer yourself to be drawn, either by the Court of Naples or yet by the Court of Vienna into a premature attitude of suspicion, much less of hostility, of the Russian agents in Italy. It is of the utmost importance to keep down, as far and as long as possible, these local cabals which may shake the main Alliance—still indispensable to the safety of Europe. . . . We cannot be too susceptible in our minor relations to the hazards of the great machine of European safety." In a circular addressed to all missions abroad he again warned British diplomatists "to discourage that spirit of petty intrigue and perpetual propagation of alarm, upon slight evidence and ancient jealousies, which too frequently disgrace the diplomatic profession, and often render the residence of foreign Ministers the means of disturbing, rather than preserving, harmony between their respective sovereigns."

Castlereagh preserved this attitude with admirable consistency during the years that remained to him. When in March 1817 Metternich through Esterhazy renewed his suggestion that Great Britain should collaborate with Austria in curtailing Russia's ambitions in Spain and the Near East, Castlereagh returned a definite refusal. He informed Esterhazy that he disliked "measures of precautionary policy upon speculative grounds." He did not consider that Metternich's insinuations regarding Russian policy were justified "either in degree or in proximity." If trouble came, then they must induce France and Prussia to join them in opposing a common barrier against further Russian encroachments. But he would only agree to such a policy in face of "a real and obvious danger." Such a danger did not, in his opinion, then exist.

It is evident that during this period Castlereagh was in agreement with Wellington in thinking that the Russian menace was partly an invention of Metternich's, partly a bogey raised by the professional diplomatist, and partly a gigantic bluff on the part of Russia herself. He was wisely convinced that if only Great Britain could avoid a head-on collision with Russia during the coming few years Russia would herself be obliged from motives of internal economy eventually to curtail her excited ambitions and to reduce her vast military establishments. He had been obliged to defend the Holy Alliance in the House of Commons and he did so in such sympathetic language that the Tsar was touched. In a further impulse of conciliation Alexander thereupon suggested to Castlereagh "a simultaneous reduction of armaments of all kinds." Metternich, as was to be expected, described this suggestion as a further proof of the Tsar's duplicity. And Alexander himself admitted to Lord Cathcart that he would in practice only consider reducing the armaments of Russia provided that Austria and Prussia first restricted their own military establishments. Nor was the proposal taken seriously by any of the other European chancelleries, since the Tsar continued on all occasions to boast that he could place a million men in the field, and since his new and reactionary Minister, Araksheiev, was at that moment organising with unexampled brutality the system of military colonies in west Russia. Yet Castlereagh, while he rejected the proposal, had at least the courtesy to send a considered reply. "It is impossible," he wrote on May 28, 1816, "not to perceive that the settlement of a scale of force for so many Powers,—under such different circumstances as to their relative means, frontiers, positions and faculties for re-arming,—presents a very complicated question for negotiation: that the means of preserving a system if once created are not without their difficulties, liable as States are to partial necessities for an increase of force: and it is further to be considered that on this, as on many subjects of a jealous character, in attempting to do much, difficulties are rather brought into view than made to disappear." His suggestion was, therefore, that each State should reduce its own armaments to the minimum which each might consider necessary; and that each State should then "explain to allied and neighbouring States the extent and nature of its arrangements as a means of dispelling alarm and of rendering moderate establishments mutually convenient."

Already, during the months which intervened between Waterloo and the Second Peace of Paris, the diplomatic kaleidoscope had shifted once again and disclosed a new pattern of combination. "The relations between the Powers," wrote Gentz on September 4, 1815, "have changed since Vienna. The friendship between Russia and Prussia has chilled considerably; Prussia today stands much closer to us and England becomes more and more estranged from each of us. Conversely, Russia, France and England stand for the moment upon the same side. It is in this manner that the foolish minds of men veer now to one side now to another; upon the shifting sands of modern politics how difficult it is to build on solid foundations!"

The Quadruple Alliance which Castlereagh had created at Chaumont, preserved during the Vienna Congress and reconstructed in Paris, thus seemed already in danger of disintegration. His just equilibrium was already threatened by the shifting of great weights. The Holy Alliance had exposed his whole system to ridicule, which was rapidly merging into apprehension and dislike. Distrust of Russia's overt and covert ambitions was creating an ever-widening breach between East and West. The conference system remained for him the only hope of maintaining the Concert of Europe. He sought to preserve that system with all the great energies of his heart and soul and mind.

He did not succeed.

16. The Failure of the Conference System

[1818-1822]

Castlereagh's conception of the Concert of Europe as "the great machine of European safety"—The fallacies of this conception—He underrated the inevitability of change even as he underestimated the force and nature of British public opinion—The original purpose of the Coalition having disappeared the Four Powers began to interpret the Quadruple Alliance in different ways—A gap widened therefore between Great Britain and the Eastern Powers—Castlereagh persisted in believing that the gap could be narrowed by repeated personal conferences—The Conference of Aix-la-Chapelle—The Tsar's suggestion of an *Alliance Solidaire* obliges Castlereagh to define the extent to which Great Britain considers herself bound by existing treaties—This definition makes it clear that our future collaboration with the Alliance will be conditioned and limited—The spread of unrest—The assassination of Kotzebue—The Carlsbad decrees—The position of the British Government weakened by the controversy regarding Queen Caroline—Revolutions in Spain, Portugal, Piedmont and Naples—The Troppau Conference—Great Britain publicly refutes the Russian claim to intervene in the internal affairs of other countries—The Greek revolt introduces the Eastern Question—The death of Castlereagh—The advent of Canning—The disruption of the Holy Alliance—The end of the Quadruple Alliance—The calm sunset of Metternich.

IN GAZING BACK across the gulf of time we are able to form a juster estimate of the merits and defects of Castlereagh's policy than was ever vouchsafed to his contemporaries. On the one hand we possess, as they did not, documentary evidence to prove his constancy of aim and purity of character. On the other hand we know which of the many tendencies of his age became the dominant tendencies; and we conclude, too readily perhaps, that he was obtuse in regarding the spread of liberalism and the rise of nationalities as distressing but momentary symptoms of the reflux of the revolutionary epoch; and in not recognising in them the twin streams of a mighty tide which was to flow for more than a hundred years.

To him the unity of the Three Great Allies was something more than a diplomatic system, something more than the corollary to the balance of power. It was "the great machine of European safety." It was the guarantee of peace, the central aim of policy, the Great Ideal, in the service of which England was in duty bound to make many sacrifices and to assume heavy obligations. "The power," he had written in 1813, "of Great Britain to do good depends not merely on her resources but upon a sense of her impartiality and the reconciling character of her influence. . . . To be authoritative she must be impartial: to be impartial she must not be in exclusive relations with any particular Court." This might well be taken as the guiding precept of all Castlereagh's policy; the consistency with which he applied that precept earned him the confidence of all foreign potentates and statesmen; it did not earn him the confidence of the British people.

The essential fallacy of Castlereagh's political philosophy was that by exaggerating the general need for "repose" he sought to enforce static principles upon a dynamic world. Obsessed as he was by the long years of struggle against French militarism, he identified liberal thought with revolution and revolution with war. He failed to realise with sufficient clarity that an alliance based upon the maintenance of the existing order could not preserve its unity in a Europe in which interests and ambitions were in a state of constant flux. He was apt to interpret the Concert of Europe in terms of the personal relations which he had himself established with the leading European statesmen, forgetting that politicians or monarchs retire, die, or change their moods. He refused to face the fact that both Metternich and the later Alexander were fundamentally averse from democratic or even constitutional thought and that whereas he desired to use the Grand Alliance to protect the small nations, they desired to exploit it for purposes of repression. Nor did he foresee that a system founded avowedly upon the combined strength of the Three Great Powers would incur the suspicion, and finally the hostility, of all those smaller Powers which had been excluded from the directorate.

More damaging, as has already been indicated, was his indifference to, and even his contempt for, parliamentary and public opinion in his own country. It never seems to have dawned upon him that in an age when communications were slow and uncertain the system of diplomacy by conference entrusted to a British plenipotentiary powers of initiative and decision which neither the Cabinet, nor the House of Commons, nor the public, would tolerate for long. He took slight pains to win the confidence of Parliament and on many occasions he was guilty of concealing important transactions, not only from the House of Commons, but from the Cabinet itself. He was too apt to regard all criticism or opposition as factious and ill informed and he failed to understand the growth or influence of a new commercial class in England, which cared nothing for dynasties or frontiers and a great deal about trade routes and markets, sugar islands and naval bases. He did not even begin to appreciate the value of a responsible and independent press, and on one occasion he suggested to Lord Liverpool that the attacks of the London newspapers might be mitigated by the payment of subsidies to their editors. "No paper," replied Lord Liverpool, "which has any character, and consequently an established sale, will accept money from the Government." Above all he underestimated the mood of isolationism which had begun to infect British public opinion and which increasingly induced men of all parties to regard as "foreign" and "un-English" a policy of continental commitments and negotiation. All this was unfortunate and even reprehensible. But when we consider the strength of Castlereagh's character, and recall the tragedy of his death, we cannot but feel indignant at the hysterical vituperation which was heaped upon him by the liberal intellectuals of his own and succeeding generations.[1] "He failed," writes Sir Charles Webster, "to associate his ideas with the deepest emotions of his age." This was a tragic, but not unworthy, failure.

[2]

History teaches us, and invariably we disregard her lesson, that coalitions begin to disintegrate from the moment that the common danger is removed. With Napoleon at St. Helena and Louis XVIII back in the Tuileries France had ceased to be a menace to the peace of Europe; it was before long agreed to withdraw the armies of occupation and to readmit France into the comity of nations. The original purpose of the Coalition having thus disappeared, it soon became evident that the three main partners to the Alliance interpreted its future in different ways. The British Government, as Metternich complained, were inclined to regard the Quadruple Alliance as a "civil contract," namely as an engagement specifically and expressly entered into for the purpose of preventing the revival of militarism in France. The Emperor Alexander viewed it as the political instrument of the Holy Alliance, and desired to extend and exploit it for the repression of revolutionary movements wherever and whenever they might appear. Metternich disliked both the legalistic view adopted by the British Government and the flexible view adopted by the Emperor Alexander: he sought for a formula which, on the one hand, would deter the Tsar from sending Russian armies of intervention across Germany, and on the other hand would prevent Great Britain from withdrawing into isolation. He thought he had found that formula in the phrase "moral solidarity." The years and the events which followed threw increasing emphasis upon the British dislike of, and the Russian desire for, intervention in the internal affairs of other countries; the gap between the two camps widened so rapidly that even a man of Metternich's outstanding agility found it impossible to keep a foot in each. Reluctantly he was compelled to join the Russian, rather than the British, camp; it was in this manner that the Coalition eventually dissolved. The five conferences which intervened (Aix-la-Chapelle in 1818; Carlsbad in 1819; Troppau in 1820; Laybach in 1821 and Verona in 1822) each marked a further widening of the gap; the strange thing is, not that the conference system was finally abandoned, but that it lasted for so long.

The Conference of Aix-la-Chapelle, which began in September and ended in November 1818, did much useful work. "Never," remarked Metternich, "have I known a prettier little congress." It arranged for the evacuation of French territory; it settled the reparation problem; it confirmed the rights of the Jews; it approved the measures being taken for the safe custody of Napoleon at St. Helena; and it addressed to Bernadotte of Sweden a sharp reminder that he must now pay to Denmark those compensations to which he had pledged himself under the Treaty of Kiel.[2]

To all appearance the Powers assembled at Aix-la-Chapelle had demonstrated the efficiency of the conference system, and the continued solidarity of the great Allies. In fact, however, this, the first of the post-war conferences, disclosed the ideological rift between the democratic and the autocratic Powers and marked, to all acute observers, the beginning of the end. Even Castlereagh was obliged to recognise, and to warn his foreign colleagues, that circumstances had changed.

At the very outset of their discussions he felt it wise to make it clear to the Tsar and Metternich that they could not now expect him to act with the same personal initiative and independence that he had been able to manifest in the great Vienna days. He would be obliged, he warned them, henceforward to refer many decisions for the approval of the Cabinet in London. This was a wise precaution. In the first place, the war now being over, Parliament was increasingly critical and alert. In the second place, whereas it had taken almost a fortnight to communicate between Vienna and London, this delay was reduced by the comparative proximity of Aix to a matter of four days; no longer could Castlereagh contend that it was a physical impossibility for him to refer for further instructions. And in the third, and most important, place, Canning had in 1816 returned to England and become a member of the Cabinet in the capacity of Chairman of the Board of Control. It was known that Canning had infected many of his governmental colleagues with his own detestation of the conference system, a system which he regarded as "new and very questionable." Such a method of diplomacy, Canning argued, would "necessarily involve us . . . deeply in all the politics of the continent, where as our true policy has always been not to interfere except in great emergencies and then with commanding force." Even Lord Liverpool, who had proved so amenable in the past, became uneasy. "We have," he wrote to Castlereagh, "a new Parliament to meet, which has not been tried, of a doubtful character, and certainly not accustomed to look at foreign questions as Parliaments were some years ago when under the impression, or immediate recollection, of some great foreign danger."

When therefore, shortly after his arrival at Aix-la-Chapelle, Castlereagh derived from his conversations with the Tsar and Capo d'Istria, the impression that some proposals more definite, more comprehensive, and more horrible even than the Holy Alliance were being contemplated by the Russians, he felt it right to render the position of the British Government unambiguous. He explained to the Emperor Alexander that "it was perhaps a misfortune in our system that we could not act upon precautionary principles so early or so easily as His Imperial Majesty, but that the only chance we had of making the nation feel the wisdom of such a course was to be free, at the moment, to urge the policy of so acting, not because we had no choice, but as having a choice." The Tsar's reply to this somewhat involved statement was curt and true. He answered that "these were ideas with which he was very little familiar."

The Russian proposal, when it came, was even worse than Castlereagh had feared. It suggested that a new and universal treaty, an *Alliance Solidaire*, should be signed under which all the States of Europe should mutually guarantee, not only each other's territories and possessions, but the existing form of government at that date therein established. Castlereagh knew that no British Government could ever consent to such a suggestion. In a statement which he made to the Conference in October, and which he subsequently embodied in a memorandum, he explained beyond all possible misunderstanding the exact extent to which the British Government considered themselves bound by the Treaties in force.

It was this statement which, by clearly repudiating the suggestion that the Coalition had the right to intervene in the internal affairs of other countries, marked the withdrawal of Great Britain from the Holy Alliance. It portended the abandonment by the British Government of the general theory of solidarity underlying the great diplomatic work which Castlereagh had accomplished from the time of Chaumont to the conclusion of the Second Peace of Paris. It is often supposed that this change of policy was only brought about when Canning succeeded Castlereagh in 1822. It is thus important, in concluding this study, to make it clear that the conference system, unwillingly perhaps and if only by implication, was in fact abandoned by Castlereagh himself before his tragic death.

Castlereagh, in his statement to the Congress of Aix-la-Chapelle, began by drawing a tactful distinction between "the benign principles" of the Holy Alliance and the political treaties actually in force. The Holy Alliance constituted the system of Europe only in so far as matters of "political conscience" were concerned. "It would be derogatory," he contended, "to this solemn Act of the Sovereigns to mix its discussion with the ordinary diplomatic obligations which bind State to State." These obligations were contained only in such treaties as had been concluded in the accustomed form, namely the First Peace of Paris, the Second Peace of Paris, and the Final Act of the Congress of Vienna. These treaties were not accompanied by any guarantee of their observance. The Treaty of Chaumont and the Quadruple Alliance signed at Paris on November 30, 1815, had as their specific purpose the defeat of Napoleon and thereafter the prevention by joint action of any future military menace on the part of France; it was not intended that they should give to the Allies the right of intervention, under unspecified conditions, in internal French affairs. If domestic disorders were to take place in France which, when "prudentially considered," might seem to constitute a menace to other countries, then all the Allies were obliged, after discussion among themselves, to furnish the "stipulated succours." The British Government must make it clear, however, that they were not prepared to stand by engagements "beyond the text and import of the treaties signed." These treaties they could loyally observe without "transgressing any principles of the law of nations or failing in the delicacy which they owe to the rights of other States." To suggest an *Alliance Solidaire* implied a system of administering Europe through a general alliance of all its States; this the British Government would not accept. "Nothing," he continued, "would be more immoral or more prejudicial to the character of government generally than the idea that their force was collectively to be prostituted to the support of established power without any consideration of the extent to which it was abused." Each State must be allowed to rely for its security upon the "justice and wisdom" of its own system, aided by such support as other States might be prepared to give. The British Government welcomed the method of holding periodical consultations between the main Allies: beyond that they were not prepared to go.

The immediate effect of this statement was to induce the Tsar to withdraw his suggestion of an *Alliance Solidaire*. Its ultimate effect was to convince the other three partners to the Quadruple Alliance that it would be a mistake in future to count upon any unconditional co-operation on the part of Great Britain. From that moment they began to contemplate separate combinations as between themselves. From that moment, in effect, the Grand Alliance and the conference system were doomed.

[3]

Meanwhile the spirit of unrest, which was the spirit of the first half of the nineteenth century, was seething in every country. It was not the lees of the old wine of 1789; it was the ferment of a new and no less inebriating vintage. It was not the rise of the internal and external proletariate; it was the rise of the internal and external bourgeoisie, the revolt of the young intellectuals. Throughout Germany the boys and girls who in

1813 had formed the resistance movement against Napoleon, and who regarded themselves as the heroes of the War of Liberation, observed with dismay the old crust forming again in the several States and Principalities. They were enraged by the spectacle of the same old men creeping back into the same old positions;—denying to Germany the promises which they had made in the hour of danger;—denying to youth those opportunities which, in the gay dawn of liberation, had seemed so glamorous. In Spain, in Portugal, in Greece, in Switzerland, young men were banding together to defy the established order. Even in England an internal revolution seemed inevitable. On August 16, 1819, a meeting addressed by Orator Hunt in St. Peter's Field at Manchester was dispersed by the military and six people were killed. The Government, with the panic assent of the Opposition, passed the Six Acts under which the traditional liberties of the British subject were suspended. And Metternich, journeying with his Emperor through Austria's Italian provinces, was appalled by the activities of the *Carbonari* and the spirit of Jacobinism which he everywhere observed.

At Mannheim, on March 23, 1819, a young theological student of the name of Karl Sand assassinated the dramatist Kotzebue[3] who was known to be an agitator in the pay of Alexander. The news of this outrage reached Metternich in Rome; he reacted to it with unusual celerity, seeing in the incident an opportunity of crushing the liberal movement in Germany and of re-establishing Austria's predominance in the Germanic body. In a hurried interview with Frederick William III at Teplitz he persuaded the Prussian monarch to accept his plans. In August the representatives of the nine German States were summoned to a conference at Carlsbad and were forced to promulgate the measures which Metternich had already drafted and which became known as the Carlsbad Decrees. They provided for the dissolution of the students' societies, the censorship of the German press, the appointment of "curators" to supervise the universities, and the creation of a commission at Mainz to investigate the conspiracy of which Karl Sand was believed to have been the tool. Metternich viewed his success with horrible complacency. "I have become," he wrote, "a moral power in Germany, and perhaps even in Europe." And in fact the Carlsbad Decrees succeeded in stifling the young German movement for twenty-nine years.

Metternich then attempted to induce his partners in the Quadruple Alliance publicly to approve his action. Castlereagh replied expressing sympathy but refusing public approval. "We are always pleased," he wrote, "to see evil germs destroyed, without the power to give our approbation openly." The British press had in fact severely criticised the Carlsbad Decrees. *The Times*, wrote Metternich on September 26, 1819, "has already begun: but this is not surprising, since it has become even more seditious and Jacobin than *The Morning Chronicle*." More interesting still was the attitude adopted by the Emperor Alexander towards Metternich's overtures; he refused to sponsor the Carlsbad Decrees and in fact let it be known that he disapproved of them. The duality of his temperament was never more apparent. At home, and in his treatment of his Polish kingdom, he was becoming increasingly autocratic. But he still at that date wished to maintain abroad the role of La Harpe's pupil, the part of the great liberator, the attitude of a Christian democrat. It still flattered his vanity to appear as the distant but all-powerful patron of all underground movements; as the unspoken friend of the *Carbonari* and the constitutionalists; and above all to display his "magnanimity" in an anti-Austrian sense to the two "liberal" German States of Würtemberg and Baden. The mutiny of the Semenovski regiment in 1818, the plot to kidnap him on his way to Aix-la-Chapelle, had done much to shake his faith in free institutions and to strengthen his belief in "the principles of order." His final conversion came in 1820 when the forces of revolution rose in every land. From then onwards, his political philosophy was moulded by the brutal Araksheiev, while his mysticism was diverted into wholly reactionary channels by the Patriarch Photinus. But meanwhile Metternich's failure to obtain the public approval of Great Britain and Russia to the Carlsbad Decrees had taught him one decisive lesson. He realised from that moment that however much Castlereagh might privately approve of repressive methods, British opinion would not permit him to support them, and, conversely, that however unstable might be the Tsar's momentary whims and attitudes, he would be forced by circumstances and his own apprehensions eventually to make common cause with the policy of order. The ravine between Great Britain and the Continent had widened into a gulf; it was spanned by a foot-bridge upon which Castlereagh, serene but unpopular, walked alone.

[4]

On January 29, 1820, George III died at Windsor and almost immediately the Tory Government were threatened with a major crisis in the shape of the divorce of Queen Caroline. Canning, who had been friendly with the Queen, resigned from the Cabinet and thereby recovered the popularity which he had lost. Castlereagh remained on in a Government weakened by internal dissensions and exposed to public obloquy. At the same time four revolutions broke out in Europe—in Spain, in Portugal, in Piedmont and in Naples. The Tsar wished to intervene by force and threatened to send a Russian army into the Peninsula. In a memorandum of May 5, 1820, Castlereagh was obliged to reaffirm in even more decided language the principles which he had advanced at Aix-la-Chapelle. Great Britain, he explained, would only consent to intervene in cases where the peace of Europe was threatened; events in Spain did not threaten the peace of Europe. The partners of the Quadruple Alliance, owing to the difference in their constitutions, "could not feel alike on all subjects." "There was," he said, "a difference of outlook and method between the autocratic, or Eastern Powers, and the democratic, or Western Powers." "The principle," he continued, "of one State interfering in the internal affairs of another in order to enforce obedience to the governing authority is always a question of the greatest moral, as well as political, delicacy. . . . To generalise such a principle, to think of reducing it to a system, or to impose it as an obligation, is a scheme utterly impracticable and objectionable."

These were strong words and did not augur well for the success of the Conference which, in the mud and wind and rain, met at Troppau in October 1820. Castlereagh absented himself from this Conference; Great Britain was represented by his half-brother Lord Stewart, at that time Ambassador in Vienna. It was then that the final breach occurred. On November 19 Metternich presented to the Conference a *Protocole Préliminaire* which had been drafted by Capo d'Istria and already approved by the three Eastern Courts. Basing itself upon the "principles of the Alliance" and the "rights consecrated by the treaties" this document established the doctrine that any State which had succumbed to revolution ceased thereby to be a member of the Holy Alliance and that the remaining members of that Alliance had the right to employ coercion, or armed intervention, in order "to bring it back to the bosom of the Alliance." The British Government replied to this by a public repudiation of the *Protocole* which would render the Holy Alliance a super-State "which would tend to destroy all wholesome national energy and all independent action" and which would constitute the Allies "the armed guardians of all thrones." His Majesty's Government, it was announced, would "never consent to charge itself as a member of the Alliance with the moral responsibility of administering a general European police of this description."

The Conference of Troppau was followed in January of 1821 by that of Laibach. Eighty thousand Austrians by then had marched into northern Italy and ninety thousand Russians had crossed the frontier into Europe. Again the British Government protested. Such principles, such action, they said, "were in direct repugnance to the fundamental laws of this country." The rupture was overt and complete.

The Great Coalition was thus finally dissolved; the Concert of Europe had disintegrated; the Holy Alliance had succeeded in destroying the Quadruple Alliance; the Conference System had failed. The just equilibrium in which Castlereagh had believed so confidently had lost its equipoise; there was no longer any balance of power; the disunity of the Three Great Allies had been manifested to all the world.

It was at that moment, on April 2, 1821, that Archbishop Germanos raised the standard of revolt at Kalavyrta. The Greek War of Independence had begun. In the shape of the Eastern Question a new and lasting controversy,—political, strategic and economic,—had come to sunder Russia from the West.

[5]

Desperately, although with failing health and confidence, Castlereagh struggled to preserve the unity of the Three Powers. The Tsar, while proclaiming his pacific intentions, began to speak of the "pressure of public opinion" and used that ominous phrase about there "being a limit to Russian patience." In October 1821 Castlereagh accompanied George IV to Hanover where Metternich joined them. They were united in feeling that if Russia were to profit by the Greek revolt to raise the whole Eastern Question she would involve the world in "the most awful dangers." It was agreed to make representations at Constantinople urging the Sultan to display the utmost moderation; Lord Strangford, our Ambassador to the Porte, devoted all his efforts to preventing Baron Stroganov from outraging the Turks and the Turks from outraging Baron Stroganov. The Sultan proved obstinate and frightened. He seemed to be under the impression that the Holy Alliance implied a *jehad*, or holy war, declared by the Christian Powers against the Moslems. He thereafter massacred all the Greeks in Chios and the conscience of Europe became inflamed.

In these circumstances it was provided that a further conference should be held in the autumn of 1822 at Verona. Castlereagh promised to attend this, the last of all the conferences, in person. He arranged to leave England on August 26.

The session in that year 1822 proved more than usually arduous; Parliament did not rise till August 6. Castlereagh had been obliged to deal with a turbulent Opposition who pressed him with questions regarding the recognition of the Greek rebels as belligerents, the assistance to be given to the revolted Spanish colonies in South America, the situation in Spain itself. The work at the Foreign Office had been overwhelming; even the indefatigable Planta complained that it had been "almost too much." It was noticed by the Foreign Office staff that Lord Castlereagh's handwriting, usually so legible, had become distorted; his accustomed urbanity was broken by moods of querulous irritation; he spoke of plots against his life; accosting a casual acquaintance in Hyde Park, he expiated with unaccustomed lack of reserve upon the "torment" of public life in present conditions. So soon as Parliament rose he went down to his house at North Cray Farm in Kent. One of his secretaries, Hamilton Seymour, observing his dejection, sought to rouse his interest by mentioning the forthcoming visit to Verona. "At any other time," said Castlereagh, "I should have liked it very much, but"—and here he placed his hand upon his forehead,— "I am quite worn out here, quite worn out; this fresh responsibility is more than I can bear."

On the following morning, August 9, he went up to London. His first visit was to King George who was about to leave for his tour in Scotland. His Majesty was so much alarmed by the disordered nature of Castlereagh's conversation that he scribbled a hurried line to Liverpool. Castlereagh then drove to Apsley House and found the Duke of Wellington in the library on the ground floor. Years afterwards the Duke recounted to Stanhope what had then occurred: "I told him, 'From what you have said, I am bound to warn you that you cannot be in your right mind.' He was sitting or lying on the sofa, and he covered his face with his hands and said, 'Since you say so, I fear it must be so.'"

Wellington was so apprehensive that he at once sent a note to Dr. Bankhead, Castlereagh's family physician. "I sincerely hope," he wrote, "that you will contrive by some pretence to go down to his Lordship. I have no doubt he is very unwell. He appears to me to have been exceedingly harassed, much fatigued, and overworked, during the last session of Parliament, and I have no doubt he labours under mental delirium. I beg that you will never mention to anybody what I have told you respecting his Lordship."

Castlereagh returned to North Cray Farm where he was joined by his wife and Dr. Bankhead. He remained in bed during the 10th and 11th; he was given sedatives and bled; Dr. Bankhead as a precaution removed his pistols and razors but was unaware of a small pen-knife which Castlereagh had concealed in the drawer of his wash-stand. Early in the morning of August 12 he sent a message asking Dr. Bankhead to come to his dressing room immediately. On entering the room Dr. Bankhead saw him standing by the window looking out, with his hands above his head, and his throat cut from ear to ear. "Bankhead," he gasped, "let me fall on your arm; I have opened my neck; it is all over."

[6]

Canning meanwhile had been offered, and had accepted, the post of Governor-General in India. His ship was already waiting, but he delayed his departure hoping that, in spite of the King's prejudice, he might be offered the succession. No message came, and on August 30 he made his farewell speech to his constituents. On September 9, however, he received from Lord Liverpool the offer of the posts of Foreign Secretary and leader of the House of Commons. On the 15th he accepted this offer. His first letter from the Foreign Office was dated 6.15 P.M. on September 16, 1822. "So here," he wrote, "I am."

There was no doubt at all, either in Canning's mind or in that of foreign observers, that he would now substitute for Castlereagh's continental policy, a policy which would be more in accord with the isolationist feelings of the British people. What Metternich described as *"la grande déviation"*—the great divergence—had begun. "For *Europe*," wrote Canning to his friend Bagot shortly after assuming office, "I shall be desirous now and then to read *England*." The antipathy between Canning and Metternich was of long standing and very marked. To the Austrian statesman Canning appeared as some "malevolent meteor" presaging chaos and convulsion. Canning's new system of democratic diplomacy, his attempts to win the support and to enlighten the understanding of the general public, struck Metternich as both wicked and undignified. "To acquire a sort of popularity," he wrote, "is a pretension misplaced in a statesman." "It was he," wrote Metternich to Esterhazy after Canning's death, "who gave to evil the frightful stimulus which we have seen it take." This dislike was reciprocated. Canning referred to Metternich as "the greatest rogue and liar in Europe, perhaps in the civilised world."

Canning was not, as Metternich supposed, a Jacobin in disguise; he was a philosophic Tory of the school of Burke. He believed that Great Britain, "whose pigmy body, animated and o'er-informed by the spirit of her free constitution" had saved Europe from Napoleon, could once again lead the world along the middle path between despotism and revolution. To do that she must dissociate herself finally from the Holy Alliance and place herself in the vanguard of the new movement of nationalism and democracy.

The methods by which he succeeded in this purpose are beyond the scope of this present volume. It suffices to summarise the stages by which Canning broke the Alliance and brought British policy into harmony with the spirit of the age. In September 1822 he informed the Conference at Verona that "come what may" Great Britain would not be a party to any intervention in Spanish internal affairs. In March 1823 he refused to accept the French theory that intervention was justifiable. In October 1823 he refused even to attend a conference on the Spanish question. In November 1824 he similarly refused to allow Great Britain to be represented at a conference on the Eastern Question. In December 1824 he recognised the independence of the Spanish colonies without any reference to the Quadruple Alliance. By taking an independent line in according to the Greek rebels the status of belligerents, he thrust a wedge between Austria and Russia. In 1825 he recognised, without consulting any of his Allies, the independence of Brazil and re-established British influence over Portugal. By 1826, as the leader and protector of world liberalism, he had finally discredited the Holy Alliance and established Great Britain as the patron of a new age.

It was on December 12, 1826, that Canning, having defied the Holy Alliance by his independent handling of the Portuguese situation, and by his recognition of Brazil, came down to the House of Commons to justify his policy. It was then that he used the well-known, but almost meaningless phrase: "I called the New World into existence to redress the balance of the Old." Observers have recorded that when he said these words there was a sudden hush, broken by one slight titter. Then the whole House rose and shouted their applause.

History does not record the name of the man who tittered. We are left wondering whether he was foolish or wise.

[7]

As the century progressed the balance of power assumed ever varying forms and one by one the great protagonists of the Congress of Vienna disappeared. Hardenberg died in 1822. On December 1, 1825, in a final act of mystification, Alexander succumbed at Taganrog on the Black Sea, "crushed," as he said, "beneath the terrible burden of a crown." His coffin, when opened forty years later, was found to be empty. In the interval the Russian tide, as Castlereagh had predicted, had temporarily ebbed. In August 1827 Canning died, to be followed the next year by Liverpool. On May 17, 1838, Talleyrand died in his house in the Rue St. Florentin, having, under pressure from his niece and the Abbé Dupanloup, made his peace with the Church. The Emperor Francis died in 1835, and King Frederick William III in 1840. On September 14, 1852, the Duke of Wellington died in his little room at Walmer Castle. Only Metternich remained.

In March 1848 the great surge of revolution at last broke over Europe. Metternich was forced to resign the office which he had graced for forty years and to escape from Vienna. Travelling under an assumed name, he passed through Olmutz,

Teplitz and Dresden until at last he found sanctuary in London in the Brunswick Hotel, Hanover Square. After spending a few months at Brighton he crossed to Brussels and was finally able to settle in his property of Johannisthal in the Rhineland. It was there that Bismarck visited him and that he expounded to the young Prussian his plans for the future of the Germanic Federation. In 1849 he was allowed to return to Vienna where he established himself in a pretty villa on the Rennweg. His self-satisfaction did not desert him for a moment. "I was not understood," he remarked. "I became a phantasm, an imaginary being, a thing without substance." He would talk for hours about the great events and personages of the past and would remind his visitors that he had outlived all his contemporaries and had been a world figure for more than half a century. "I ruled Europe sometimes," he would sigh, "but I never governed Austria." His opinion was invited, but seldom followed, on all important diplomatic occasions: the young Emperor Franz Josef treated him with deference and respect.

The final portrait of Metternich comes to us from the pen of Count Hübner, who visited him in his villa on the Rennweg on May 25, 1859. "Our conversation," he records, "was lively and stimulating. On my leaving him he said to me again and again with emphasis, 'I was a Rock of Order.' I had already closed the door behind me when I opened it again softly to take one more look at the great statesman. There he sat at his writing desk, pen in hand, glancing upward contemplatively, erect, cold, proud, distinguished, just as I had formerly often seen him in the Chancellery when in the full glow of his power. The shadow of death which I had noticed in these latter days was gone from his countenance. A sunbeam lighted the room and the reflected light transfigured his noble features. After a time he noticed me at the door, fixed upon me a long look of profound benevolence, turned away and said half aloud, half to himself, 'A Rock of Order.'"

On June 5 following, Metternich learnt that the nephew of the great Napoleon had defeated the Austrian armies at Magenta and had entered Milan. He died on June 11, 1859. He was spared the news of Solferino.

Appendix I: Notes

[1] *Russian campaign*, 1812. The main dates are as follows: June 24, Napoleon crosses the Niemen south of Kowno: June 28, takes Vilna: August 17, takes Smolensk: September 7, Battle of Borodino: September 14, enters Moscow: September 14-16, burning of Moscow: Napoleon retires to Petrovski Palace in the suburbs: September 18, he returns to Kremlin: October 5, sends Lauriston in hopes of concluding armistice with the Tsar; no result: October 18, Napoleon leaves Moscow, retreat begins: November 9, reaches Smolensk: November 28-29, crossing of the Beresina: December 3, issues 29th Bulletin: December 5, abandons army at Smogorni: December 18, midnight returns to Paris.

[2] *Caulaincourt, Armand Louis de, Duc de Vicence* (1773-1827). Born of an ancient feudal family at the Château de Caulaincourt near St. Quentin. His father had known Josephine as a girl and to this he owed his appointment in 1802 as one of the First Consul's aides-de-camp. In 1804 he was sent to Willstadt in Baden to arrest certain émigrés and British agents at the same moment as Ordener was sent to the neighbouring Ettenheim to kidnap the Duc d'Enghien. At the age of 31 made master of the horse to Napoleon. 1807-1811, Ambassador in Russia, created Duke of Vicence. Accompanied Napoleon on 1812 campaign. Served as his representative at Pläswitz (May 1813) and Prague (July 1813). November 20, 1813, appointed Foreign Minister. January 1814, Napoleon's representative at Congress of Châtillon. Conducted negotiations for Napoleon's abdication and Treaty of Fontainebleau (April 1814). With return of Bourbons retired into private life. During Hundred Days he rejoined Napoleon and was with him when he re-entered Tuileries. March 21, 1815, again appointed Foreign Minister. He received Napoleon at the Elysée when he returned from Waterloo. He urged him to fly to the United States. He remained in Paris when the Allies

entered and was then allowed to retire into private life. In February 1827 he died at his house in the Rue St. Lazare, Paris. The Château de Caulaincourt, which he did much to embellish during his last years, was completely destroyed by the Germans in 1917.

³ *Alexander I, Emperor of Russia* (1777-1825). Son of the mad Tsar Paul I and Maria, daughter of Frederick of Würtemberg. At the age of sixteen he was forced by his grandmother Catherine II to marry Princess Maria of Baden, who took the Orthodox name of Elizabeth Feodorovna. At the age of twenty-three became Tsar of Russia on the murder of his father Paul I. He at once reversed Paul's policy, made peace with England, and ranged himself with Napolecn's enemies. Under influence of La Harpe he tried to introduce social and educational reforms into Russia but these were later abandoned. Allied himself with Prussia and Austria. When Austria was beaten at Austerlitz and Prussia at Jena, Alexander still remained Napoleon's enemy until routed at Friedland (June 13 and 14, 1807). Met Napoleon on a raft at Tilsit (June 25, 1807) and fell completely under his spell. At their second meeting at Erfurt (October 1808) his first enthusiasm for Napoleon had waned. In 1809 Alexander seized Finland from the Swedes. He was enraged by Napoleon's creation of Grand Duchy of Warsaw and Napoleon was hurt by the Tsar's refusal to give him the hand of the Grand Duchess Anne. Then followed the campaign of 1812 and the events recorded in the text. Alexander died in mysterious circumstances at Taganrog on December 1, 1825. It was popularly believed that, succumbing to religious mania, he had become a hermit. He was in fact supposed to have been the Siberian hermit, Feodor Kusmitch, who died near Tomsk on February 1, 1864.

⁴ "They believe him to be weak," Caulaincourt had written to Napoleon, "but they are wrong. Doubtless he puts up with many annoyances and knows how to conceal his feelings. But this facility of character has its limits and never goes beyond the circle he has traced for it; and that circle is of iron and will never yield. For underneath his appearance of good-will, frankness and natural loyalty, there is a core of deep dissimulation which is the mark of an obstinacy which nothing can move."

⁵ It should be realised that the Napoleonic Empire at its summit embraced practically the whole of Europe, from the Ems to the Adriatic and from the Baltic to the Ebro. Rome, Barcelona, Hamburg, Cologne, Geneva, Lübeck, Trieste, Genoa and Ragusa were

all French towns. Napoleon's satellites included Italy, Spain, Naples, Westphalia, Sweden, Switzerland, the Confederation of the Rhine, and the Duchy of Warsaw. As vassal States were Denmark, Bavaria and Saxony. Austria was his ally, Prussia his victim. Russia was engaged in war with Turkey. Except for Portugal, whose dynasty had been obliged to escape to Brazil, not a European Government was on Great Britain's side.

It is not surprising that Napoleon should have regarded British resistance as illogical, treacherous and hypocritical. "With France as I conceived it," he said at St. Helena, "England would have become little more than an appendix. Nature devised her to be one of our islands, just as Oléron or Corsica are French islands. . . . If in place of the expedition to Egypt I had landed in Ireland; if a few nugatory impediments had not interfered with my preparations for invading Britain at Boulogne, what would England be today? What would the Continent be today? What the world?"

[6] *Stein, Baron vom und zum* (1757-1831). Born at Nassau, entered Prussian service: 1804, Minister for Trade: quarrelled with Frederick William after Jena but was appointed First Minister after Tilsit (October 1807): responsible for the Edict of Emancipation and other internal reforms: proclaimed an enemy of France, December 16, 1808: escaped to Brünn where he lived till May 1812 when he was summoned to St. Petersburg by Alexander: after Tauroggen appointed by Tsar provisional administrator of East Prussia: organised the Landwehr and the Landsturm: entered Leipzig with the Allies (October 1814): at Congress of Vienna he tried, but failed, to create a United Germany: thereafter retired into private life.

[7] There were five main coalitions against France, all but the last two of which disintegrated under separate defeats: (1) *First Coalition*, 1792-1797. Austria, Prussia, and Sardinia subsequently joined by Great Britain, Spain, Portugal, Naples, Tuscany and the Papal States. The Netherlands were overrun by France; Prussia made a separate peace in April 1795, Spain in July 1795, Sardinia in May 1796, and Naples in October 1796. Austria was defeated and concluded the peace of Campo Formio in October 1797. Russia never took the Coalition seriously. In 1797 Great Britain stood alone. (2) *Second Coalition*, 1799-1801. Great Britain, Russia, Turkey, Austria, Naples and Portugal. Russia withdrew in 1800. Austria, defeated at Marengo and Hohenlinden, was forced to conclude Treaty of Lunéville in February 1801. Great Britain remained alone.

(3) *Third Coalition*, 1805-1806. Russia, Austria, Sweden, Great Britain and later Prussia. After Austerlitz Austria forced to make peace of Pressburg (December 1805); Prussia completely knocked out at Jena (October 14, 1806). Russia, after hanging on for six months, made alliance with Napoleon at Tilsit (July 1807). Great Britain remained on alone. (4) *Fourth Coalition*, 1812-1814. Great Britain and Russia. Prussia joined February 1813. Austria joined June 1813. Würtemberg, Baden, Hesse joined subsequently. Battle of Leipzig October 16, 1813. Treaty of Chaumont (March 9, 1814) established the Quadruple Alliance which lasted for twenty years. (5) *Fifth Coalition*, 1815. Established at Vienna on news of Napoleon's escape from Elba. Ended at Waterloo.

CHAPTER 2

[1] The main dates in the Peninsular War (1808-1814) are as follows. On the instigation of Canning an expeditionary force was sent under Sir A. Wellesley to the peninsula in July 1808: on August 21, 1808, Wellesley defeated Junot at Vimeiro but was superseded by Sir Hew Dalrymple who concluded the Convention of Cintra. Both Dalrymple and Wellesley were then recalled and the command left to Sir John Moore who on January 16, 1809, was obliged to evacuate the expeditionary force from Corunna. In April 1809 the British army, again under the command of Wellesley, landed for a second time at Lisbon. After winning the battle of Talavera in July he retreated to the lines of Torres Vedras behind which he remained entrenched till 1811. He then began his great advance and there followed the battles of Ciudad Rodrigo, Badajoz, Fuentes de Onoro and Albuera, culminating in Salamanca (1812) and Vitoria (1813). Soult was driven out of Spain and the battle of Toulouse in April 1814 put an end to the war.

[2] *Frederick William III, King of Prussia* (1770-1840). In 1793 married Louise of Mecklenburg Strelitz: succeeded his father, Frederick William II, November 1797: totally unable to cope with the Napoleonic hurricane and after Jena (1805) and Tilsit (1807) was despoiled of half his kingdom. Under his wife's influence, however, he supported the domestic and military reforms of Stein, Scharnhorst and Gneisenau. Queen Louise died in July 1810. Forced by public opinion in 1813 to join Alexander against Napoleon he promised in the excitement of the moment to grant his country a constitution. He

thereafter developed reactionary tendencies and his promise was never fulfilled. Died June 7, 1840. A weak, unintelligent, rigid and honourable man.

[3] *Frederick Augustus I, King of Saxony* (1750-1827). Succeeded his father, the Elector Frederick Christian, at the age of thirteen. Began to reign in 1768. In 1806 joined Prussia against Napoleon but after Jena concluded peace at Posen (December 11, 1806) and joined Confederation of the Rhine under the title of King of Saxony. After Tilsit (July 1807) he was created Grand Duke of Warsaw but his sovereignty over the Grand Duchy was never more than nominal. In 1809 he fought on Napoleon's side against Austria. In April 1813 he was tempted by Metternich to join Austria in her efforts to mediate; he received an ultimatum from Napoleon and, after Lützen, he rallied in panic to Napoleon's cause. After Leipzig he was taken prisoner by the Allies and interned at Schloss Friedrichsfelde, near Berlin. After the Congress of Vienna he regained his freedom after having been forced to surrender three-fifths of his kingdom to Prussia. He returned to Dresden on July 7, 1814, resumed his horticultural pursuits, and died on May 5, 1827. He was honest, industrious but lamentable.

[4] There were three partitions of Poland, namely those of 1772, 1792 and 1795. Under the first partition Russia obtained the regions bounded by the Dvina and the Dnieper and including the districts of Polotsk, Vitebsk and Mogilev: Austria obtained southern Galicia, including Przemysl and Lemberg: Prussia obtained what subsequently became known as "the Polish corridor," including the city of Danzig. Under the second partition of 1792 Russia obtained a vast area of White Russia, running from the neighbourhood of Dvinsk to the frontier of Bessarabia: Prussia obtained the district of Posen, including Plock, Kalisch and Lodz. Under the third partition of 1795 what remained of Poland was taken over by the three neighbouring Powers: Russia absorbed the Duchy of Courland and advanced her frontier to the Niemen, obtaining at the same time Vilna and vast areas of Lithuania and Volhynia: Austria (who had obtained nothing under the second partition) acquired under the third the whole of western Galicia, including Lublin, Radom and Cholm: Prussia obtained the remainder of Poland including Warsaw.

CHAPTER 3

[1] *Metternich, Prince Clément Wenceslaus Lothaire Nepomucène*
(1773-1859). The main dates in Metternich's long life are as follows: Born at Coblentz, May 1773: his tutor John Friedrich Simon
who ended by being a Jacobin terrorist: educated at Strassburg and
Mainz universities: influence of Professors Koch and Vogt who
preached the importance of "the just equilibrium": holidays at Brussels where he came under influence of the French émigrés and in
England where he met Pitt, Fox and Burke and formed a friendship
with Prince of Wales (George IV), "one of the most handsome
men that I have ever met." In 1795 he married Countess Kaunitz.
In 1797 he represented the Westphalian Counts at the Congress of
Rastadt: 1801-1803, Austrian Minister at Dresden: 1803-1806,
Minister at Berlin: 1806-1809, Ambassador in Paris: in 1809 at
the age of 36 he was appointed by the Emperor Francis Minister
for Foreign Affairs, a post he held till 1848. On the death of his
first wife he married Antoniette von Leykam and on her death the
young and indiscreet Countess Mélanie Zichy-Ferraris. On the death
of Francis in 1835 his position became more difficult: in March 1848
a revolution took place in Vienna: Metternich and his wife escaped
to the Brunswick Hotel, Hanover Square, London, and subsequently
to Brighton. In 1840 he retired to his property at Johannisthal,
where Bismarck visited him. He then returned to Vienna, established
himself in his villa on the Rennweg and was befriended by the young
Emperor Franz Joseph. On June 4, 1859, came the battle of
Magenta. A week later Metternich died.

[2] *Francis I* (1768-1835). Emperor of Austria, son of Leopold II
and Maria Louisa, daughter of Charles III of Spain. Educated by
his uncle Joseph II who bullied him and implanted in him an abiding
sense of inferiority. On the death of his father in 1792 he became
Roman Emperor under title of Francis II but in 1804 he abandoned
the claim to be head of the Holy Roman Empire and became only
Emperor of Austria, with the title of Francis I. He married four
times. His greatest quality was the long-suffering patience which
enabled him to withstand the tribulations of his reign. He was not a
man of great intelligence, but he possessed some literary culture and
was much beloved by his subjects.

[3] *Cathcart, William Shaw, tenth Baron and first Earl of Cathcart*

(1755-1843). Served in America against the Colonies and in Germany: in September 1807 he commanded the Army of the Baltic which bombarded and captured Copenhagen: in 1812 he was appointed Ambassador to Russia and British Commissioner at the Tsar's headquarters: after 1815 he was Ambassador to Russia for five years and thereafter retired into private life. He died at the age of eighty-eight.

[4] *Stewart, Sir Charles, subsequently third Marquis of Londonderry* (1778-1854). Lord Castlereagh's half-brother: served in Ireland and in Holland: entered the Union Parliament as member for Derry: in 1807 he became Under Secretary for War: served under Sir John Moore in Spain: and subsequently in Portugal under Wellesley, when he distinguished himself by reckless courage. In April he was appointed British Minister at Berlin "specially charged with the military superintendence, so far as Great Britain is concerned, of the Prussian and Swedish armies." He was present at Lützen and Bautzen; and at the battle of Leipzig he captured a battery at the head of the Brandenburg Hussars. In 1814 he accompanied Lord Castlereagh to Allied headquarters and subsequently to the Congress of Vienna; he represented Great Britain at the Congress of Troppau (1820) and Laybach (1821) and accompanied Wellington to Verona (1822). By his second marriage he acquired the Vane Tempest estates in Durham and devoted much of his later life to the construction and improvement of Seaham harbour. He was a vain, quarrelsome and ostentatious man who often incurred the ridicule and dislike of his contemporaries; but even Wellington, who admitted that "he was not particularly partial to the man" considered him an efficient diplomatist.

[5] The immense effect produced at Prague by the news of the battle of Vitoria is well conveyed in Gentz's letters to Pilat. The first news arrived in Prague on July 16. On July 22 Wellington's own account of the battle was received. "Lord Wellington's despatch," Gentz wrote, "is written with his usual modesty, which one cannot help admiring—and with a simplicity which, although almost irritating at moments, is none the less elevated and noble."

CHAPTER 4

[1] *Bernadotte, Jean Baptiste, Prince of Ponte Corvo and subsequently King Charles XIV of Sweden* (1763-1844). Born at Pau; entered

the French army and made a Marshal in 1804; fought at Ulm, Austerlitz and Wagram: in 1810, on the death of the Crown Prince of Sweden, he was unexpectedly elected as his successor to the throne, and adopted by Charles XIII under the title of the Crown Prince Charles John. In order to distract the attention of Sweden from Finland he conceived the idea that she should incorporate Norway; with this in mind he made an agreement with the Emperor Alexander at Abö in 1812 and with the British Government in March 1813. Under the latter agreement Bernadotte, in return for the promise of Norway, was to send an army into northern Germany. He kept his head after Lützen and Bautzen and although he sought to spare his Swedish forces as much as possible he did in fact render useful assistance to the Allies during the Leipzig campaign. In 1818 on the death of Charles XIII he succeeded to the throne of Sweden and Norway. He was popular with the Swedes and his jubilee was celebrated with much enthusiasm in 1843. He died at Stockholm on March 8, 1844.

[2] *Maritime Rights*. A phrase employed by Great Britain to designate what other countries called the freedom of the seas. The British contention was that a belligerent had the right to visit and search neutral vessels on the high seas. The opposed contention was that neutrality carried exemption from interference on the principle of "free ships, free goods." Britain claimed that if this principle were admitted no naval blockade would prove effective since any blockaded country could import goods in neutral bottoms. The others said that to extend British maritime supremacy to the point of interference with legitimate neutral commerce was against the Law of Nations. The smaller Powers were in fact united in their indignation at British procedure and Napoleon's appeal to them to "smash the tyranny of the oceanic Rome" found some echo in their hearts. It led to such combines as Armed Neutrality and explains why Napoleon's scheme for "conquering the sea by land" was not at first so ill received by the continental Powers. This controversy, which dates from the Treaty of Utrecht and extends to November 1918 (if not beyond), is outside the scope of this study and is infinitely more complicated and technical than this note might suggest.

[3] *Gentz, Chevalier Friedrich von* (1764-1832). Born at Breslau and studied under Kant at Königsberg. Entered the Prussian service but in 1802 transferred himself to Vienna. From 1812 onwards he became Metternich's secretary and publicity agent. He acted as

Secretary General at the Vienna Congress and at all subsequent congresses until Verona. He was a man of wide knowledge and considerable political acumen. Although self-indulgent in his private life and corrupt in regard to bribes, he was essentially a man of intellectual integrity and his memoirs and letters are on the whole reliable as well as brilliant. He was one of those rare men who are universally mistrusted and yet esteemed.

⁴ *Murat, Joachim, King of Naples* (1767-1815). He was the second son of an inn-keeper at La Bastide-Fortunière (Lot). He first met Bonaparte in 1795, assisted him during the events of the 13th Vendémiaire, and became his aide-de-camp in Italy. He thereafter accompanied him to Egypt and it was his leadership of the charge at the Battle of the Pyramids which established him as the most dashing cavalry leader in Europe. On the return from Egypt it was he who brought the Grenadiers into the Orangery at St. Cloud on the 16th Brumaire and dispersed the Council of Five Hundred. He became Captain of the Consular Guard, married Napoleon's youngest sister Caroline in 1800, was made a Marshal in 1804 and Grand Duke of Cleves and Berg two years later. He fought in most of Napoleon's most famous battles and in 1808 was made King of Naples. He commanded the cavalry in the Moscow campaign and fought again at Leipzig. On his return to Naples in November 1813 he sought to open negotiations with the Allies, offering to abandon Napoleon if Austria and England would guarantee him his throne. A treaty to this effect was signed with Austria on January 11, 1814, with the knowledge and tacit approval of Castlereagh. This treaty was not, however, approved of by the other Allies and his position was much undermined by Talleyrand during the Vienna Congress. On Napoleon's escape from Elba, Murat tried to raise Italy on his behalf but on May 2, 1815, his forces were routed by the Austrians at Tolentino. Murat escaped to France and offered his services to Napoleon who refused them with contempt. Napoleon at St. Helena regretted this action and asserted that had Murat led the charge at Waterloo the battle might have been won. Murat, who had taken refuge in Corsica, attempted after Waterloo a further *coup de main* in Italy. Landing at Pizzo in Calabria on October 8, 1815, he was captured and court martialled. He was executed on October 13. His eldest son escaped to the United States where he became the eponym and postmaster of Lipona, Jefferson County, and died in 1847.

⁵ *Pozzo di Borgo, Carlo Andrea, Count* (1764-1842). Born in

Corsica and became Corsican deputy to French Legislative Assembly. On his return to Corsica he joined Paoli and became estranged from the Bonaparte family. When Napoleon occupied Corsica he escaped to England and thereafter accompanied Lord Minto on his embassy to Vienna where he remained six years. He was protected by Adam Czartoryski and by his influence was in 1804 admitted into the Russian diplomatic service. After Tilsit he was dismissed from Russian service, lived for a while in Vienna until Napoleon insisted on his extradition, and then again escaped to England. In 1812 he was summoned to Russia by the Tsar, was instrumental in persuading Bernadotte to join the Allies, and on the Bourbon restoration became Russian Ambassador in Paris, where he remained till 1835 when he was appointed to London in succession to Prince Lieven. He suffered much from the English climate, retired in 1839 and died in Paris in 1842.

CHAPTER 5

[1] *Wilson, Sir Robert* (1777-1849). As a cornet in the 15th Light Dragoons, he took part in the famous cavalry charge of April 24, 1794, in which the Emperor of Austria was rescued from imminent capture at Villiers-en-Couché. He later served with Sir Ralph Abercromby in Egypt and on his return to England he published an account of the campaign in which he accused Bonaparte of having ill-treated prisoners at Jaffa. In 1807 he accompanied the King of Prussia to Memel and joined the Russian headquarters after Eylau. After serving in the early stages of the Peninsular War he was sent to Constantinople in 1812 with Sir Robert Liston and thereafter attached to the headquarters of the Emperor of Russia. He took part in the battles of Lützen and Bautzen. In September 1813 he was transferred from the Russian to the Austrian army and served on Prince Schwarzenberg's staff at the battle of Leipzig. He was known to be corresponding behind the back of his chiefs with the Whig leaders in London and was therefore, much to the fury of the Russian and Austrian Emperors, transferred to Italy, Lord Burghersh being appointed in his place. In January 1816 he was concerned with the escape from prison of Count de LaValette and was condemned by a French court to three months' imprisonment. He entered Parliament in 1818 but was dismissed from the army for his intervention in a riot on the occasion of Queen Caroline's funeral. On the accession of

William IV he was reinstated in the army with the rank of lieutenant-general. In 1842 he was appointed Governor of Gibraltar, a post he held until 1848. He died suddenly in a hotel in Oxford Street in May 1849.

[2] This distinction between "natural" and "ancient" limits loomed so large during the negotiations which followed that it is useful to make quite clear what was meant by these two epithets. By "natural limits" was meant the frontiers of the Pyrenees, Alps and Rhine. If France retained these she would have included within her territory not only Alsace-Lorraine but also what we now call Belgium, including Brussels and Antwerp. By "ancient limits" was meant the frontiers as they had stood in 1792, which included Alsace and Lorraine but not the Belgian areas and under which the northern limit of France would have followed much the same line as the Franco-Belgian frontier today.

[3] At St. Helena Napoleon confessed that he never imagined the Austrians would proceed to extremes since that would mean rendering Russia the dominant Power in Europe. To the end of his days he sought, somewhat uneasily, to defend the attitude which he had adopted towards the Châtillon Conference. "I had to refuse," he said. "I well knew what I was about. Even on this rock, even in the midst of all this misery, I do not repent of my decision."

CHAPTER 6

[1] The Comtesse de Boigne in her memoirs records that one evening in the spring of 1814 Nesselrode pulled from his pocket a crumpled scrap of paper which he handed to her with the words: "Would you like to see the document which determined us to advance on Paris?" It was a message in Talleyrand's handwriting which had got through the lines. "You are groping about like children," it said, "you ought to stride forward on stilts. You are in the position to achieve anything that you wish to achieve."

There is no reason to doubt the authenticity of this tale of Talleyrand's treachery.

[2] *Talleyrand-Périgord, Charles Maurice de* (1754-1838). The main dates in Talleyrand's life are as follows: Born in Paris, February 13, 1754, he was permanently crippled by falling out of a chest of drawers at the age of four. He thereby forfeited his rights of primogeniture and was obliged to enter the Church; he became

Bishop of Autun on March 13, 1789, and in the States General he took the revolutionary side; at the festival of July 14, 1790 ("The Feast of Pikes") he celebrated Mass at the altar in the Champ de Mars and voted for the civil constitution of the clergy. In January 1791 he resigned his see and in March was placed under the ban of the Church by the Pope. In 1792 he was sent on a diplomatic mission to London and was well received by Pitt. On the execution of Louis XVI on January 21, 1793, he was expelled from British soil and sought refuge in the United States where he remained till 1795. In 1797 he was appointed Foreign Minister by Barras but foreseeing the fall of the Directory he resigned in 1799. He assisted Bonaparte during the Brumaire coup d'état in 1799 and was rewarded by the post of Minister for Foreign Affairs which he held from December 1799 till 1807. In 1803 he at last married his mistress, Madame Grand. With the establishment of the Empire in May 1804 he was made Grand Chamberlain and in 1806 he was given the title of Prince of Benevento. He resigned his office after Tilsit in 1807 but accompanied Napoleon to Erfurt in September 1808. When the Allies entered Paris on March 31, 1814, Talleyrand remained behind and received the Emperor Alexander in his own house; on April 1, he convened the Senate and on April 2 forced them to vote for the deposition of Napoleon. In 1814-1815 he served as the representative of the Bourbons at the Congress of Vienna and in July 1813, he became Foreign Secretary and President of the Council to Louis XVIII. He resigned this post in the following September and became Grand Chamberlain. During the July revolution of 1830 he urged Louis Philippe to assume the throne, refused his offer of the Foreign Ministry and accepted instead the post of Ambassador in London where he remained till the autumn of 1834. He died on May 17, 1838, having made his peace with the Church, and was buried at Valençay.

[3] *Marmont, Auguste, Duke of Ragusa* (1774-1852). Born at Châtillon-sur-Seine, July 1774. Entered the artillery and served with Bonaparte at Toulon: became Bonaparte's aide-de-camp and followed him to Italy and Egypt. Made a general of division for his services at Marengo. Fought at Ulm in 1805 and for five years was Governor of Dalmatia. In 1808 made Duke of Ragusa and Governor-General of the Illyrian provinces. Succeeded Massena in Spain in 1810 and was wounded at Salamanca. He served in the campaign in France in 1814 and deserted Napoleon at Essonnes. Under the Restoration he

was made a peer of France and General of the Royal Guard. In 1830 he opposed Louis Philippe and went into exile with Charles X. He finally settled in Vienna and became tutor to Napoleon's son. He died in Venice in March 1852.

⁴ *The Comte d'Artois,* subsequently Charles X, and known as Monsieur, was the brother and successor of Louis XVIII. Born in 1757 he escaped from France in 1789 and sought asylum in Holyrood Palace, Edinburgh. On the restoration of his brother he headed the reactionary party of the ultra-royalists and on succeeding to the throne behaved with such narrow stupidity that he was mainly responsible for the Revolution of July 1830. He then retired again to Holyrood and died at Goritz in 1836. "The Comte d'Artois," wrote Lady Holland, "is a man of slender abilities with violent passions; before the Revolution he was weak and volatile; he is now weak and revengeful."

⁵ The first and conditional abdication in favour of the King of Rome ran as follows: "The Allied Powers having proclaimed that the Emperor Napoleon was the sole obstacle to the re-establishment of peace in Europe, the Emperor Napoleon declares that he is ready to abandon the throne, to leave France and even to sacrifice his life" in favour of his son, the King of Rome. The second and unconditional abdication, after a similar preamble, continued: "The Emperor Napoleon, remaining faithful to his oath, declares that he renounces for himself and his heirs the thrones of France and Italy and that there is no personal sacrifice, even that of his life, that he would not be ready to make in the interests of France. . . ."

It is curious to note that the first abdication, that of April 4, was dated from "*our* palace of Fontainebleau," whereas the second, that of April 11, is dated from "*the* palace of Fontainebleau."

⁶ From 1808 onwards Napoleon had worn round his neck a small heart-shaped satchel containing a poison prepared according to a formula given by Cabanis to Condorcet. In 1812 he substituted for this a prescription prepared for him by Dr. Yvan; it was this dose which failed him in 1814. In 1815 he carried with him, attached to his braces, a far more potent poison; he did not use this after Waterloo on the ground that he "must fulfil his destiny."

CHAPTER 7

[1] *Kosciuszko, Tadeusz* (1746-1817). Born at Mereczowszczyno. Completed his military education in Germany, Italy and France. In 1776 joined the armed forces of the American Colonies as a volunteer and distinguished himself at Yorktown. Accorded rank of brigadier-general by Congress with United States citizenship. Returned to Poland in 1791 and sought to enlist sympathy of the French Jacobins for Poland's cause. In 1793 invited by Polish insurgents to take command. On April 3, 1794, he defeated the Russians at Raclawice; on October 10 his armies were annihilated and he himself wounded and taken prisoner. He was released and returned to the United States where he lived till 1798. He refused to join Napoleon and retired to his cottage at Berville near Fontainebleau. Thereafter he exiled himself to Solothurn where he died on April 2, 1817.

[2] *Louis XVIII* ("Louis le Désiré") (1755-1824). Third son of the Dauphin Louis, son of Louis XV, and Maria Josepha of Saxony. Until the birth of a son to Louis XVI he was regarded as the heir to the throne and known as Monsieur. At the time of the flight to Varennes he managed to escape with his favourite, Count d'Avaray, to Brussels. After Valmy he escaped to Hamm in Westphalia from where he was driven successively to Brunswick and then to Mittau in Courland. On being expelled from Mittau he spent three years in Warsaw. After Tilsit he took final refuge in England, first at Gosfield, a property of the Earl of Buckingham, and finally at Hartwell in Buckinghamshire, belonging to Sir George Lee.

CHAPTER 8

[1] Lady Castlereagh, for all her virtues, was a stupid woman; she had been handsome as a girl but became stout in middle age. Lady Bessborough has left a portrait of her which is so vivid and so devastating that it deserves to be recorded: "No one was ever so invariably good-humoured yet she sometimes provokes me; there is a look of contented disregard of the cares of life in her round grey eye that makes me wonder if she ever felt any crosses or knows the meaning of the word anxiety. She talks with equal indifference of Bombardments and Assemblies, the Baby and the Furniture, the

emptiness of London and the massacre of Buenos Ayres, Lord Castlereagh's increasing debility and the doubtful success of Mr. Greville's
new opera—all these succeed each other so quick and with so exactly
the same expression of voice and countenance that they probably hold
a pretty equal value in her estimation."

[2] *Hardenberg, Prince Charles Augustus*, born at Hanover, 1750.
Served the courts of Hanover, Brunswick and Baireuth. Entered
Prussian service 1791. In 1804 became Prussian Foreign Secretary.
Retired after Tilsit but in 1810 appointed Prussian Chancellor.
Died 1822.

CHAPTER 10

[1] More detailed figures can be given as follows, with the reservation that all such statistics are only approximate. Under the first
partition of 1772 Russia obtained 34,616 square miles of Polish territory with a population of some 550,000. Austria obtained 32,045
square miles with a population of some 816,000. Prussia obtained
14,025 square miles with a population of 378,000. Under the second
partition of 1793 Poland was reduced to one-third of her original
area and population, Russia obtaining a further 96,751 square miles
and Prussia obtaining the rich areas of Thorn and Danzig. Under
the third partition of 1795-1796 Poland was wiped off the map,
Austria obtaining Cracow and western Galicia, Prussia obtaining
Warsaw, and Russia the rest. Even when "Congress Poland" was
eventually constituted at Vienna in 1815, Prussia retained the Posen
area with a Polish population of some 810,000 and Austria retained
Galicia with a Polish population of some 1,500,000.

[2] *Ligne, Charles Joseph, Prince de* (1735-1814). Born in Brussels,
served in Seven Years' War and in War of the Bavarian Succession;
the intimate friend of Joseph II and Catherine II; a Marshal of both
Austria and Russia. As early as September 1814 he remarked to
Chambonas that *"le congres ne marche pas: il danse."* He repeated
this remark on every successive occasion until on December 13 he
died in his house on the Mölkerbastei from a cold contracted while
waiting for an amatory assignation at a street corner in his eightieth
year. His joke about the Congress, which was first made before the
Congress had even assembled, has received undue publicity.

CHAPTER 11

[1] During the panic of the Hundred Days the text of the treaty was left behind by the Comte de Jaucourt in his writing table at the Tuileries. It was found there by Napoleon, who obligingly sent an authenticated copy to the Emperor Alexander.

CHAPTER 12

[1] It is interesting to observe how ill-instructed the Whigs were by their political friends abroad. Sir Robert Wilson in particular sent them copious information which was almost invariably incorrect. They were quite positive that Wellington would be defeated in Spain; that the Allies would be defeated in the 1814 campaign; that Murat would prove invincible in Italy; and that England had lost the battle of Waterloo. In 1812, for instance, Creevey, after the battle of Salamanca, could write that "our ultimate discomfiture is merely a question of time." The Hon. H. Bennet, writing to Creevey, well describes the scene which took place at Brooks's Club in July 1815. "Nothing could be more droll than the discomfiture of our politicians at Brooks's. The night the news of the Battle of Waterloo arrived Sir Robert Wilson and Grey demonstrated satisfactorily to a crowded audience that Boney had 200,000 men across the Sambre and that he must then be at Brussels. Wilson read a letter announcing that the English were defiling out of the town by the Antwerp Gate, when the shouts in the street drew up to the window and we saw the chaise and eagles. To be sure we are good people and sorry politicians."

[2] *Bentinck, Lord William* (1774-1839). Second son of third Duke of Portland. Attached to Marshal Suvaroff's armies in Italy, 1799-1801. Governor of Madras from 1803-1807, from which post he was recalled by the directors of the East India Company. Was with Sir John Moore at Corunna, served for a while under Sir Arthur Wellesley in Spain and in 1811 was sent as envoy to the Court of Sicily. In 1813 he was in command of a division of Anglo-Sicilian troops in Spain and suffered a defeat in the pass of Ordal. He returned to Sicily and conducted with Murat the negotiations recorded in the text. From 1814 to 1827 he remained unemployed but in the latter year was appointed Governor-General of Bengal. He adopted on the whole a liberal attitude, and was responsible for the abolition

of *suttee*. In 1833 he became Governor-General of India but returned for reasons of health to England in 1835. He entered Parliament but died in Paris in June 1839.

³ The main dates in the contemporary history of Naples and Sicily, known as the Kingdom of the Two Sicilies, are as follows. In 1738 Don Carlos of Bourbon, son of Philip V of Spain, was recognised as King of the Two Sicilies. In 1759 Carlos abdicated in favour of his son Ferdinand who married Maria Carolina, daughter of the Empress Maria Theresa and a woman of strong character. In 1798 she persuaded her husband to declare war on France with the result that in January 1799 a French army entered Naples and proclaimed the Parthenopaean Republic. Ferdinand and Maria Carolina escaped to Sicily but were brought back to Naples in 1802 from where they had again to escape in 1805 and establish themselves at Palermo. Jerome Bonaparte was then proclaimed King of Naples but transferred his throne to Murat in 1808. In Sicily meanwhile a conflict arose between the Court and the Constitutionalists. Lord William Bentinck, the British Minister at Palermo, forced Ferdinand to appoint his son as regent, to exile Maria Carolina, and to grant a constitution. In 1815 Ferdinand entered Naples under the protection of an Austrian army and, with Castlereagh's consent, abolished the constitution.

⁴ The general background of the Swiss problem as it presented itself to the Congress of Vienna was as follows. In August 1291 the three cantons of Uri, Schwyz and Unterwalden had united to form "the three forest cantons." They were joined by Lucerne in 1332, by Zürich in 1351, and by Berne in 1353. At the battle of Sempach on July 9, 1386, the Hapsburg domination over Switzerland was broken. By 1501 there were thirteen cantons members of the League, but in fact they were divided into three conflicting groups, (*a*) the aristocratic cantons of Berne, Lucerne, Fribourg and Soleure, (*b*) the democratic cantons of Uri, Schwyz and Unterwalden, and (*c*) the guild cantons of Basle, Zürich and Schaffhausen. In 1798 the French invaded Switzerland and proclaimed the Helvetic Republic. By the Act of Mediation of 1802 Napoleon revived the old Diet, recognised the sovereignty of the cantons, and proclaimed a perpetual alliance with France. On December 21, 1813, the Allies, much against Alexander's wishes, violated the neutrality of Switzerland and, on the revolt of the aristocratic cantons, imposed the Federal Pact of September 12, 1814. Hans von Reinhard, the Landemann of Zürich, summoned an extraordinary Diet (*Tagsatzung*) which declared the

Act of Mediation abolished, but Bern retorted by summoning a "legitimate Diet" to which five of the other cantons adhered. It was this confused situation which the Congress was called upon to settle.

CHAPTER 13

[1] *Isabey, Jean-Baptiste* (1767-1855). Born at Nancy and became the pupil of David. He was employed at Versailles by Marie Antoinette, and lived to receive the Legion of Honour from Napoleon III. He devoted much of his time to lithography and to designs for court costumes and ceremonies. He designed the setting for the coronation of Napoleon as well as for the coronation of Charles X. He had already been in Vienna in 1811 when he had painted many portraits of the Austrian royal family. His most famous painting is that of Napoleon at Malmaison. It was Talleyrand who persuaded him to come to Vienna to paint the official picture of the Congress and during his sojourn there he was officially attached to the French delegation.

[2] *The Slave Trade*. This trade had developed during the later half of the eighteenth century until it had reached the proportions of a world scandal. Slaves were obtained from Africa, sometimes by kidnapping, sometimes through professional Arab slave traders, sometimes by bribing local chiefs with casks of brandy. By 1770 British traders alone were exporting 40,000 to 60,000 slaves annually; the boats in which they were taken to America or the West Indies were of an average of 150 tons; each boat carried as many as 600 slaves who were chained to shelves below deck throughout the voyage. The profit on each slave sold was £2 to £3.

In Great Britain protests had early been raised against this practice. Bishop Warburton protested in 1766; the Quakers launched an organised anti-slavery campaign; in 1774 John Wesley published his *Thoughts on Slavery*. In 1787 the Anti-Slavery Committee was formally constituted; they enlisted the support of Thomas Clarkson and Wilberforce and obtained the approval of Pitt. On May 12, 1789, Wilberforce brought forward the first of his many motions in the House. It was defeated in a debate in which Alderman Newnham asserted that to abolish the trade would "render the City of London one scene of bankruptcy and ruin." In 1791 Wilberforce's second motion was again defeated. On March 16, 1792, King Christian VII of Denmark issued a decree under which no Danish subject would be allowed to take part in the trade after January 1, 1803. In the same year, after a magnificent speech by Pitt, the House of Commons accepted a resolution providing that the trade should be abolished by stages. In spite of the war Wilberforce persisted. In 1795 he would have secured the passage of a private bill had not twelve of his supporters gone to the opera to witness Portugallo's performance in *I due Gobbi*. Finally in 1804 Wilberforce's motion was approved by the House of Commons although deferred by the upper house. In 1806 Fox brought in a resolution which was carried. In 1807 a definite Bill was presented which, on May 23, 1808, became law. The United States passed a similar act the same year. The task of Castlereagh was to induce other European Governments to prohibit their own nationals from engaging in this trade.

It should be remembered that these early efforts were devoted, not to the abolition of slavery, but to the abolition of the slave trade. It was not till 1833 that slavery itself was abolished throughout the British Empire at the cost to the taxpayer of twenty million pounds.

CHAPTER 14

[1] The Duke of Wellington's romantic affection for the Bourbons was not a lasting affection. "We made a tremendous mistake," he confessed to Princess Lieven in January 1821, "in getting rid of Napoleon. He is the man we ought to have had. As long as the Bourbons hold four thrones there will be no peace in Europe. None of that family is any good." Napoleon shared the Duke's opinion although not for the same reasons. He was himself more impressed by the Russian than by the Bourbon menace. He regarded Alexander as "sly, false, cunning and hypocritical." "It is he," said Napoleon to Las Cases at St. Helena in March 1816, "who will be my real heir in Europe. I was the only man who could have stopped him and his flood of Tartars. The menace for the continent of Europe, especially for Constantinople, is serious and will endure." "If I were the Tsar," he added, "I should march on Calais and then I should find myself the master and arbiter of Europe."

[2] *Ney, Michel, Prince of the Moskowa* (1769-1815). Born at Saarelouis, the son of a cooper. Fought in the armies of the Revolution. Became one of Bonaparte's most ardent supporters and won the Battle of Elchingen which led to the capitulation of Ulm. After the Battle of Friedland was given by Napoleon the title of "Bravest of

the brave." In the Russian campaign he took a leading part in the Battle of Borodino and rendered magnificent service during the retreat. At the first Restoration he made his peace with the Bourbons and on Napoleon's landing at Fréjus he assured Louis XVIII that he would bring back the "usurper in an iron cage." He was thus sent to bar Napoleon's advance on Paris but deserted to him at Lons-le-Saunier. He fought with Napoleon at Waterloo, failed to escape thereafter, and was arrested on August 5. In spite of Louis XVIII's attempts to save him the ultra-royalists, inspired by the Duchess d'Angoulême, demanded his execution. He was court martialled and shot in the Luxemburg garden on December 7, 1815.

CHAPTER 15

[1] *The Treaty of Bucharest* (May 28, 1812). At the beginning of 1812 Russia was engaged in war with Turkey. Napoleon hoped to keep her so occupied and sent Andreossi to Constantinople to conclude an alliance with the Sultan. Largely owing to British mediation (very ably conducted on the spot by the young British chargé d'affaires, Stratford Canning) the Reis Effendi was dissuaded from listening to these overtures. The Russians at the same time were induced to offer comparatively moderate terms of peace. They agreed to abandon their claim to Asiatic territory and even to the Principalities. They accepted, for the moment, the frontier of the Pruth. Thus at the time of Napoleon's invasion important Russian armies were liberated for action on the home front.

CHAPTER 16

[1] Castlereagh pretended, with pathetic self-deception, to be indifferent to the misrepresentation to which his policy was exposed. "Unpopularity," he stated in 1821, "is more convenient and gentlemanlike." He was temperamentally incapable of explaining his motives to the House of Commons or to the public generally; he possessed none of Canning's remarkable gift for public relations. "Lord Castlereagh," said the Duke of Wellington, "possessed a clear mind, the highest talents, and the most steady principles; more so than anybody I ever knew—he could do everything but speak in Parliament. That he could not do."

His personal unpopularity was largely due to the cold reserve of his manner which induced Bulwer-Lytton to refer to him as "Stately in quiet, high-bred, self-esteem." His political unpopularity was due, partly to his responsibility for the Irish Union, which led men like O'Connell and Tom Moore to regard him as "the assassin of his country"; partly to his advocacy of the Six Acts of November 1819, which inspired the famous lines introduced by Shelley into *The Masque of Anarchy:*

> I met Murder on his way,
> He had a mask like Castlereagh,

and partly to his identification with the Holy Alliance and the repressive policy of Metternich.

Byron, who took an emotional view of politics, owed his detestation of Castlereagh to the influence of Moore, Hobhouse and his Italian friends, such as the Gambas, who were incensed by the betrayal of Genoa. The insults which he hurled at Castlereagh both during his lifetime and after his death did much to affect the popular estimate of the dead statesman. These insults were varied, frequent and intense. Byron referred at different times to Castlereagh as "a wretch never named but with curses and jeers"; as "the intellectual eunuch Castlereagh"; as "the cold-blooded, smooth-faced, placid miscreant"; as "the vulgarest tool that Tyranny could ever want"; as "a bungler even in his disgusting trade"; as "a tinkering slave-maker"; as "a second Eutropius." He also devoted much time, and some wit, to ridiculing the "Mrs. Malaprop" style of Castlereagh's speeches and despatches. In Canto IX of *Don Juan* there was, for instance, a sharp reference to Castlereagh's "parts of speech," and to "that long spout of blood and water—Castlereagh."

[2] *The Treaty of Kiel* (January 14, 1814). In 1812 Bernadotte of Sweden had joined the Allies whereas Frederick VI of Denmark had fought with Napoleon. It was thus decided to reward Bernadotte and to punish Frederick by detaching Norway from Denmark and giving her to Sweden. This arrangement was embodied in the Treaty of Kiel. The Norwegians strongly objected to this transference. The British Government sought to overcome this reluctance by assisting Russia in blockading the coast of Norway; for this action they were strongly attacked by the Opposition in Parliament. In the end the Norwegians surrendered and accepted the Act of Union with Sweden which was maintained till 1902. It was Bernadotte's attempts to evade the compensations which he had promised to Den-

mark under the Treaty of Kiel which led to the matter being raised at Aix-la-Chapelle.

[8] *Kotzebue, August von* (1761-1819). Born at Weimar. Entered the Russian service, and became assessor in the Court of Appeal at Reval. Wrote novels, historical works, and comedies. In 1817 he returned to Germany as a Russian spy with a salary of 15,000 roubles. He produced a weekly journal (the *Literarisches Wochenblatt*) in which he ridiculed the liberal ideas of the young German generation. As he was unpopular at Weimar, and as Goethe much disliked him, he moved to Mannheim where he was stabbed by Karl Sand on March 23, 1819. Sand was executed and the Carlsbad Decrees resulted.

Appendix II: List of Books Consulted

Alison, Sir A., *Lives of Lord Castlereagh and Sir Charles Stewart*, 3 vols., Blackwood, 1861.

Arblay, Madame d', *Diary and Letters*, Colburn, 1846, 7 vols.

Atteridge, A. Hilliard, *Joachim Murat*, Methuen, 1911.

Aubry, Octave, *St. Helena*, Gollancz, 1937.

Basily Callimaki, Mme. de, *J.-B. Isabey, sa Vie et son temps*, Paris, 1909.

Belloc, Hilaire, *The Campaign of 1812*, Nelson, 1924.

Berry, *Journals and Correspondence of Miss Berry*, Longmans, 3 vols., 1865.

Bertuch, Carl, *Tagebuch von Wiener Kongress*, Berlin, 1916.

Bessborough, Earl of, *Lady Bessborough and Her Circle*, Murray, 1940.

Boigne, Countess of, *Mémoirs*, Plon Nourrit, 1907, 2 vols.

Bonnefons, *Un Allié de Napoléon*, Fred. Auguste, King of Saxony.

Bourienne, M. de, *Mémoirs of Napoleon*, London, 1836, 4 vols.

Bryant, Arthur, *Years of Victory*, Collins, 1944.

Buckland, C. S. B., *Friedrich von Gentz's Relations with the British Government*, Macmillan, 1934.

——, *Metternich and the British Government*, Macmillan, 1932.

Burghersh, Lady, *Correspondence with the Duke of Wellington*, Murray, 1893.

——, *Correspondence*, edited by Lady Rose Weigall, Murray, 1893.

Burghersh, Lord, *Correspondence*, edited by Rachel Weigall, Murray, 1912.

Cambridge History of British Foreign Policy, 3 vols., Cambridge, 1922.

Cambridge History of Poland, edited by W. F. Reddaway, Cambridge, 1941.

Cambridge Modern History, vol. IX, 1906.

Campbell, General Sir Neil, *Napoleon at Fontainebleau and Elba*.

Castlereagh, Viscount, *Correspondence*, 12 vols., Murray, 1853.

Caulaincourt, Marquis Louis de, *Mémoires*, edited by J. Hanoteau, Plon, 1933.

Cooper, Rt. Hon. Duff, *Talleyrand*, Cape, 1932.

Coudray, R. du, *Metternich*, Cape, 1935.

Creevey Papers, The, edited by Sir H. Maxwell, Murray, 1903.

Croker Papers, The, 3 vols., Murray, 1884.

Dino, Duchesse de, *Souvenirs*, Calman Lévy.

Festing, Gabrielle, *John Hookham Frere*, Nisbet, 1899.

Ford, Clarence, *Life and Letters of Madame de Krüdener*, Black, 1893.

Foster, Vere, *The Two Duchesses*, Blackie, 1898.

Fournier, August, *Der Kongress von Châtillon*, Tempsky Verlag, 1900.

Gentz, F. von, *Briefe an Pilat*, Leipzig, Vogel Verlag, 1868, 2 vols.

——, *Dépêches inédites aux Hospodars de Valachie*, Paris, 1876.

Gruyer, Paul, *Napoléon, Roi de l'Ile d'Elbe*, Hachette, 1906.

Herman, Arthur, *Metternich*, Allen and Unwin, 1923.

Holland, Lady, The Journals of, edited by the Earl of Ilchester, Longmans, 1908.

Jaucourt, Comte de, *Correspondance avec Talleyrand*, Plon.

Junot, Madame, *Memoirs*, London, 1893, 4 vols.

La Garde-Chambonas, Comte Auguste Louis Charles de, *Souvenirs du Congrès de Vienne*, Paris, 1901.

Las Cases, Comte de, *Mémorial de Sainte-Hélène*, 4 vols.

Lieven, Princess, Private Letters of, edited by Peter Quennell, Murray, 1937.

Lockhart, J. G., *The Peacemakers, 1814-1815*, Duckworth, 1932.

Macunn, F. J., *The Contemporary English View of Napoleon*, Bell, 1914.

Maitland, Rear-Admiral Sir F., *The Surrender of Napoleon*, Blackwood, 1904.

Marriott, Sir John, *Castlereagh*, Methuen, 1936.

Masson, Frédéric, *Revue d'Ombres*, Paris, Ollendorf, 1921.

Metternich, Prince de, *Mémoires*, Plon, 1880, 2 vols.

——, *Lettres à la Comtesse de Lieven*, edited by Hanoteau, Plon, 1909.

Napoléon, Correspondance de, Imprimerie Impériale, Paris, 1858.

Nicolas Mihailovitch, Grand Duke, *Scenes of Russian Court Life*, Jarrolds, 1917.

Nicolas Mihailovitch, *L'Empereur Alexandre Ier*, St. Petersburg, 1912.

Oman, Carola, *Britain against Napoleon*, Faber, 1942.

Paléologue, Maurice, *The Enigmatic Tsar*, Hamish Hamilton, 1938.

Pares, Richard, *Colonial Blockade and Neutral Rights*, Clarendon Press, 1938.

Petrie, Sir Charles, *Life of George Canning*, Eyre and Spottiswoode, 1930.

Philips, W. Alison, *The Confederation of Europe*, London, 1914.

Piggot, Sir Francis, *Freedom of the Seas*, F. O. Handbooks, 1920.

Salisbury, Marquess of, *Biographical Essays*, London, 1905.

Satow, Sir Ernest, *A Guide to Diplomatic Practice*, 3rd edition, Longmans, 1932.

Ségur, Comte de, *History of the Expedition to Russia*, London, 1825, 2 vols.

Seton-Watson, Dr. R. W., *Britain in Europe*, Cambridge, 1937.

Sorel, *L'Europe et la Révolution Française*, Paris, 1904, vol. VIII.

Stenger, Gilbert, *The Return of Louis XVIII*, Heinemann, 1909.

Talleyrand, *Mémoires*, Griffith Farren, 1891, 3 vols.

——, *Correspondence inédite*, edited by G. Pallain, Paris, 1881.

Temperley, Professor Harold, *The Foreign Policy of Canning*, Bell, 1925.

Tisenhaus, Countess (Madame de Choiseul-Gouffier), *Memoirs of the Emperor Alexander I*, Kegan Paul, 1904.

Vandal, Albert, *Napoléon et Alexandre Ier*, 1891, 3 vols.

Vitrolles, Baron de, *Mémoires*, Paris, Charpentier, 1884.

Waliszewski, K., *Le règne d'Alexandre Ier*, Plon, 1923, 3 vols.

Webster, Sir Charles, *The Congress of Vienna*, London, Bell, 1937.

——, *The Foreign Policy of Castlereagh*, Bell, 1931, 2 vols.

Weil, Commandant, *Les dessous du Congrès de Vienne*, Payot, 1917, 2 vols.

——, *Le revirement de la politique autrichienne à l'égard de Joachim Murat.*

Wellington, Duke of, *Despatches*, London, 1847, vol. XII.

——, *Supplementary Despatches*, vol. VIII-XI, London, 1860.

Woodward, E. L., *Three Studies in European Conservatism*, 1929.

Index

Aberdeen, George Hamilton Gordon, 4th Earl of (1784-1860): His precocity, 59; appointed Ambassador to the Emperor of Austria, 59; Gentz's opinion of, 60; affected by Metternich's charm, 60; approves the Frankfurt Proposals, 61-63; Castlereagh's attitude toward, 68, 206; at the Congress of Châtillon, 72, 79; in Paris, 100; his impulsiveness, 189

His opinion of Metternich, 37; and of Nesselrode, 131

Adams, John, President of the United States (1735-1836), 212

Aix-la-Chapelle, Conference of (September-November 1818), 261-64

Alexander I, Tsar of Russia (1777-1825): Main dates of his life, 276; during the invasion of Russia, 12; his early unpopularity, 13; his unwillingness to invade Europe, 20; he negotiates the Treaty of Kalisch (February 1813), 26-27; his Polish ambitions, 27-31, 82; his courage after Lützen, 33; after Bautzen, 34; he rejects the Frankfurt Proposals, 63; at Langres, 65, 71; his determination to capture Paris, 75, 84; during the crisis of Troyes, 78-80; his entry into Paris, 85-86; attitude towards Bourbon restoration, 87; he negotiates the Treaty of Fontainebleau, 91-97; mistakes in his policy after the abdication of Napoleon, 102-103; his attempts to conciliate the Poles, 105-106; his interview with Louis XVIII at Compiègne, 108-109; his assistants during the Vienna Congress, 131; his attitude towards the Polish problem at the outset of the Congress, 149-150; he regards himself as the sole plenipotentiary, 158-59; his social indulgences, 162; his handling of the Polish problem at Vienna, Chapter 11 *passim;* his intrigues with the London Whigs, 202, 247; Secret Service reports on, 203; on learning of Napoleon's escape from Elba, 225; is informed of secret Treaty of January 3, 1815, 229; he leaves for Paris, 242; he rejects the Treaty of Guarantee, 243; his Eastern ambitions, 243-44; his meeting with Baroness von Krüdener, 246-48; his intrigues in Germany, Turkey, and Spain, 252; his proposal for a General Disarmament Treaty, 254; his suggestion of an *Alliance Solidaire,* 262-64; his attitude toward the Carlsbad Decrees, 266; his increasing reactionary tendencies, 266-67; wishes to send a Russian army into Spain, 267; his attitude on outbreak of Greek War of Independence, 269; his death, 273